RESISTING THE NEWS

Resisting the News brings together unique insights from activists and alternative-media users to offer a distinctive perspective on the problems of journalism today—and how to fix them.

Using critical-cultural theory and, in particular, the conceptual frameworks of ritual communication and interpretive communities, this book examines how audiences filter their interpretations of mainstream news through the prisms of their identities and experiences with alternative media and political protest. Jennifer Rauch gives voice to alternative-media audiences and illuminates the cultural resources, values, assumptions, critical skills, and discursive strategies through which they make sense of their news environments. Drawing on a 15-year research project, Rauch employs a variety of qualitative, quantitative, and quasi-ethnographic methods, including focus groups, media-use diaries, close-ended surveys, and open-ended questions, to paint a layered portrait of liberal and conservative critiques of journalism.

Shedding new light on popular theories about "how news works" and about "mass" audiences, this book will be useful to students, scholars, and teachers of political communication, journalism studies, media studies, and critical-cultural studies.

Jennifer Rauch is a professor of journalism and communication studies at Long Island University Brooklyn and a visiting professor of journalism and media studies at Linfield University. She was honored with a Silver Nautilus Book Award for her book *Slow Media: Why Slow Is Satisfying, Sustainable and Smart*.

In the early 2000s, this parody of a World-War II propaganda poster circulated widely through anti-corporate activist media, including the zine shown here.

RESISTING THE NEWS

Engaged Audiences, Alternative Media, and Popular Critique of Journalism

Jennifer Rauch

Routledge
Taylor & Francis Group

NEW YORK AND LONDON

First published 2021
by Routledge
52 Vanderbilt Avenue, New York, NY 10017

and by Routledge
2 Park Square, Milton Park, Abingdon, Oxon, OX14 4RN

Routledge is an imprint of the Taylor & Francis Group, an informa business

Library of Congress Cataloging-in-Publication Data
A catalog record for this book has been requested

ISBN: 978-0-367-44117-3 (hbk)
ISBN: 978-0-367-43017-7 (pbk)
ISBN: 978-1-003-00772-2 (ebk)

Typeset in Bembo
by Apex CoVantage, LLC

To everyone who has ever put aside a writing project.
Maybe you didn't recognize its value;
maybe other dimensions of life beckoned.
Go back and read it again.

CONTENTS

TABLES

ACKNOWLEDGMENTS

This page is traditionally called "Acknowledgments." A more appropriate word would be "Gratitude." I deeply appreciate the panoply of people who have nurtured me as an academic, a writer, a social agent, and a human being. In the hustle and bustle of our distracted world, I am grateful for their gifts of time and attention.

First and foremost, I feel deep appreciation for the wonderful activist-discussants, students, and alternative-media survey respondents who participated in this research with me. I hope I've done justice to their compelling, complex, and contrarian attitudes toward mainstream news. Thanks to all of these audience participants for "looking at it sideways."

I will always be thankful to my dissertation committee at Indiana University, who helped set me on the path of scholarship that I have followed for nearly two decades. The breadth and depth of knowledge of Dave Nord, my advisor, never ceased to amaze me. His keen eye once detected that I had misplaced my main thesis in a footnote on page 7 of a research paper. Carol Polsgrove's passion for alternative media and social progress were models for my own. Tom Gieryn's originality of thought and clarity of expression also served as beacons. Chris Ogan set high standards for intellectual rigor and personal integrity to which I aspire. For their patience and advice I am much indebted.

I also extend thanks to other Indiana University faculty members who engaged me in research and teaching projects, including Randy Beam, Dave Boeyink, Susan Tyler Eastman, Betsi Grabe, Paul Voakes, and Dave Weaver. And to earlier professors at Temple and Penn State, who left an indelible mark on my thinking: George Gerbner, Vince Norris, Ed Trayes, Angie Valdivia, and Barbie Zelizer.

Thanks to John Downing and Chris Atton for tilling and sowing the field of alternative media studies that I now tend and harvest. Both have provided me with inspiration, feedback, and encouragement at multiple points in my career. Fellow scholars of alternative media, activism, and audiences like Joshua Atkinson, James Hamilton, Tony Harcup, Linda Jean Kenix, and Radhika Parameswaran offered perceptive insights reflected in this book.

A fine cadre of editors and scholars shared crucial comments with me at various stages of this research: Anthony Giffard, Daniel Kreiss, Julian Matthews, Paul Mihailidis, Victor Pickard, Colin Sparks, Nikki Usher, Teun Van Dijk, and anonymous reviewers. Thanks to the terrific team at Routledge who shepherded this project from proposal to production—among them Emma Sherriff, Sheni Kruger, and Erica Wetter.

To Kappa Tau Alpha, the national journalism and mass communication honor society, for the honor of being a member, the pleasure of being a chapter adviser, and the research grant that supported some of this work.

To Peter Laufer and Jack Lule for their friendship as well as Douglas Rushkoff, for sharing his incredible talent, mind, and heart with all of us on Team Human.

Finally, to my ananda gurus, my compassionate friends and family, and my irresistible husband, all of whom keep me engaged in the things that matter.

1

POPULAR THEORIES OF MAINSTREAM AND ALTERNATIVE NEWS

The power of alternative news sources to sway mainstream political communication has long remained hidden, subtle, and underestimated. Many people who make, use, and study the news once assumed that alternative media exerted little public influence; even those who wished the genre *were* consequential lamented its limited impact. Such media were often viewed as marginal, perhaps obsolete, descendants of the revolutionary, abolitionist, labor, socialist, ethic, underground, gay, and feminist press. Until recently, alternative media were widely presumed to have a liberal or progressive disposition toward issues such as civil rights, women's equality, pacifism, and environmental protection; that is, until the U.S. presidential campaign of 2016 revealed the extent to which a right-wing media ecosystem bolstered by nontraditional sources like partisan blogs, niche publications, and conspiracy websites could dominate the mainstream news agenda and shape electoral outcomes.[1] Manipulative actors sometimes plant stories in alternative media to give them a sheen of legitimacy and draw the attention of legitimate journalists, a practice called "trading up the chain."[2] Alternative media also serve as testing grounds where political actors develop and refine new ideas to see what resonates with audiences. Those concepts and arguments then move into mainstream arenas through press releases, op-ed columns, talk radio, and TV news roundtables.[3] It is clear that alternative media, mainstream journalism, political communication, and citizen knowledge are deeply intertwined in the public sphere.

Alternative news sources—which can be hyper-partisan or centrist or bounce across the ideological spectrum—have grown in prominence to become key vectors of information for many citizens. Mainstream journalism from corporate entities such as ABC, CNN, NBC, the *New York Times*, and the *Washington Post*—as well as from public broadcasters like BBC, NPR, and PBS—featured prominently among favored U.S. sources for 2016 campaign news,[4] and so did news from digital-native organizations such as *BuzzFeed, Drudge Report, Huffington Post,* and Reddit, as well as from "outrage outlets" such as Fox News and MSNBC.[5] Partisan blogs like the *Blaze, Daily Kos, InfoWars, Newsmax,* and *Salon* attracted between 5 million and 15 million viewers monthly.[6] In the 2020 election cycle, news purveyors such as the *Atlantic, Common Dreams, Daily Beast, Daily Caller, Washington Times,* Breitbart, and Reddit were among the most popular online publishers, alongside more traditional sources.[7]

In parallel with the rise of non-legacy news sources in the 21st century, trust in mainstream journalism has dropped among audiences of all ideological stripes.[8] Confidence in institutions like government and business stayed relatively steady, yet confidence in the press declined precipitously from 1973 to 2008.[9] Mainstream broadcast and cable TV news networks remain among the most watched by Americans, but they are among the least trusted media sources.[10] At the same time, alternative news sources such as the *Atlantic,* BBC, *Democracy Now!, Drudge Report, Instapundit, Politico, Powerline,* PBS, *Vox,* and *Young Turks* have risen into the ranks of most trusted.[11]

When faced with a choice between different messages and different sets of "facts" offered by mainstream and alternative media, people continually choose to consume and trust certain sources over others. Why do alternative-media enthusiasts turn to news sources such as *Brietbart, Daily Kos, Mother Jones,* or the *Weekly Standard* instead of ABC, CNN, *Newsweek,* or the *New York Times?* What values and ideals do these audiences associate with the genre called "alternative media," and how do they distinguish it from oft-derided "mainstream media" (nicknamed MSM)? Why do alternative-media users—many of whom are avid political activists—feel distrust or even antipathy toward the legacy press?

This book offers answers to these questions to help us better understand how and why people make such news choices. *Resisting the News* extends our knowledge of alternative media's role in the news ecosystem by closely examining the attitudes and behaviors of their audiences, about whom we know relatively little. It explores the dynamic interplay between alternative media and mainstream journalism by probing the values and assumptions that engaged audiences bring to their news encounters. It illuminates the discursive resources and strategies through which people make sense of the news. And, it reconfigures our definition of "alternative media" by viewing this category from the perspective of audiences, rather than that of scholars, journalists, or alternative news creators.

Alternative Media Matters

Other. Alternate. Another. Different. These are common synonyms for alternative. It seems self-evident that some media are different from others. The term "alternative media" contains a multitude of meanings—from a simple understanding of this category as opposing "mainstream media" to complex definitions that are more problematic, contentious, and slippery. John Downing, who helped found this area of research, described alternative media as both a form of resistance to power structures in society and a voice of social movements.[12] Another key figure is Chris Atton, who described alternative media in terms of their organizational processes and participatory production as much as by their content.[13] This sphere of work takes into account a panoply of alternative forms and genres: public-access television, community radio, activist websites, zines, and other radical, citizens, or grassroots media—even street theater, flyers, graffiti, and buttons.[14] Research on the evolution of U.S. alternative media has focused on radical communication, social movements, and the dissident press spanning from revolutionary days to the present.[15] People often bestow the moniker "alternative" upon particular media based on the roles those projects play in their individual lives or in the broader culture.

Scholars and practitioners who once conceived of alternative/mainstream as a dichotomy now tend to view these media genres on a spectrum or a continuum, with many hybrids and few "pure" instances.[16] Many audience members have similar difficulty distinguishing between the two. In some ways, there is now more overlap between the content, forms, and practices of alternative and mainstream media than there used to be; in other ways, we have become more cognizant of similarities that have always existed but were often overlooked. The goal of placing all media into two categories, alternative and mainstream, disregards the ways in which these interdependent genres resemble, influence, interact, and compete with each other. While recognizing the limitations of a binary conception of alternative-mainstream, I use it in this book as an organizational and analytical device. For me, the terms "alternative media" and "mainstream media" express two ideal types, not empirically distinct phenomena. I strive to use this vocabulary in ways consistent with the discourse of my informants, which will be shared anon.

In the minds of alternative-media admirers, a major distinction between alternative and mainstream media is that the former produces critical content with the primary goal of promoting social change (with financial considerations taking a back seat), while the latter is mainly motivated by the pursuit of profit (with little regard for the social impact of news). Empirically, as well as subjectively, there are particular producer motives and content attributes that support this characterization of alternative media. Research shows that many alternative creators share with activist consumers the goal of struggling for a better world. Mainstream journalists might sometimes be driven by a desire for social change, but they are rarely as explicit and vocal about this motivation as alternative news producers are. Mainstream content is also less likely to express ideologies as radical as those in alternative media—to wit, leftist publications that frequently put forth visions of a world beyond capitalism.[17]

Resisting the News focuses primarily on a particular subset of alternative media that my study participants found integral to their lives: alternative *news* media, the alternative *press*, and alternative *journalism*. The latter label is typically applied to "alternative media practices that involve reporting and/or commenting on factual and/or topical events, as opposed to wider cultural or artistic forms of alternative media," Tony Harcup explained.[18] This category encompasses a wide range of newspapers, pamphlets, magazines, broadcast stations, blogs, social networking platforms, and other media spaces that "are primarily informed by a critique of existing ways (the dominant practices) of doing journalism."[19] This conception of alternative media is widespread in the United States, the United Kingdom, and other liberal democratic contexts with high levels of economic development, technological access, and press freedom—in contrast with nations enjoying less development, access, and freedom.[20] Elements of popular critique that this book will examine include news sourcing and framing routines, the commercial model of journalism, the professional norm of objectivity, and modes of addressing audiences.

My research participants deemed not only a wide array of media "alternative"—particularly legacy alternative press institutions, public broadcasting, foreign sources, and political blogs and websites, but also satirical news, social media, and partisan commentators. These audience-derived definitions of alternative media guided discussions and analyses throughout this book. Experiences with other radical, ethnic, or community media appeared less frequently in their responses. The range of alternative media you will encounter in the conversations and analyses to follow encompasses sources such as

- the legacy alternative press (e.g., *Alternet, Counterpunch, Democracy Now!, Human Events, Mother Jones,* the *Nation, National Review,* the *New American,* the *Progressive,* the *Washington Spectator, Z Magazine*);
- political blogs and political news websites (e.g., *Altercation, Bretibart News, Common Dreams, Crooks and Liars, Daily Kos, Drudge Report, NewsBusters, Patriot Post, Politico, Talking Points Memo, Think Progress, Townhall, Truthdig, Truthout*); and
- partisan broadcasters and commentators (e.g., Alex Jones, Ann Coulter, Fox News, Glenn Beck, Laura Ingraham, Michael Medved, Michael Savage, Michele Malkin, MSNBC, Rachel Maddow, Rush Limbaugh, Sean Hannity)—what Jeffery Berry and Sarah Soberiej have called "outrage media."

These engaged audiences reported also using daily newspapers, newsweeklies, news magazines (e.g., the *New Yorker, Atlantic, Harper's*), public broadcasters with a centrist orientation (*National Public Radio, PBS, C-SPAN*), noncommercial campus and community sources, foreign-language media, CNN, and British news sources (the *BBC, Economist, Guardian*).[21] They attended to news from watchdog and advocacy organizations such as American Family Association, Americans for Prosperity, Center for American Progress, Family Research Council, Heritage Foundation, and Media Matters. Admittedly, it is challenging to ascribe these news sources to categories, a fact that emphasizes the extent to which our media system is hybridized.[22] Whither to place outlets such as the *Huffington Post* and *The Daily Show*—which might not seem like "alternative media" to some people but are viewed as such by members of these communities? The audience perspectives shared in future chapters explain why they categorize media genres in the way they do.

Ritual Approaches to News Consumption

News is significant not only as a source of information but also as a social resource, a glue that helps construct and maintain a shared reality. Our experiences with journalism shape our personal identities and our sense of being bound to other people in communities of imagination and interpretation. Audiences are communal in complicated senses, as Martin Barker explained. Sometimes we perform our "audiencing" in groups—a gerund that helps capture the active nature of news consumption. But even when we watch, listen, and read alone, we carry in us "a sense of belonging to different discursive communities—some real, some imaginary."[23]

For several centuries, journalism has punctuated readers' daily rhythms and incited them to form community attachments and engage in civic life, as David Nord noted.[24] The daily ritual of reading newspapers—of simultaneously receiving media content across a spatial expanse—contributed to the rise of nation-states by spurring people to recognize themselves as part of an "imagined community," in Benedict Anderson's influential conception.[25] News coverage of Olympic Games, state funerals, and other public events not only reflects social and national identities but also helps create them.[26] When newspapers briefly became unavailable during a 1945 strike, readers said they didn't miss the content so much as the pleasure of reading and the provision of topics for conversation.[27] "People use news as a catalyst for much broader, social discussion," said media anthropologist Elizabeth Bird. "Its ritualistic, community-building role allows us to interrogate morality and dialogue with others about shared values."[28]

The concepts of *ritual* and *transmission* communication are essential to understanding alternative news audiences, as James Carey elucidated. Ritual communication can be thought of as "a symbolic process whereby reality is produced, maintained, repaired, and transformed."[29] Both our sense of reality and reality itself are formed through the ritualistic creation and dissemination of meaning, which blends subjective experience and intersubjective agreement. Transmission refers to instrumental or goal-oriented communication: "the extension of messages across geography for the purpose of control." (Note the transportation metaphor, following a linear model of sender–message–receiver.) The first conception of communication emphasizes its relationship to meaning, culture, and the maintenance of society in time, whereas the second stresses information, power, and the efficacy of communication across space. The two modes are not mutually exclusive and are frequently interwoven. News audiences need facts and information, but they also need discursive and interpretive resources to aid them in forming opinions, following arguments, understanding other people's viewpoints, and debating goals that a community might formulate and pursue.

I first became attuned to the importance of ritual communication when studying independent publishers of *zines*, idiosyncratic publications that espouse do-it-yourself aesthetics and participatory ethics.[30] The vast majority of zine producers who talked with me undertook their projects as labors of love. They made zines mainly for affective reasons and not instrumental ones, such as earning money or spreading a message. Members of this interpretive community immersed themselves in acts of not only ritual zine production and reception but also ritual *circulation*—a media phenomenon that receives less attention. They enjoyed the sense of community that sprang from exchanging zines in face-to-face interactions where they could see their creations enter someone's everyday life, as well as with people they never met in person. Myriad rituals in zine communities help individuals feel like part of a social group whose members share their views, beliefs, and values. The same is true of alternative-media fans.

This book considers alternative-media audiences as imagined communities as well as *interpretive communities*, groups that share understandings of social reality, intersubjective meanings, and strategies for decoding media texts. Interpretive communities can form around media production, circulation, and consumption. Sometimes they are naturally occurring groups of people who gather in discrete locations such as the home or workplace to consume media together; sometimes they do not assemble physically or interact or even know each other.[31] People can belong to several—even seemingly incompatible—interpretive communities at once. The alternative-media devotees studied here were members of intersecting coteries with similar orientations toward and experiences with media.

Research taking cultural, ritual, and interpretive approaches to news audiences remains somewhat unusual. "Journalism scholars rarely tackle reception of news in other than quantitative, text-response ways," Bird noted, "while cultural-studies scholars primarily focus on entertainment genres."[32] Those sociological and cultural ethnographies of news that do focus on people tend to study producers—and mainstream ones, at that—rather than audiences and niche or alternative news sources. One provocative study of online news fans, who participated in lively discussion forums, confirmed that journalism consumption interlaces emotion, ritual, and information.[33] This research showed that audiences interpret the meaning of "the story" in relation to the competing views of other audience members, as well as journalists and politicians—not just the specific news report.

A similar void exists in knowledge of how audiences and readers use alternative media, which Downing called "an urgent one to fill" given the global growth of giant media corporations and anti-corporate sentiment and action, alongside the multiplying social roles of alternative media.[34] People in alternative-media communities once imagined themselves to be lone guardians of many ideals and practices of democratic communication: horizontal relationships, two-way flows, interactivity, collaboration, participation, and peer-to-peer networks. In the early aughts—a time when digital devices and social networks allowed virtually anyone to create, distribute, and access media texts—an argument arose that alternative media were obsolete. Nearly two decades after Downing's call, little empirical attention has been paid to the perspectives and practices of people who choose to read, watch, or listen to alternative-media products.

In addition to my own work, a handful of studies have helped fill this lacuna. Atton's research found that readers valued an alternative weekly for its honesty, credibility, independence, nonprofit orientation, mobilizing information, and coverage of protest actions and radical cultural events.[35] Jacqui Ewart and her coauthors found that alternative-media audiences viewed community radio and TV as telling local stories and talking with people in the community in ways that redefined "news" and contested traditional journalistic values and practices.[36] Joshua Atkinson found that activists associated alternative-media content with a liberal critique of corporatism. He also observed that those participating in discussions with alternative-media producers were typically media creators themselves; rarely did any nonproducing activists report sharing feedback.[37] Harcup found that readers of a local blog were dissatisfied with mainstream media and saw alternative media as better helping them make sense of the world.[38] Summer Harlow and Dustin Harp found that Latin American activists, like ones in the United States, trusted alternative news sources more than mainstream ones.[39]

We have only scratched the surface in our efforts to understand the meanings and practices of these audiences that exercise agency in their daily lives by routinely choosing alternative media over dominant ones. This overarching neglect likely results from two clusters of biases among researchers: mental ones against audiences in favor of media creators and methodological ones toward data that can be efficiently gathered and analyzed. While some were proposing that the idea of "alternative media" was meaningless in the digital age, others were consigning audiences to the dustbin of history.[40]

Audiences Fall Out of Fashion

When people think of alternative and activist media, they often gravitate toward practices related to producing and disseminating messages—as embodied in phrases like "We Media," "Be the Media," and "Become the Media."[41]

Such slogans were eagerly touted at the turn of the millennium by everyone from punk rockers and political activists, to communication professors and tech gurus, to media critics and professional journalists.[42]

One-time Green Party presidential candidate (and Dead Kennedys singer) Jello Biafra ranted against globalization in a 2000 album called *Become the Media*. The motto was claimed as *nom-de-plume* by self-publisher Jen Angel, who was inspired by the Seattle WTO protests to launch the radical cultural magazine *Clamor*. People marching in Rome in 2002 in support of Indymedia Italia emblazoned their placards with the slogan "Don't hate the media! Become the media!"[43] Journalism expert Dan Gillmor touted citizen journalists and bloggers in his 2004 book *We the Media*, which helped popularize the notion of the "former audience."[44] And the 2009 handbook *Be the Media*, whose logo depicts an upraised fist clutching a microphone, features contributions and endorsements from the likes of Ben Bagdikian (author of *The New Media Monopoly*), Jeff Cohen (founder of liberal watchdog group Fairness and Accuracy in Reporting, aka FAIR), Robert McChesney (founder of media reform group Free Press), Craig Newmark (the namesake founder of Craigslist), and media theorist Douglas Rushkoff (author of *Throwing Rocks at the Google Bus*).[45]

The novel productive and distributive capacities of digital media and networks momentarily distracted many people from envisioning audiences as media recipients and consumers to seeing them, instead, as newly empowered media participants and producers. First-wave audience researchers of the 1980s were criticized for overstating the power of media users to resist the ideological messages "encoded" into content and, instead, to make their own meanings. Paradoxically, a subsequent wave of scholars in the 2000s celebrated the resistant power of "the people formerly known as the audience" to make their own media.[46] Awkward neologisms like *produser*, a mash-up of producer and user, were duly coined to express this apparent redistribution of power.[47] Yet reports of the audience's death have been greatly exaggerated.

In this book, I consider my engaged subjects as *alternative-media audiences*— and alternately as *users, fans, consumers, enthusiasts, devotees*, and *admirers*. This is because, to some extent, "everyone is audiences all the time," as Nick Abercrombie and Brian Longhurst observed.[48] People spend more time immersed in media than they do working, studying, or sleeping. We are both audiences and performers, sometimes in oscillating moments and sometimes simultaneously. In a media-saturated environment, diffused audiences like these alternative-media fans make their enthusiasms known partly through their uses of media and partly by performing their media use, as we shall see. Audience uses of alternative media (and performances of that media use) represent instances wherein individuals have chosen, from the vast array of available media, to receive and interpret messages relevant to alternative social and political visions. After all, the lesson of 1960s activism was not just that people were recording what happened but that the whole world was watching it, too.[49] With news sources proliferating in a fragmented media environment, audience attention is a highly valuable resource. Paying attention, yet alone paying money, "is a deliberate vote of confidence during an era of infinite choices."[50] If we are to "become the media," Downing urged, we must consider the question: "Who will actually have the stamina to listen to this myriad of popular communicators pounding out their messages?"[51]

I don't mean to imply that people are always *only* news audiences. They are also citizens, voters, media creators, news subjects, participants in reporting processes, and much more. Many audience members are, at other moments, media producers or distributors. Yet few audiences do, in fact, "become the media." Rates of active participation in online media are generally estimated between 10 percent and 20 percent. While creator-to-consumer ratios vary widely by platform, one rule of thumb posits that 10 percent of online users create, edit, or contribute content (such as posting comments) while the remaining 90 percent only view content.[52] There's also the Pareto principle, a widely applied power-law distribution stating that 20 percent of a group produces 80 percent of any given activity. (It is reasonable to say that alternative-media users are conspicuous among participants though still a minority.) There is often a "veneer of participation" wherein organizations that try to engage the public in conversations get frustrated with always encountering "the usual suspects" rather than "genuinely" ordinary people.[53]

The fact that more people now participate in media production and dissemination does not justify forever narrowing the scope of audience activities to that limited vignette. Much scholarship and public conversation has tended to reify the idea of "creating media creators."[54] Some theorists go further in criticizing such reductionist understandings of media participation, even deeming them "vulgar."[55] We are ignoring important questions of ownership of platforms/companies, collective decision-making, profit, class, and distribution of material benefits when we overstate the creativity and activity of media users.[56] In her essay "Are We All Produsers Now?" Bird proposed that the academy's enthusiastic embrace of Web 2.0 practices as a model of audience agency blinds us to non-web-based audience practices and the continuing structural power of media industries.[57]

Amid the fashionable talk about online audiences being more "active" than allegedly "passive" TV viewers and about interactive texts posing unprecedented interpretive challenges, the decades-old argument about active audiences seems forgotten.[58] The lack of attention to what Harcup called the "original active audience"—be it mainstream and/or alternative, analog and/or digital—is all the more remarkable "when rhetoric about an active and empowered audience is being used even in relation to mainstream media in the digital age."[59] These intellectual trends have coalesced to create a gap in our knowledge of alternative-media users—at exactly a time when we needed to know more, not less, about such audiences.

Obstacles to Qualitative Audience Research

Why such a weak appetite for user research in the realm of alternative media, as Downing asked? If people who make alternative media neglect to examine how their own audiences think about and use their products, it's easy enough to justify the oversight. Such media creators expend tremendous time, energy, and money in creating and sustaining their projects, leaving little to study users. Some of these producers might be stuck in cultural niches, whether by unconscious habits or deliberate choices not to engage with people outside their own group.[60] Some of them might disapprove of the commercial and marketing mentalities that sometimes underlie audience research. Those alternative news producers who *do* study audiences often focus on instrumental goals such as improving outreach, increasing revenue, or expanding readership. For these reasons, the task of examining the social, cultural, and ritual aspects of alternative media falls to politically engaged academic researchers—who face their own conceptual and practical obstacles.

The dearth of scholarship on alternative news audiences is striking though unsurprising, in light of the multifarious hurdles to pursuing such work.[61] It's hard to identify news audiences for study because people are receiving and circulating news all the time, attending to it intermittently and from multiple sources.[62] It's challenging to even identify "news," which is diffused through everyday life and blurs with other genres; by contrast, entertainment content is often experienced in discrete places and times. Once you've defined both news and an audience, you need to gain access to informants at times and in places when they engage in interpretive actions and interactions with media. It helps if you can pay respondents, an option not always feasible for underfunded scholars. As I can attest, it's easier dealing with inanimate texts than with live human beings.

Studying the close readings of audience members is "sufficiently daunting to make its undertaking exotically infrequent," as W. Russell Neuman puts it. Field research is time-consuming, labor-intensive, and expensive. Many scholars feel uncomfortable talking with the public, imposing on busy people's time and privacy, or treating audience members as objects of study.[63] To these cognitive biases, add the tasks of recording, transcribing, reducing, organizing, and analyzing discursive data. To boot, some cultural analysts are vaguely suspicious of data collection "that may seduce" them "into an awkward and inexcusable scientism," Neuman notes, in championing a convergence of empirical and critical research.

Other, subtler forces have contributed to academic neglect of news audiences. These include a shift from empirical to theoretical work in the field of reception studies; a heightened expectation of research productivity that can discourage time-intensive audience work; and a devaluation of qualitative methods against quantitative data among scholarly as well as broader cultural values. Yet traditional quantitative research tends to treat people as isolated, objective individuals and thus ignores the social, subjective nature of human experiences with media. Qualitative methods, on the other hand, are well equipped to address the social and cultural circumstances in which we interpret media.

A conservative, quantitative methodological consensus similar to the current one in mass communication research once dominated political communication research. That field was long "premised on surveys, experiments and content analysis that only permit narrow questions to be asked" about "how citizens, journalists, and elites interact, experience, and engage in political communication."[64] Studies of why Americans hate the media and of asymmetrical consumption of partisan propaganda are excellent examples of the quantitative approach. The complementary value of qualitative approaches has been displayed in studies of how reporters and activists view the democratic process and how citizens talk and avoid talking about experiences with government and media.[65] These projects yielded great insights into the roles played by identity, narratives, and emotions in shaping public beliefs and behavior. Another crucial study in this vein asked why audiences turned to sensational, personality-based programs such as Sean Hannity and Ed Schultz instead of more subdued sources such as the *Weekly Standard* or *Nation*.[66] Like mine, that analysis looked beyond information to capture interactions among media content and audience experiences, social contexts, feelings of pleasure and satisfaction, and the desire to belong to a like-minded, albeit dispersed community.

Ritual communication is culturally and contextually specific; it can only be understood, first, as a process and, second, from the point of view of the people involved. My interdisciplinary work, which connects scholarship taking place in the fields of alternative media and political communication as well as audience studies and media sociology, strives to do just that. My approach contrasts with the dominant research paradigm that puts "the methodological cart ahead of the theoretical horse," in Todd Gitlin's trenchant phrase.[67] "Or rather: It has procured a horse that could pull its particular cart." Unlike the prevalent mode in journalism studies, I examine alternative-media audiences from a cultural-studies perspective that highlights subjective, demand-side phenomena; that considers culture as a co-determinant, rather than a cause or an effect; that focuses on consumer-agents rather than producer-providers; and that stresses self-representation and popular emancipation.[68]

Overview of the Book

Resisting the News brings together and expands upon my 15-year project examining people of varying political commitments who use alternative and mainstream news sources. The research shared here employs a range of qualitative, quantitative, and quasi-ethnographic methods, including focus groups, media-use diaries, close-ended surveys, and open-ended questions, to provide a more layered account of how audiences engage with, interpret, and resist the news. I had two primary aims. The first was to see how an interpretive community of alternative-media fans interpreted mainstream news content in light of their experience with diverse other sources of information. The second, building on the first, was to explore how a broader swathe of alternative-media devotees defined "alternative media," how they distinguished this genre from "mainstream media," and how they described the problems with mainstream news sources that, in their eyes, necessitated alternatives.

The research for this book took place in two distinct stages. In the first phase, I watched and discussed a mainstream news program with groups of college students and then did the same with groups of activists who appreciated alternative media. Those findings are presented in more detail in Chapters 3, 4, 5, and 7. In the second phase, I conducted a survey of alternative-media users that asked which news sources they used, why they valued those media, and what they didn't like about mainstream media. Those findings are described in Chapters 8 and 9. These men and women offered keen insights into the central concern of this book: why people resist mainstream sources and embrace alternative media. These theoretical and methodological frameworks resulted in intriguing discoveries about news audiences. I collected information about media use from the alternative audience through diary data, as well as group conversations. And, I gathered both quantitative and qualitative data in the survey to capture the respondents' own language. This enabled triangulation of data where responses to interview questions could be checked against diary entries. (Methods are addressed more fully in the relevant chapters and appendices.)

Let us briefly tour the layout of the book. **Chapter 2** delves deeper into the critical-cultural theories that informed my research. It synthesizes enduring questions about news reception, interpretive power, cultural resistance, and semiotic democracy raised by qualitative audience scholars like Bird, Fiske, and Jenkins, as well as Stuart Hall, David Morley, Janice Radway, and others. You will meet the cast of extraordinarily thoughtful informants whom I recruited to share their interpretations of mainstream and alternative media. This chapter describes the design of the first phase of research: the quasi-ethnographic study that combined focus-group interviews, an experimental stimulus, and media-use diaries.

Chapter 3 discusses patterns of variation between two audience groups' interpretations of a mainstream newscast. It begins by describing the prime-time TV program that all discussants watched with me. My analysis of their discourse was guided by Kim Christian Schrøder's reception model that captures dimensions of the audience experience related to *comprehension* of, *discrimination* in, and perception of a *position* in a news text. The alternative-media groups claimed to understand the program, discerned it as a socially constructed product involving power relations, and consciously rejected its perceived viewpoint. By contrast, the student groups showed some awareness of the newscast being socially constructed but claimed they could not make sense of the program, while seeming to accept its worldview. Through intertextual references, the alternative-media fans frequently invoked broader lay theories about the structure of mainstream news—especially its corporate, commercial model, which they contrasted with their vision of alternative media—than the comparison group did.

Chapter 4 details how this alternative-media audience articulated the *third-person effect*, a perception that others are more influenced by media content than one's self is. This interpretive community compared its own responses to the mainstream news program with those of an imaginary conventional audience assumed to be naive about "how media works." While the research design provided a comparison case for alternative interpretations of news by using students as control group, the activists brought along their own control group, in their minds. This chapter provides compelling evidence of the third-person effect alongside participant explanations of why they believed "other people" were more susceptible to the powerful influence of news messages to which they perceived themselves being immune. It describes conversational strategies through which they situated themselves as simultaneously a part of and apart from a presumed mass audience.

Chapter 5 describes the structural critique of mainstream news voiced by liberal users of alternative media, which distinguished them from both the student groups and the conservative users of alternative media. Through an analysis of what these viewers said "they" were "trying to do," I illuminate their perception of newsmakers' political-economic motives for psychologically manipulating viewers. These alternative viewers understood corporate power, profit orientation, and commercial advertising (Big Media) as corrupting mainstream news, constraining the agency of journalists, and undermining civic life. They rejected market-driven journalism that entertains consumers in favor of a public-service model that informs citizens and associated the latter goal with alternative media.

Taking a short detour from empirical discussion, **Chapter 6** looks closely at the interplay between alternative media and social-movement activism. I consider how activists comprise an interpretive community with shared understandings of social reality and strategies for decoding news texts, due in great part to their experiences as both audiences for and actors in protest reportage. I address the important role of alternative media as a public sphere that offers more sympathetic coverage of social-change issues and events. This discussion pays special attention to the theories, practices, and implications of news framing, including the influence of Gitlin and other movement scholars. In this worldview, mainstream journalism fails its public responsibilities by treating audiences as passive spectators, instead of inspiring people to take civic action.

Chapter 7 returns to my research findings, expanding earlier discussion of alternative news audiences by comparing this group discourse with media diaries kept by its individual members. By integrating this new data source, I shed light on their omnivorous news consumption and their identity as a hybrid audience, rather than "pure" devotees of alternative media. You'll see how these alternative viewers ritually characterized their personal consumption of corporate media as fleeting and episodic in conversation with peers but in diaries reported using a wide range of not only alternative but also mainstream sources; indeed, they consumed more of the latter than the general populace did. I explain how members of this interpretive community performed the role of "alternative reader" by rejecting mainstream media, which serves as a marker of individual taste and group belonging. I describe these alternative audience practices as rituals of interaction and integration within their community, as rituals of separation from mainstream values and practices, and as rituals of abstention from corporate news. The activists' symbolic, principled resistance to mainstream news is contrasted with the actual resistance of students and other people, who avoid news for different reasons.

In Chapters 8 and 9, we delve into the survey phase of this research. **Chapter 8** presents a range of evidence supporting the argument that alternative media continues to be a meaningful, high-status genre to people who read, watch, and listen to such content. I describe what the contested term "alternative media" means to people who champion this genre and discuss gaps between their idealized views of alternative media and some realities of alternative media practice. My analysis of survey data shows that this omnivorous, hybrid audience considered a wide array of media "alternative": political blogs, public broadcasting, foreign sources, radical institutions, even—surprisingly—many corporate-owned, advertiser-supported outlets. I investigate some reasons why they scorned most (but not all) corporate, commercial news outlets. This chapter illustrates their distinction between alternative media that produce critical content to spur social change and mainstream media motivated by profit with little regard for social consequences.

Chapter 9 expands the scope of this book by considering survey research on conservative audiences that uproots long-standing liberal assumptions about the political orientation of alternative media. This chapter compares the press criticism of left-wing and right-wing media users, whose perspectives on mainstream and alternative news sources converge and diverge in intriguing ways. While liberals-progressives fixated on structural, economic influences on mainstream news, conservatives focused on individual, political factors—with some provocative exceptions that reveal differences in how much power journalists are perceived in having over the content they produce. I discuss the paradoxical audience views on media bias, objectivity, and partisanship revealed in a side-by-side analysis of qualitative and quantitative responses. Here, I explore asymmetries between liberal and conservatives in their levels of news omnivorousness, their dislike of the MSM business model, and their visions for improving mainstream news systems.

Chapter 10 explores the interplay of lay theories about "how media works" with long-standing public misperceptions about the news, including assumptions that news producers simply give audiences what they want and that partisan influences outweigh economic motives. I situate my findings in the context of a century-old debate spanning progressive reformers, mass-culture theorists, and contemporary scholars who offer competing views of what news audiences are and could be. This chapter argues that a more diverse "toolkit" of cultural resources could be promulgated to help more audiences "resist the news" in constructive ways, rather than unproductive ones like tuning it out. I propose positive actions that foster a turn from criticism of and cynicism toward journalism to instead support a range of alternative, public-oriented, and nonprofit approaches to news that have been proliferating in the past decade.

This book's spotlight on two distinct groups of U.S. alternative-media users—one interviewed, one surveyed—is designed to provide in depth what it may lack in breadth. The data and discussion here are products of a particular historical moment: the first decade of the 21st century, a critical period of development in the hybrid media system that saw dramatic changes in the interplay of mainstream and alternative outlets as well as in U.S. audience orientations toward news. Publications such as *Mother Jones*, the *Nation*, *In These Times*, *National Review*, and others saw their circulation and ad rates jump around the time my research began, following the September 11 terrorist attacks and a U.S. military invasion of Iraq.[69] Alternative media practices in the United States and Europe experienced "exponential growth" in this era, as crises in Western democratic systems, the growth of social and environmental justice movements, and other global changes made oppositional approaches to journalism perhaps more pressing than ever.[70] Such trends continue to this day.

The ethos of my work echoes one espoused by many alternative news outlets: to produce meaningful knowledge that can inform social action. I hope this book will be useful to people practicing alternative and mainstream journalism who want to better comprehend and earn the trust of their audiences as well as those studying journalism, political communication, and social movements in the academy. *Resisting the News* holds lessons for educators seeking to promote news literacy; for activists seeking systemic media reform; for anyone who circulates and consumes mediated messages about current issues and events; and for everyone who cares about understanding and improving our rich, dynamic, and complex news environment.

Resisting Mainstream News, Imagining the Alternatives

This book provides new evidence that some audiences respond to both the content *and* the structure of news in ways that can be characterized as resistant. When I say that alternative-media users *resist* mainstream news, I mean that most of the people I encountered depicted themselves as opposing it, withstanding the effect of it, refraining or abstaining from it. This follows common-sense definitions of "resist" and "resistant." Scholarly conceptualizations of resistance or opposition—especially in regard to audience interpretations of media texts—are much more complicated. Theorist Michel de Certeau considered resistance to be inherent in daily practices of life, including reading the news. For him, seemingly passive consumers could be active, autonomous, self-determined producers who resisted and reconfigured the dominant cultural order by "poaching" and playing with materials from it. The original French title of his book, *L'Invention du Quotidien: Arts de Faire*, captures this sense of everyday creativity and inventiveness better than the English translation, *The Practices of Everyday Life*, does. The question of how my research is informed by scholars of media resistance such as Hall, Morley, Fiske, Radway, and Jenkins will be addressed in due course.

Resisting the News acquaints readers with fascinating "lay theories" about how mainstream journalism works, which both resemble and diverge from the theories of media scholars and news professionals. The term "lay" is used to compare and contrast the theories held by "amateur" or "ordinary" social actors with those published by professionals and academics.[71] It does not imply any negative judgment or condescension toward the theories expressed by informants, who indeed might be familiar with academic or professional iterations of such ideas. Ellen Seiter used the concept "lay theories of news media effects" to explain parents' and teachers' perceptions of the impact of media on children.[72] In studying a network of activists—who avidly consumed alternative media content as well as created and distributed it—Patrick McCurdy discovered that they had existing knowledge, experience, and assumptions about "how news media work" that informed and influenced their social-change actions.[73] The activists in his study held lay theories addressing the motivations of news media personnel, the structural context of news production, and the influence of news values on media representations of reality—ideas foreshadowing some of the narratives told here by alternative-media users.

Susan Herbst, who examined political activists' opinions about democratic society, noted that her informants had fairly sophisticated ideas about "how media work." Indeed, the views of people in her study were consistent with theories about media held by academics and industry professionals. This finding underscored just how complex people's lay theories or mental models of the media really are. She described lay theories as "powerful and dynamic processes of culture and interpretation" that are "very much a product of media exposure, conversation, and internal dialogue."[74] Lay theories reflect interpretations of media experience that are simultaneously individual and cultural. The concept helps us examine audience members' assumptions about media, including about what kind of news to accept and reject.[75]

The corpus of theories, interpretations, and practices described in the chapters that follow has important implications for journalism as well as for democratic citizenship. Lay theories of news matter because they guide how people not only think about but also interact with media, as well as with society. My conversations with alternative-media fans about mainstream news offer evidence that elite media criticism and tabloid-style coverage together contribute to cultivating mistrust of journalists. Audiences are often lambasted for not being adequately engaged with "real" journalism—either for being entrenched partisans who gravitate toward bias-confirming sources or for being apathetic lay-abouts who can't be bothered to "follow the news." What if it's not just the public's fault, but also the media's? What if the system is broken, as well as the users? This research demonstrates that it's time for news organizations to repair their structural foundations and win back audiences. If journalism is to survive and thrive, it needs public support in doing so. And vice versa.

Notes

1 Yochai Benkler, Robert Faris, and Hal Roberts, *Network Propaganda* (Oxford and New York: Oxford University Press, 2016).

2 Ryan Holiday, *Trust Me, I'm Lying* (New York: Portfolio, 2013); Alice Marwick and Rebecca Lewis, *Media Manipulation and Disinformation Online* (New York: Data and Society Research Institute, 2016).

3 Chip Berlet, "Who's Mediating the Storm? Right-Wing Alternative Information Networks," in *Media, Culture, and the Religious Right*, eds. Linda Kintz and Julie Lesage (Minneapolis: University of Minnesota Press, 1998).

4 Pew Research Center, "Trump, Clinton Voters Divided in Their Main Source for Election News," January 18, 2017.

5 Jeffrey Berry and Sarah Soberiej, *The Outrage Industry* (New York and Oxford: Oxford University Press, 2014).

6 So as not to overstate the status of alternative media, let's note that all but two of the 20 most heavily trafficked news websites are produced by mainstream, legacy, traditional organizations.

7 Per Alexa.com on March 28, 2020, the usual suspects included CNN, the *New York Times*, the *Guardian*, the *Washington Post*, CNBC, Bloomberg, the *Wall Street Journal*, *Forbes*, Fox News, *USA Today*, Reuters, NBC News, the *New York Post*, U.S. News and World Report, ABC News, *Time*, CBS, National Geographic, *San Francisco Gate*, *Newsweek*, and the *Los Angeles Times*. See also Benedict Nicholson, "These Were the Top Publishers on Facebook in January 2020," *Newswhip*, March 2, 2020. The *Washington Times* is owned by the Unification movement, colloquially called "Moonies" after its leader Sun Myung Moon.

8 Jonathan Ladd, *Why Americans Hate the Media and How It Matters* (Princeton, NJ: Princeton University Press, 2012).

9 By 2017, public trust in government officials, business executives, nonprofit organizations, and other people had begun to decline in tandem. Trust remained significantly higher among the "Informed Public" (defined as college-educated, top 25 percent in terms of household income, reporting significant media consumption; about 13 percent of the total global population; resembling engaged citizens of my research) than among the "Mass Population." See "2017 Edelman Trust Barometer," January 21, 2017.

10 As the media environment became more fragmented, audience ratings for U.S. network evening news programs declined from 36 percent in 1970 to 19 percent in 2009. Yet 21.3 million people still watched network news nightly in 2019, in addition to 3.9 viewers of prime-time cable news. See Ladd, *Why Americans Hate*, and

A.J. Katz, "Evening News Ratings, Week of May 6," *Adweek*, May 14, 2019. On trust, see Reynolds Journalism Institute (RJI), "Trusting News Project Report," July 25, 2017.

11 RJI, "Trusting News."

12 John Downing et al., *Radical Media* (Thousand Oaks, CA: Sage, 2001).

13 Chris Atton, *Alternative Media* (Thousand Oaks, CA: Sage, 2002).

14 For more on global, small-scale media initiatives, see Clemencia Rodriguez, *Citizens' Media Against Armed Conflict* (Minneapolis: University of Minnesota Press, 2011).

15 See David Armstrong, *A Trumpet to Arms* (Boston, MA: South End Press, 1981); Lauren Kessler, *The Dissident Press* (Thousand Oaks, CA: Sage, 1984); and Rodger Streitmatter, *Voices of Revolution* (New York: Columbia University Press, 2001).

16 Tony Harcup, *Alternative Journalism, Alternative Voices* (Abingdon, UK, and New York: Routledge, 2013); and Linda Jean Kenix, *Alternative and Mainstream Media* (London: Bloomsbury Academic, 2011).

17 Some research confirming distinctions between alternative and mainstream producers, intentions, and content includes Downing et al., *Radical Media*, and Atton, *Alternative Media*, as well as Linus Andersson, "There Is No Alternative," *tripleC* 10, no. 2 (2012); Chris Atton and Emma Wickenden, "Sourcing Routines and Representation in Alternative Journalism," *Journalism Studies* 6, no. 3 (2005); Nina Eliasoph, "Routines and the Making of Oppositional News," *Critical Studies in Mass Communication* 5, no. 4 (1988); Christian Fuchs, "Alternative Media as Critical Media," *European Journal of Social Theory* 13, no. 2 (2010); and Sarah Platon and Mark Deuze, "Indymedia Journalism," *Journalism* 4, no. 3 (2005).

18 Tony Harcup, "Asking the Readers," *Journalism Practice* 10, no. 6 (2016): 684.

19 Chris Atton and James F. Hamilton, *Alternative Journalism* (Thousand Oaks, CA: Sage, 2008).

20 For concise overviews of existing approaches to alternative media, see Gabi Hadl, "Alternative, Community, Citizens, Radical, Autonomous, Tactical, or Civil Society Media?" International Association for Media and Communication Research, 2009 Congress, Mexico City; and Jennifer Rauch, "Are There Still Alternatives?" *Sociology Compass* 10, no. 9 (2016).

21 While NPR's editorial tone is liberal, it adheres to mainstream journalistic norms in reporting. In that regard, NPR is "more like a liberal version of the *Wall Street Journal*, than like Fox News or MSNBC," per Benkler et al., *Network Propaganda*, 316.

22 Andrew Chadwick, *The Hybrid Media System* (New York and London: Oxford University Press, 2013).

23 Martin Barker, "I Have Seen the Future and It Is Not Here Yet," *The Communication Review* 9 (2006).

24 David Nord, *Communities of Journalism* (Champaign-Urbana: University of Illinois Press, 2001).

25 Benedict Anderson, *Imagined Communities* (New York: Verso, 1991).

26 Eric Rothenbuhler, *Ritual Communication* (Thousand Oaks, CA: Sage, 1998).

27 Bernard Berelson, "What Missing the Newspaper Means," in *Communications Research 1948–49*, eds. Paul Lazarsfeld and Frank Stanton (New York: Harper, 1949).

28 S. Elizabeth Bird, "Seeking the Audience for News," in *The Handbook of Media Audiences*, ed. Virginia Nightingale (New York: Wiley-Blackwell, 2014).

29 James Carey, *Communication as Culture* (Boston, MA: Unwin Hyman, 1989), 43.

30 Jennifer Rauch, "Hands-On Communication," *Popular Communication* 2, no. 3 (2004). See also Stephen Duncombe, *Zines and the Politics of Alternative Culture* (New York: Verso, 1997).

31 An example of an interpretive community that only interacts online is Jonathan Gray, "The News: You Gotta Love It," in *Fandom*, 2nd ed., eds. Jonathan Gray et al.

(New York: NYU Press, 2007). An example of one in which members did not know each other or directly interact is Ang's 1985 study of Dallas fans, which placed an ad in a Dutch women's magazine asking viewers of the show to write to her and explain why they were fans; Ien Ang, *Watching Dallas* (London: Metheun, 1985).

32 Bird, "Seeking the Audience for News."

33 Gray, "The News: You Gotta Love It!," 213.

34 John Downing, "Audiences and Readers of Alternative Media," *Media, Culture and Society* 25, no. 5 (2003): 626.

35 Atton, *Alternative Media.*

36 Jacqui Ewart et al., "Through the Ears of the Audience," paper presented to the Journalism Education Conference, Griffith University, November–December, 2005.

37 Joshua Atkinson and Debbie S. Dougherty, "Alternative Media and Social Justice Movements," *Western Journal of Communication* 70, no. 1 (2006); Joshua Atkinson, *Alternative Media and Politics of Resistance* (New York: Peter Lang, 2010).

38 Harcup, "Asking the Readers."

39 Summer Harlow and Dustin Harp, "Alternative Media in a Digital Era," *Communication and Society/Comunicación y Sociedad* 26, no. 4 (2013).

40 Circa 2006, these trends were disheartening to someone who had just completed her dissertation on *audiences* for *alternative media*—two entities that supposedly no longer mattered, if they even still existed.

41 For more discussion of how ritual and reception relate to the study of activist audiences, see Jennifer Rauch, "Participation Beyond Production," in *Audience and Interpretation in Media Studies*, ed. Radhika Parameswaran (Oxford: Wiley-Blackwell, 2013).

42 This genre includes Shayne Bowman and Chris Willis, *We Media* (Reston, VA: The Media Center at the American Press Institute, 2003).

43 For a detailed analysis of how Independent Media Centers employ the "Be the Media" slogan, see Victor Pickard, "Assessing the Radical Democracy of Indymedia," *Critical Studies in Media Communication* 23, no. 1 (March 2006).

44 Dan Gillmor, *We the Media* (Cambridge, MA: O'Reilly Media, 2004). I like to use the acronym TPFKATA, in homage to TAFKAP, The Artist Formerly Known as Prince. Another well-known proponent of the idea, Jay Rosen, defines TPFKA as "those who were on the receiving end of a media system that ran one way, in a broadcasting pattern, with high entry fees and a few firms competing to speak very loudly while the rest of the population listened in isolation from one another—and who today are not in a situation like that *at all*" (emphasis in original). See Rosen, "The People Formerly Known as the Audience," *PressThink* (blog), June 27, 2006.

45 David Mathison, *Be the Media* (Tiburon, CA: Natural E Creative, 2009).

46 Rosen, "People Formerly Known as the Audience."

47 Axel Bruns, *Blogs, Wikipedia, Second Life, and Beyond* (New York: Peter Lang, 2008).

48 Nick Abercrombie and Brian Longhurst, *Audiences* (Thousand Oaks, CA: Sage, 1998).

49 Todd Gitlin, *The Whole World Is Watching* (Berkeley: University of California Press, 1980).

50 Jake Batsell, *Engaged Journalism* (New York: Columbia Journalism Review Books, 2015), 80.

51 Downing, "Audiences and Readers of Alternative Media," 632.

52 Christian Fuchs, "Against Henry Jenkins," May 30, 2011. See also José van Dijck, "Users like You?" *Media, Culture, and Society* 31, no. 1 (2009): 211–31.

53 John Clarke, "In Search of Ordinary People," *Communication, Culture, and Critique* 6 (2013).

54 Mitzi Waltz, *Alternative and Activist Media* (Edinburgh: Edinburgh University Press, 2005), 33.

55 Fuchs, "Against Henry Jenkins."

56 Fuchs, "Against Henry Jenkins."

57 S. Elizabeth Bird, "Are We All Producers Now?" *Cultural Studies* 25, nos. 4–5 (2011).

58 Sonia Livingstone, "Giving People a Voice," *Communication, Culture, and Critique* 3 (2010).

59 Harcup, "Asking the Readers."

60 Downing et al., *Radical Media*.

61 For more on the difficulties of audience research, see Bird, "Seeking the Audience for News."

62 Karin Wahl-Jorgensen and Thomas Hanitzsch, "Introduction," in *The Handbook of Journalism Studies*, eds. Karin Wahl-Jorgensen and Thomas Hanitzsch (London: Routledge, 2008).

63 Livingstone, "Giving People a Voice."

64 David Karpf et al., "The Role of Qualitative Methods in Political Communication Research," *International Journal of Communication* 9 (2015).

65 Herbst's informants included three categories of political actors: staffers at a state legislature, reporters on the state legislative beat, and state party activists. See Susan Herbst, *Reading Public Opinion* (Chicago, IL: University of Chicago Press, 1998); Nina Eliasoph, *Avoiding Politics* (New York: Cambridge University Press, 1998).

66 Jeffrey Berry and Sarah Soberiej, *The Outrage Industry* (New York and Oxford: Oxford University Press, 2014).

67 Todd Gitlin, "Media Sociology," *Theory and Society* 6 (1978).

68 Wahl-Jorgensen and Hanitzsch, "Introduction."

69 Ta-Nehisi Coates, "Four More Years?" *Village Voice*, August 24, 2004.

70 Chris Atton and Nick Couldry, 2003; Mark Deuze, "Ethnic Media, Community Media, and Participatory Culture," *Journalism* 7, no. 3 (2006): 262–80.

71 Adrian Furnham and Helen Cheng, "Lay Theories of Happiness," *Journal of Happiness Studies* 1, no. 2 (2000).

72 Ellen Seiter, *Television and New Media Audiences* (Oxford: Oxford University Press, 1999).

73 Patrick McCurdy, "Mediation, Practice, and Lay Theories of Media," in *Mediation and Protest Movements*, eds. Bart Cammaerts, Alice Mattoni, and Patrick McCurdy (Bristol, UK, and Chicago, IL: Intellect Ltd., 2013).

74 Herbst, *Reading Public Opinion*, 21–2. See also Seiter, *Television and New Media Audiences*.

75 Furnham and Cheng, "Lay Theories of Happiness."

2

THE PROBABILITY OF RESISTANCE IN EMPIRICAL NEWS AUDIENCES

It was the 4th of July, and thousands of activists were gathered in Philadelphia, the birthplace of the nation, to rally for democracy, justice, and peace.[1] Their banners, chants, flyers, costumes, and conversations promoted a range of issues. They opposed the U.S. military presence overseas, the death penalty, racism, tax cuts for the wealthy, and threats to civil liberties. They supported environmental protection, workers' rights, reproductive choice, universal healthcare, and electoral reform, among other aims. The protesters shared declarative statements in this public forum:

> "Fund mass transit—not war for empire," read posters stapled to telephone poles all over the city.
>
> "Shut down the School of the Americas," stated an invitation to future protests at Fort Benning, Georgia, where a federal training site for military personnel from South and Central America has been linked to human-rights abuses.
>
> "Raise the minimum wage! Abolish the death penalty! Defend women's access to abortion!" demanded a campaign flyer for local third-party candidates.
>
> "Stop the Deportation of 13,000 Muslim, Arab, and South-Asian Immigrants!" said a handout from opponents of racial profiling in the "war against terrorism."

The activists' slogans not only advanced liberal and progressive political and social goals but also condemned the information environment in which modern discourse about politics and society occurs. Some participants accused the news media of oppressing the populace by withholding the truth, in the service of elite power. This view was articulated in radical texts like these:

> "Looking for truth in a world of unjust war, censorship, patriotic hype, and lies?" asked the subscription form for a revolutionary publication.
> "You write what you're told! Thanks, corporate news! We couldn't control the people without you," joked a satirical zine made by anarchist artists.[2]

Censorship, hype, lies. These words convey a strong mistrust of "corporate news." Given this aversion to mainstream journalism, one wonders where these engaged citizens learned about issues such as those advocated at this demonstration. (In turn, many of them believe that mainstream media are hostile toward them and other people pursuing social and political progress.) What sources do they regularly use to follow the news? Do they read, watch, or listen to the same information as the general public? Do they consume different news sources than the population at large? Why do they consider some news sources credible and others less so? Do they interpret mainstream media content differently than other people do, and if so, how?

These are some questions that guided my research. Assuming that people who used alternative media would be well represented at the protest, I had come to the "Justice in July" event to recruit participants for focus-group interviews. Independent, grassroots, and community media commonly serve as logistical resources for protest actions, provide spaces where activists speak to each other about their work, and have a less antagonistic relationship to social movements and the issues they organize around than mainstream media do. To my mind, people who resisted and criticized state power through real-world action seemed likely to generate resistant and critical readings of the news.

This chapter situates my study of alternative-media enthusiasts in the context of existing empirical research on news audiences. First, I introduce some essential critical-cultural theories of resistance, semiotic freedom, polysemy, and extra-textuality that guided my analysis. Then, I preview some findings, which will be detailed later, about interpretive agency and the structural factors that enabled or constrained these readers' ability to understand and take a position on news.

Trends Toward Reception and Resistance

Scholars in a range of fields have questioned assumptions that audiences passively "receive" messages from media producers who (wittingly or unwittingly) attempt to persuade the public to support the existing power structure. One fount of such work was Stuart Hall's seminal 1973 encoding/decoding model, which proposed that media professionals embed messages favorable to social-political elites into news stories and that readers take those messages at face value and readily accept them. This theory presumes that dominant groups maintain power in part by controlling news discourse that presents the existing social order as natural or inevitable and that subordinate groups largely accept those representations. This is sometimes described as the "incorporation/resistance paradigm," or IRP, in which audiences can either be incorporated to the status quo or resist it.

According to this model, *preferred* (you could say *dominant, hegemonic,* or *mainstream*) readings help maintain the existing social order while *oppositional* (or *resistant, critical, alternative*) readings support social change.[3] Preferred and oppositional are two of the four ideal types of meanings that Hall proposed; the other two are *professional* readings—that is, the interpretations of intermediary journalists, publishers, and broadcasters—and *negotiated* readings in which audience members (presumably amateurs) mix preferred and oppositional elements. Hall encouraged scholars to conduct empirical research to see whether audiences do interpret texts in the way supposedly preferred by media elites or, instead, in an oppositional way that challenges dominant ideologies. His theory took into account social differences between viewers to some extent. Hall proposed that audiences who profited from the status quo would accept the preferred meanings of news; that those who would benefit from social change would produce oppositional readings; and that those situated somewhere in-between would read the text in a "negotiated" way. For example, Hispanic and working-class audiences would oppose and criticize the (supposedly) intended meanings of news stories while women (presumably white, elite ones) would negotiate and reinterpret those meanings somehow to accommodate their personal interests.

One milestone foray into audience research that applied the encoding/decoding model was David Morley's study of people who watched the BBC's *Nationwide* documentary series. He and coauthor Charlotte Brunsdon concluded that some viewers took the news program at face value while others read it critically.[4] Morley deemed the readings created by audiences to be oppositional by comparison with his own interpretation of the preferred reading. As Hall's theory predicted, Morley found that active trade-union members saw the news as rabidly anti-union and objected to right-wing propositions they perceived in the program, while young trainee managers thought the show had a heavy pro-union bias and were opposed to its alleged socialist slant. (This reflects the common audience perception called "hostile media bias," wherein partisans perceive media as hostile toward their own viewpoint. The protest banners cited previously, as well as the frontispiece to this book, colorfully convey this perception.)

The encoding/decoding model and the *Nationwide* study had profound impacts on audience research and invigorated debates about how much autonomy people might (or might not) have in interpreting news messages. Morley and Brunsdon's study is "regarded as the closest attempt to show the many meanings that can be made from television news," according to Elizabeth Bird. Her comment alludes to a phenomenon called "polysemy" in which one text can be interpreted in diverse ways by people who bring their own identities, experiences, and personal knowledge to their experiences of media.[5] In other words, audiences are not uniformly dominated, persuaded, or manipulated by ideological messages that elite media professionals might (or might not) send the public intentionally (or unintentionally) through news stories.

However, Morley's assumption that he was singularly able to decode the preferred meaning is problematic. How could he know whether producers "really" wanted *Nationwide* to support right-wing ideas or socialist ones? Indeed, how could he determine that the program had a single, fixed meaning at all? If an analyst takes polysemy seriously, he or she cannot assert that a news story "really" has a single meaning—which would be proposing monosemy, as Russell Neuman reasoned. Also troubling was the assumption that viewers would not be able to detect the intended meaning. Morley himself found fault in the ways he had chosen to (1) establish a preferred reading with which to compare alternative ones, (2) overemphasize class in relation to other social factors, and (3) neglect the conceptual frameworks that respondents themselves used in making sense of the program.[6] He observed that the "so-called oppositional responses of audiences cannot be left to stand alone; moments of apparent opposition and resistance at the site of reception need to be placed into other social contexts in order to assess their real power."[7]

Morley ultimately questioned the usefulness of dominant ideology theory. In this view, the news is de facto produced by capitalist owners and commercial advertisers; journalists are just promoting elite interests, whether they know it or not. Many scholars interested in political empowerment, as Hall and Morley were, professed that readers have some power to accept or reject the ideological domination of mainstream journalism. Nonetheless, they viewed the ideology in news so forceful (or audiences so easily manipulated) that most people could not resist decoding these messages in the preferred way.

Some go farther in criticizing the encoding/decoding model. Notable among detractors are Nick Abercrombie and Brian Longhurst, who saw the incorporation/resistance paradigm as reducing the complex phenomenon of news interpretation to a matter of reinforcing or opposing dominant ideologies.[8] The IRP overlooks other significant dimensions of audience interpretive experiences beyond meaning—such as emotional responses and physical pleasures.[9] Abercrombie and Longhurst proposed a contrasting "Spectacle/Performance Paradigm" incorporating Erving Goffman's 1959 insight that social interaction entails people to continually present themselves to others—in effect, to perform.[10]

Another critical response to encoding/decoding was offered by Kim Christian Schrøder and his colleagues, who thought that Hall's theory held "a canonical status far beyond what is warranted by its modest intentions, complete lack of empirical foundation for its argument, and the political narrowness of its Marxist perspective."[11] He argued that a *preferred reading* was not a master interpretation of a media text but rather a property or product of the audience. Schrøder proposed an alternative model of media reception that captures complex factors beyond ideology (the only element in encoding/decoding theory) when analyzing qualitative audience data.[12] His model includes dimensions of reading such as *comprehension, discrimination, position*, and *motivation*. This framework allows for the possibilities that audiences might understand (or not) a news story, might recognize (or not) a news story's social constructedness—for example, that producers have particular intentions and motives—and might (or might not) take a position such as accepting or rejecting the viewpoint that they perceive in the story.

The audience position isn't necessarily fixed or binary, Schrøder said; it can vacillate between accepting and rejecting the producers' stance. Viewers who accept the perceived stance "normally do so unawares: their response appears not to be based on careful deliberation," he observed. By contrast, viewers who reject the producers' perceived stance are bound to consciously realize it, Schrøder says, because "the very recognition of attitudinal difference produces an awareness of the power relations inherent in communication: the existence and struggle of conflicting perceptions of social and cultural phenomena." It is in this latter dimension of news interpretation, position, that the possibility of oppositional and resistant readings lies.

From Ideological Manipulation to Semiotic Freedom, and Back Again

Qualitative studies of media audiences were hot in the 1980s and 1990s. In that era, empirical reception research was "uniformly motivated by a desire to empower media audiences and explore ways in which audiences already possessed empowering potential," theorists have said.[13] Such studies tended to conclude that audiences were critical consumers of media who produced oppositional decodings, often by reference to alternative frames of understanding.[14] The pendulum swung from considering audiences to be dopes or dupes controlled by the media establishment—as many Marxists and critical scholars from the Frankfurt School and the early Birmingham School, such as Hall and Morley, were (and are) wont to do—to recognizing people as agents with the potential to resist domination.

Cultural studies scholars such as Bird, John Fiske, Henry Jenkins, and Janice Radway conducted in-depth studies exploring how audiences made their *own* meanings from the media texts they watched and read. Of these, Fiske is most closely associated with theories about audiences' resistant interpretations and uses of media. With an emphasis on fictional entertainment over nonfiction genres like news, he proposed that audiences found pleasure in resisting and "playing" with TV texts. Viewers were not victims of domination, he said, but rather participants in a *semiotic democracy* with relative freedom to "rewrite" TV texts to their own liking. To him, television was a more semiotically democratic form of media than others: "The pleasure and the power of making meanings, of participating in the mode of representation, of playing with the semiotic process—these are some of the most significant and empowering pleasures that TV has to offer."[15]

Fiske's influential work inspired a legion of scholars, including Jenkins, who studied fan audiences that literally rewrote popular-media texts such as Star Trek to create their own slash fiction, fan zines, and "filk" music.[16] (Filk is a folk-inflected genre spawned by science fiction, fantasy, and horror fans.) Along with Ien Ang and others, Jenkins was critical of the IRP that viewed audiences as chumps being brainwashed into accepting mainstream worldviews. Such research has unearthed and celebrated hidden creativity and resistance among media audiences, stressing their power to play with texts and construct their own meanings. For instance, Jenkins' work revealed the imagination of Star Trek enthusiasts who used the show as source material for both making their own media and creating their own subcultural communities. He also noted that fans' resistant readings occurred within rather than outside the framework provided by the program, suggesting that their interpretations were constrained and not fully autonomous.[17]

Even when scholars acknowledge the limits placed on audience freedom, others sometimes overlook those caveats. Another example is Radway, whose book *Reading the Romance* explained how some romance-novel readers used books of this oft-disparaged genre in liberating ways: to protest and escape patriarchal culture. The women in her interpretive community described the act of romance reading as a "declaration of independence" from their self-abnegating, other-directed roles as wives and mothers. Though often cited as evidence of audience resistance, Radway's work also suggests boundaries to her readers' contestation. She recognized that the act of reading romances provided a release valve that helped these women cope with patriarchal culture, that reinforced and capitulated to the practices and beliefs from which they sought temporary escape, without doing anything to alter their reality.

Bird's book *For Enquiring Minds*, a cultural study of supermarket tabloid readers, provides another useful counterexample. She found that people liked sensationalist papers such as the *National Enquirer* because these publications fed existing narratives and reassured readers that their own lives were better than those of the rich and famous. Such interpretations supported the status quo of income inequality rather than challenging it; why pursue social change to alter wealth distribution, when more money will likely make you less happy? As Bird concluded, we should be wary of assumptions that merely consuming news content empowers audiences to resist cultural subordination in their daily lives.[18]

Indeed, a systematic review of qualitative audience research offers at least as much evidence that people consent to dominant media frameworks as it does that they resist those frameworks.[19] The facts of audiences being active and of texts being ambiguous do not necessarily diminish media's influence; those realities might "simply make that influence more complex and diffuse."[20] It goes without saying that media producers do have substantial power to influence how audiences interpret content.[21] A notable example is Andy Ruddock's focus groups with members of a local church who demonstrated frustration with—not quite opposition or resistance to—the U.S. news program *Nightline*.[22] He found that viewers' ability to interpret the news in resistant ways was constrained by the content of the news text as well as by their information environments. People said they wanted and needed more information so that they might reach an informed opinion about current events depicted in the news.

Cultural studies analysts long dominated the canon of audience research, but a tight focus on them obscures a longer, more diverse history of reader-reception studies. Until recently, many communication scholars overlooked strong commonalities and convergent findings between studies in the field's humanistic and media-effects traditions.[23] Yet earlier pioneers such as Elihu Katz and his colleagues generated important insights about resistant readings well before the 1980s–1990s heyday of reception work. Katz and Paul Lazarsfeld were early advocates of the notions that media power was overstated and that audiences were active, critical, autonomous actors who respond to communications in different ways, depending on their prior beliefs, attitudes, and social networks.[24] In the 1955 book *Personal Influence*, they portrayed society as a honeycomb of small groups able to resist elite domination and media control through interpersonal communication with friends, family, and coworkers. Their body of work challenges common misperceptions that social scientists ignored culture until the field of cultural studies emerged. Active audience theory was not quite the disruption of past communication scholarship that some imagined it to be.

In the 1970s, Katz preceded James Carey in criticizing the transportation model of communication that conceived of messages as moving in one direction: from media producers to their audiences. He saw media's influence as permeating culture rather than existing as an independent variable that could be identified, tracked, and measured. In the 1980s, he observed that meanings were created through interactions between audiences and content—that polysemous media messages offer multiple possible interpretations while also circumscribing the individual's power to choose among those meanings. By 1990, Katz viewed the relationship between audiences and media as circular and systemic.[25] Like Carey and others, he saw media playing a ritual role in binding social groups together and sustaining collective identities.

In a landmark study exploring global popularity of the U.S. television series *Dallas*, Katz and Tamar Liebes showed that Israeli responses to the soap opera were powerfully influenced by viewers' disparate cultural frameworks and social experiences.[26] Recent settlers from the USSR concentrated on ideological themes and leitmotifs in the program; Kibbutzniks responded to it primarily in psychoanalytical terms; and Moroccan Jews and Arab Israelis focused on its linear, sociological narrative. The scholars also found long-term cultural impacts of media use such as fostering or weakening national identities, promoting or undermining integration into political systems, and advancing or delaying social change.[27] Katz and Liebes took from this study a relatively optimistic lesson that social groups are able to resist cultural colonization through television by calling upon collective resources.

Other scholars of political communication and media sociology have helped illuminate how audiences actively interpret the news by interweaving its content with their own life experiences, political beliefs, and popular wisdom. William Gamson analyzed how people constructed and negotiated shared meanings of a newscast using their own, natural vocabulary.[28] His work identified "issue framing" as the factor that invoked audiences to accept or reject the news; some journalistic frames resonated with audience sensibilities while others did not. Especially intriguing for our purposes is the fact that his discussants interpreted the news through frames that weren't even featured in the stories they watched; viewers drew on frames from elsewhere in their experiences beyond the news. With Marion Just and Ann Crigler, Neuman also explored differences between the news frames spontaneously invoked by audiences and the analysts' own perception of the producers' intended framing.[29] Discussants in their audience groups ignored prominent stories deemed irrelevant to their lives while expressing deep concern about issues barely addressed in news coverage. Viewers rarely framed public issues as political conflicts or competitions, even when a news story had done so. They also frequently framed news issues as moral lessons about good and evil, a subjective approach that journalists almost always eschewed as unprofessional.

By the turn of the millennium, these scholars and a host of others had amply demonstrated that audiences are active, critical agents who make sense of mediated messages rather than simply ingesting them. These landmark studies depict people drawing upon information and cultural resources from their personal lives as they interpret media content in complex, sophisticated, contradictory, and sometimes subversive ways.

The Puzzle of Polysemy

As a result of such groundbreaking work, scholars now accept the notion of a *polysemous* or *polyvalent* news text—that media messages are open, ambiguous, underdetermined, and thus can be (and are) interpreted in many different ways. Polysemy is a property of openness or ambiguity in a media text that allows readers to interpret the text's meaning in a range of ways. It is a fundamental characteristic of human communication that remains, in the words of Russell Neuman, something of a "structural puzzle" for scholars of communication.

Polysemy is particularly puzzling in regard to the genre of journalism, which practically begs audiences to use extratextual resources and interpretive strategies. News is "almost by definition incoherent. It is a daily sampling of a rushing flow of occurrences and observations, which has no beginning and no end," journalism historian David Nord wrote. "Readers must find (create, actually) coherence through connection, interpolation, and inference."[30] Indeed, the information provided in a single news story is usually insufficient for audiences to make sense of what is happening, so they must fill in the gaps with their own knowledge, beliefs, and experiences.

The polysemous quality of news stories was ably demonstrated by John Corner and Kay Richardson's analysis of audience responses to a BBC documentary about being out of work. Viewers with firsthand experience of unemployment reported feeling more sympathetic toward jobless people featured in the program than did viewers who had never been unemployed.[31] This audience attributed manipulative motives to producers and perceived "intended" meanings in contrary ways; some thought the documentary showed approval of the government's unemployment policies, while others thought it criticized those policies. In addition, the viewers mused about how other, absent people—for example, "my mother" or "people from Basingstoke"—might interpret the news program.[32] Viewers' interpretations drew upon "their own social knowledge of what might be 'true' to speculate on what was *not* shown, what audiences were *not* told," Corner and Richardson explained. Many viewers assumed other people lacked extratextual access to sufficient information—in this case, about unemployment—to interpret the news "correctly." The researchers called these interpretations "displaced readings," an ideal type that supplements Hall's classification.

Another study involving unemployment narratives helps illustrate the extent to which a TV newscast can be ambiguous and confusing. When a story about unemployment on the British program *News at Ten* neglected to give data on the number of "jobs created" and "jobs lost," people critical of the government asserted this absent statistic as proof that unemployment was spreading, while government sympathizers suggested jobless numbers must have gone down.[33] On the basis of such findings, Justin Lewis concluded that the narrative structure of news, rooted in newspapers, transfers poorly from print journalism to the televisual medium. He deemed televised news an "ideological octopus"— an apt and evocative metaphor for polysemy.[34]

We need to better understand the sometimes dramatic variances in interpretation of complex mediated messages among audience members—both the central tendencies of responses and the conditions under which responses vary. This means analyzing the "structure of variations" in audience-constructed meanings as well as the social, cultural, economic, and political factors that influence those variations. Both social sciences and cultural studies acknowledge the importance of institutions that create mass-mediated messages, though neither pays enough attention to them. Many questions are empirical: how does a particular media depiction at a particular historical moment generate a mixture of preferred and oppositional responses? What are the historical and structural conditions of acceptance and resistance? The answer is "rarely a dichotomous either-or of acceptance or resistance," per Neuman, "but almost always a culturally rich, polysemic distribution of views and interpretations."

While scholarship on textual polysemy and audience resistance has received extensive attention, it has also garnered criticism. One objection points to an elision of polysemy and opposition, which are related but theoretically distinct processes. Schrøder describes polysemy as a "multiplicity of meanings that arises all the time from encounters with media content, usually without the individual's conscious awareness." By contrast, opposition to a perceived textual position in media content is less frequent and cannot happen without the audience member's conscious awareness. "[Opposition] necessarily occurs in the face of a position that one acknowledges and then rejects," he said. "An oppositional reading is thus what Corner calls 'an active, aware reading *against* the rhetorical grain of the text'."[35]

Corner, Celeste Condit, Kevin Carragee, Robert McChesney, and others have found the prevalent work on resistant and oppositional readings to be unsatisfying.[36] Corner viewed Hall's encoding/decoding model as mixing together elements of comprehension and evaluation that needed to be disentangled, as Schrøder later attempted to do. Condit and Carragee suggested that most texts have stable meanings that are perfectly clear to most readers; they argued that interpretations differ mainly because audiences judge texts through the lenses of their own values and interests. McChesney, for his part, thought analysts blunted the critical edge of U.S. cultural studies tradition by focusing on audience resistance and neglecting the problematic political-economic structures of mainstream institutions that produce news.[37]

Fiske, in particular, has been accused of presenting a romantic and populist vision of semiotic freedom. Detractors said he took democracy too lightly by considering it the context of pleasure, play, and entertainment such as Madonna songs, video games, soap operas, and game shows. For decades, his arguments were often oversimplified and misrepresented to the point that people tend to portray him as an "evil 'Pied Piper'" who led audience scholars astray.[38] Some argued that semiotic "pseudo-power" gives a false sense of viewers' agency disconnected from their actual ability to affect change in the world—and might even distract audiences from efforts to gain "real" power. (Let's recall Bird's finding about romance readers.) This attitude risks underestimating Fiske's significant contributions to our understanding of media audiences. To such flak, Fiske responded that we should not underestimate the extent to which subjective interpretations can foster political identities. He thought the power to construct media meanings, pleasures, and identities—though ultimately "autonomous"—was closely related to political, economic, and social power.[39] Resistant readings "do not translate directly into oppositional politics of social action," he said, but "the absence of a direct political effect does not preclude a more general political effectivity."[40] In other words, resistant meanings should be considered not apolitical but rather, at a minimum, pre-political.

If Fiske tended to downplay ideological domination in favor of semiotic freedom, others have certainly erred in the direction of overplaying it. In the end, the choice is not, as Morley puts it, a binary one between (1) "the politics of false consciousness" where powerful media always dupe the vulnerable masses and (2) "all audiences everywhere" constantly producing oppositional readings of media. While audiences do not exercise their interpretive power over media meanings in an ideal democratic context—we don't get to "vote" for whatever meanings we want, from an infinite roster—it's not a dictatorship, either.

Between and Beyond Media Texts

Another useful concept Fiske discussed is *intertextuality*, the idea that we make sense of a media text not from its content alone but also in relation to other information, conversations, and personal experiences. (It also embraces the idea that media producers create texts that explicitly or implicitly refer to other media texts, as anyone who has watched *The Simpsons* or *BoJack Horseman* will know.) When we watch a TV show, or use any media product, we don't interpret its messages in isolation and take them at face value. When we interpret a media experience, our minds conjure up an amorphous amalgam of information, memories, and fabrications derived from stories, radio programs, social media, dreams, discussions, blog posts, advertisements, opinion polls, press releases, commentary, criticism, interpersonal communication, gossip, music, even Internet memes. Thanks to a mental phenomenon called "source amnesia," we often recall bits of information without remembering where they came from and how credible those sources were.

"Context" is an apt word for describing these intermingled factors. The term derives from the Latin roots *con*, "together," and *texere*, "to weave." Interpreting a media text means weaving together extratextual meanings from other experiences to create a fabric of understanding. Every texture is unique, although disparate fabrics often share patterns. Experience with alternative media is one contextual factor that enables or constrains interpretations of news content. Other factors include the words and images in the news text, the cultural climate that shaped it, our level of comprehension and educational capital, preexisting belief and tastes, socioeconomic class, other demographic factors, and our degree of experience with and level of dependency on mainstream media.

People who are less dependent on mainstream news sources are more prone to criticize journalism's portrayals of social reality, research shows. When exploring audience reception of a news story about a miners' strike in Britain, Greg Philo followed a similar methodology to the *Nationwide* study. He found that viewers who rejected mainstream news coverage of the event had direct experience of the strike, were personally acquainted with participants, or had access to alternative sources of information.[41] In her research on news reception in Greece, Mirca Madianou observed a "discursive oscillation" between the interpretations of more critical viewers—who had alternative resources, including foreign-language media, for learning about world events—and those dependent on mainstream sources, who found it more difficult to challenge the news.[42]

In the absence of a competing narrative or personal experience that contradicts mainstream news content, the ability of audiences to produce oppositional readings is much less than a semiotic democracy, according to Bird.[43] (Then again, democracy is often much less than a democracy, too. Voters can only choose from the menu of candidates offered, according to electoral systems designed to quickly narrow options, if they are not felons and have registered in advance and can submit their ballot to the appropriate place during a limited time frame.) Audiences have some power over their interpretation of the news but cannot compete with what Morley called the "discursive power of centralized media institutions to construct the texts"[44]—paralleling concerns about domination voiced by critical scholars like Hall and McChesney as well as Theodor Adorno and Max Horkheimer.

By building on this profound body of empirical and theoretical insights, we can better understand the social contexts and structural conditions that foster audience interpretive agency, as well as those that limit semiotic freedom. We know that news texts are interpreted in multiple fashions and that audiences construct different readings—some critical, some less so—in accord with their social positions, political identities, and cultural contexts. In other words, we know that audiences are active. It is also well established that some audiences are more active than others. Yet empirical evidence remains lacking as to how those more active audiences arrive at oppositional readings of news and what intertextual and extratextual resources they draw on to construct those resistant interpretations. That's what the first phase of my study investigated.

Taking Cues From the Reception Canon

My research looked at the conditions under which those texts are accepted more or less at face value and those under which they are opposed in various ways by various groups. This makes it somewhat unusual. Even in traditions that, like cultural studies, revere reception studies grounded in real-world interactions with actual audiences, research that moves beyond critique of mainstream media texts is "extremely rare," Neuman noted. The work of Morley, Radway, Liebes, and Katz is "inevitably cited, universally praised, and extensively commented upon in the cultural studies literatures but almost never imitated," for reasons I have elucidated elsewhere. Taking Hall seriously, Neuman said, means "moving out from documenting once again the perceived inauthenticity of . . . cultural depictions they have dutifully recorded and analyzed and move into the field to assess the contours of real-world polysemy."[45]

A quick word on "conceptual hygiene," as Schrøder called it. Like many researchers, I use the terms "reader reception" and "media ethnography" almost interchangeably. Strictly speaking, reader reception usually refers to in-depth interview-based studies of how people "think out loud" as they interpret the content of a specific media product (like a TV program or magazine) or genre (like romance novels or fanzines); this research takes place not in "natural" contexts of informants' daily lives but in social situations that are, at best, quasi-realistic. Media ethnography usually refers to studies embedded in people's normal, everyday lives that are based on participant observation, supplemented by interviews; it resembles the work of cultural anthropologists who immerse themselves in a situated group to observe and participate in local practices. In reality, however, this strain of research frequently combines the two approaches as well as various other qualitative and quantitative methods. Thus, reader reception and media ethnography are not mutually exclusive categories. While I value the distinction and rate my own research closer to the reception end of the scale, I alternate between the two terms in this book.

This study incorporated a range of techniques from cultural studies, media sociology, and political communication. In designing this research, I made several key decisions. First, I recruited participants at the aforementioned protest, considering this a sure way to find people who consumed a substantial amount of alternative media. (This resembled Gamson's method of approaching people in public areas like malls and asking them to participate in his study.) Second, I met with informants in small groups, with the expectation that these conversations would be more productive and more naturalistic than talking one-on-one. Third, I started the group sessions by watching a TV news show together to provide a concrete, shared experience with media that would stimulate conversation.[46] (In the interest of brevity, I removed commercials from the show— which would have interesting implications for our conversations. More on that to come.) Fourth, I conducted similar focus groups with college students, who watched the same program with me, to provide a basis for comparison with the alternative-media users' interpretations. Fifth, I asked participants to keep a journal of their media consumption and mediated communication for one week to get a sense of the discursive resources—alternative media, mainstream news, interpersonal conversations, and so forth—upon which they drew in interpreting and discussing the program.

Because my primary method was focus-group interviews, the data and findings reported in the following chapters should be considered jointly constructed by the discussants and me. I wanted these activists to see me as a collaborator who shared their interests rather than an intruder in the lives; to that end, I conducted sessions in my home. With these group interactions, I created an opportunity to document complex processes through which alternative-media enthusiasts expressed, negotiated, and applied communal norms and meanings. The open-ended interviews helped educe not only their opinions and experiences but also the linguistic terms and categories through which they understood and defined their own media practices. I hoped the group discussions would produce unpredictable insights that would enrich my analysis, so I tried to let discussants describe things their way, with a minimum of direction.[47]

This phase of the study comprised two group interviews with students and seven group interviews with alternative-media users, with four or five participants (plus me) in each group. The student groups included a total of 24 undergraduates, aged 18–22, from a selective liberal-arts college near Philadelphia, PA.[48] While bright and diligent, most of the students showed negligible interest in and knowledge about the current events and sociopolitical issues portrayed in the newscast.[49] The students consumed information from a narrow range of mainstream sources—similar to the U.S. population as a whole, with comparably low levels of exposure to news, according to their media diaries. Because the students reported not following the news regularly, they represented not quite the "average" or representative *news* audience (which is significantly older, with the median viewer age of network news around 60) but rather an "ordinary" or typical *media* audience, in the sense that traditional journalism sources accounted for a relatively small proportion of their overall consumption, which leaned toward entertainment and tabloid-style news. This student audience resembled other under-40 adults nationwide in attending to media generally more so than to news specifically.

The second group comprised 24 self-described and de facto alternative-media users, most of whom lived in the Philadelphia media market and had access to similar regional news sources. I recruited them by attending the demonstration described earlier, introducing myself to strangers, and telling them about the project. I approached people of various ages, genders, and ethnicities involved with a range of causes: political, environmental, feminist, anarchist, and so forth—judging by shirts, hats, badges, banners, and other material signifiers. I gave everyone a flyer describing the research and solicited e-mail addresses or phone numbers from 30 people, whom I later contacted. Fifteen of those original prospects were subsequently available and agreed to participate, with a token financial incentive for their time and effort; nine additional informants got involved through invitations shared with activist discussion groups, the Philadelphia Independent Media Center (aka Indymedia), and a local student environmental action group, as well as through referrals. A few of them brought a friend.[50] Recruitees included people advocating for welfare rights, peace, ecological protection, and the like; a few not attending under the banner of any group; as well as a legal observer, a volunteer photographer, a pastor, and some atheism proponents.

This audience aggregation was involved in a wide range of liberal causes, as depicted earlier. Some issues and groups with which they were particularly active included women's healthcare and abortion rights, separation of church and state, the Religious Society of Friends (aka Quakers), human rights and peace coalitions, a local anarchist bookshop, grassroots organizing, Indymedia, and climate-change action. In our discussions, participants labeled their political orientations as "leftist," "democratic," "liberal," "radical," and, less often, "progressive." Most of the time, however, they referred to themselves as "activists,"— that is, in terms of participatory action rather than political disposition.

As a group, the alternative-media devotees were somewhat older, and perhaps more knowledgeable about how the world works and about how the media work than the other group. Sixteen of them were in their twenties or younger, four were in their thirties, two were in their forties, and two were 60.[51] These engaged citizens were a "most-likely" case: both most likely to interpret the meanings of mainstream news in a critical or resistant manner and most likely to consume alternative news sources that informed their opposition. According to self-reports, they attended to both mainstream and alternative media at a higher rate than either the students or the population at large, as Chapter 8 will probe in detail. The interview format gave me access to the criteria, distinctions, linguistic terms, and categories through which alternative-media enthusiasts defined and understood their own practices and decisions. The open-ended approach let them narrate how they experienced, felt, and reasoned about mainstream media with a minimum of direction.

My hunch was that students would take the mainstream news program at face value, finding its verbal and visual discourse to be a more or less accurate representation of political and social life. By contrast, I expected the alternative viewers to construct a critical interpretation that disputed claims made in mainstream news by referring to information they had gathered from alternative media, as well as insights gained from personal experiences such as participating in protests and talking with other activists. You might say that I was expecting discussants to employ a transmission mode of communication rather than a ritual one. My hypothesis was confirmed, but not quite in the way I had anticipated.

Sources and Voices of Resistance

In essence, the first part of this study examined whether and, if so, how an activist audience using alternative media created an oppositional or resistant meaning of the news, while students using mainstream news constructed a preferred one—that is, one aligning closely to the meanings apparently intended by producers. I took a different approach than Morley did to establish a basis for contrasting how different audience groups responded to the news. Instead of evaluating reader insights against my own perception of what the news was "supposed" to mean, I aimed to explain interpretive differences through a cross-case analysis using two sets of structural conditions. This entailed constructing an "ordinary" rather than a preferred reading for news. Instead of taking extratextual factors for granted, I collected diaries logging participants' media use and communication activities to map more fully their social knowledge and cultural resources. As expected, alternative media constituted a significant chunk of their information diets.

I had anticipated that the alternative fans' critique of news would rely on *bias* and *inaccuracy*, principles common among liberal claims that mainstream media distort or omit crucial information.[52] That was not what happened, as the following chapters illustrate. Instead of simply looking for contradictions and omissions, they displayed a sophisticated understanding of media representations that went beyond comparing the "facts" presented in this televised news program with the "facts" they had learned from alternative media or acquired in their lives pursuing social change. They not only analyzed the content of the news but also criticized the structural conditions of production, where they sometimes saw conspiratorial forces at work that resulted in a kind of structural censorship. Akin to Corner and Richardson's viewers, this alternative-media audience attributed manipulative motives to producers and formed displaced readings about the interpretations that absent viewers might have. The following chapters illustrate not just *that* people decode news texts in resistant ways but also *how* they do it.

In addition to sharing my analysis, interpretations, and findings about these alternative-media users and their resistance to mainstream news, I am providing a great deal of my informants' own discourse. This contributes to remedying an underrepresentation of audience voices in extant scholarship on news generally and alternative media specifically.[53] Nick Couldry proposes that we are amid a crisis of voice, where human beings are treated as if they were not able "give an account of themselves and of their place in the world."[54] Our political, economic, and cultural domains are organized in ways that ignore people's voices or assume they do not matter. When scholars do attend to media audiences, they tend to translate informants' ideas into their own words rather than letting people speak for themselves.[55] By contrast, qualitative audience research strives to offer people a voice in research. Talking with informants reveals the linguistic terms and categories through which people understand their own activities. This discursive approach is well suited for investigating polysemy. Clifford Geertz famously described it as "thick description" from the "native's" point of view—which is, of course, the analyst's own interpretation and representation of informants' representations of how they interpret their own cultural activities. My research addresses, to boot, how informants represent their interpretations of other people's cultural activities. Turtles all the way down.

The alternative-media users who participated in this study were highly media-aware and politically aware—not ordinary readers and viewers but rather news fans, as well as critics. Alternative-media fans are a skilled subculture of news audiences with technical, analytical, and interpretive abilities relevant to the consumption, processing, sharing, and creation of news content.[56] John Downing called such people "in a sense the most active segment of the so-called 'active audience.'"[57] These audiences enact agency in several senses, following Henry Jenkins' explication: in their reception of media texts, in their interpretive practices, in their production of alternative texts, and in building alternative communities.[58] My informants fit this bill: they actively selected media to consume (and, importantly, not to consume), actively interpreted those media, actively produced media of their own, and actively created communities of like-minded people. This profile contrasts markedly with broader depictions of a disengaged, apathetic public that resist news by tuning out and avoiding it.

The conversations shared in the following chapters will convey the richness and subtlety of human communication about news, mediated politics, and popular culture. They demonstrate how people arrive at resistant readings, including through games of interpretation and strategies of emotional detachment from the news. You will see evidence not just that news stories are ambiguous, polysemous, and confusing but also that some audience members recognize them as such. You will learn how some people describe themselves as being simultaneously vulnerable and resistant to the manipulative and persuasive techniques that they see in mainstream news. You will hear how some people distinguish themselves from so-called ordinary viewers and why they feel alternative media gives them superlative interpretive resources. In their own words, audience members explain why they prefer and trust alternative media more than mainstream media.

Fiske considered audiences to be "already equipped with the discursive competencies to make meanings and motivated by pleasure to want to participate in the process."[59] The next chapter shares my comparative analysis of these two groups' responses to an episode of ABC's *World News Tonight*, which partially supports this perspective. The good news is: some viewers are equipped with the extratextual resources, social experience, and training necessary to acquire discursive competences for understanding, evaluating, and taking a critical stance on mainstream journalism. The bad news is: some viewers are not.

Notes

1 This U.S. antiwar rally in Philadelphia, PA, was one of more than 600 demonstrations held in cities around the world in late 2003–early 2004, when tens of millions of people protested the U.S. invasion of Iraq. The event took place amid both a Sunoco-sponsored "America's Birthday" celebration and a gala opening of the new National Constitutional Center in that city.

2 That slogan is featured in the frontispiece illustration of this book.

3 Stuart Hall, "Encoding and Decoding in the Television Discourse," edited version published in *Culture, Media, Language,* eds. Stuart Hall et al. (London: Hutchinson, 1980[1973]).

4 David Morley and Charlotte Brunsdon, *Everyday Television* (London: British Film Institute, 1978); David Morley, *The Nationwide Audience* (London: British Film Institute, 1980).

5 S. Elizabeth Bird, "Seeking the Audience for News," in *The Handbook of Media Audiences,* ed. Virginia Nightingale (New York: Wiley-Blackwell, 2014).

6 David Morley, "The Nationwide Audience," *Screen Education* 39 (1981). Morley's work since the *Nationwide* study has paid much more attention to context; see David Morley, *Television, Audiences, and Cultural Studies* (London: Routledge, 1992). For more reappraisal of that work, see Mark Dworkin et al., "Sense-making and Television News," *The Electronic Journal of Communication / La Revue Electronique de Communication* 9, nos. 2, 3, 4 (1999).

7 Quoted in Andy Ruddock, "Scientific Criticism?" *Atlantic Journal of Communication* 6, no. 1 (1998).

8 Nick Abercrombie and Brian Longhurst, *Audiences* (London: Sage, 1998).

9 Andy Ruddock provides ample discussion of the Incorporation/Resistance Paradigm and the Spectacle/Performance Paradigm in *Understanding Audiences* (London: Sage, 2001). He notes that Morley preempted much subsequent criticism in his 1981 [1992] postscript.

10 Erving Goffman, *The Presentation of Self in Everyday Life* (Garden City, NY: Anchor Books, 1959).

11 Catherine Murray et al., *Researching Audiences* (London: Bloomsbury, 2003).

12 Kim Christian Schrøder, "Making Sense of Audience Discourses," *European Journal of Cultural Studies* 3, no. 2 (2000). His model also features two "implication" dimensions, *evaluation,* and *implementation,* not employed here.

13 Catherine Murray et al., *Researching Audiences,* 136–7.

14 For example, see Ien Ang, *Watching Dallas* (London: Metheun, 1985); Philip Drummond and Richard Paterson (eds.), *Television and Its Audience* (London: British Film Institute, 1988); Dorothy Hobson, *Crossroads* (London: Methuen; 1982); Klaus Jensen, *Making Sense of the News* (Aarhus, Denmark: Aarhus University Press, 1986); and James Lull (ed.), *World Families Watch Television* (Newbury Park, CA: Sage, 1988).

15 John Fiske, *Television Culture* (New York: Routledge, 1987), 239.

16 Henry Jenkins, *Textual Poachers* (New York: Routledge, 1992).

17 Jenkins, *Textual Poachers,* 263.

18 S. Elizabeth Bird, *For Enquiring Minds* (Knoxville: University of Tennessee Press, 1992).

19 Ann Gray, "Reading the Audience," *Screen* 28 (1987).

20 Justin Lewis et al., "Images of Citizenship on Television News," *Journalism Studies* 5, no. 2 (2004): 68.

21 A good starting point in the large body of work substantiating media influence over audience interpretations is Greg Philo, *Seeing is Believing* (London: Routledge, 1990).

22 Ruddock, "Scientific Criticism?"

23 W. Russell Neuman, *The Digital Difference* (Cambridge, MA: Harvard University Press, 2016).

24 James Curran and Tamar Liebes, *Media, Ritual and Identity* (London: Routledge, 2002); see also Elihu Katz and Paul Lazarsfeld, *Personal Influence* (Abingdon, UK, and New York: Routledge, 2017 [1955]).

25 Daniel Dayan and Elihu Katz, *Media Events* (Cambridge, MA: Harvard University Press, 1992), 225.

26 Tamar Liebes and Elihu Katz, *The Export of Meaning* (Oxford: Oxford University Press, 1991).

27 Dayan and Katz, *Media Events*; Curran and Liebes, *Media, Ritual, and Identity.*

28 William Gamson, *Talking Politics* (Cambridge, UK: Cambridge University Press, 1992).

29 W. Russell Neuman et al., *Common Knowledge* (Chicago, IL: University of Chicago Press, 1992).

30 David Nord, *Communities of Journalism* (Urbana: University of Illinois Press, 2001), 254.

31 John Corner and Kay Richardson, "Documentary Meanings and the Discourse of Interpretation," in *Documentary and the Mass Media*, ed. John Corner (London: Edward Arnold, 1986).

32 Corner and Richardson, "Documentary Meanings."

33 Justin Lewis, *The Ideological Octopus* (New York: Routledge, 1991).

34 Lewis continues the analogy by calling audience research "a messy and slippery business" and comparing interview analysis to "wrestling with a jellyfish: it squirms in so many different directions simultaneously that it seems impossible to control," *Ideological Octopus*, 73, 115.

35 John Corner, "Codes and Cultural Analysis," *Media, Culture, and Society* 2 (1980): 80.

36 Celeste Condit, "The Rhetorical Limits of Polysemy," *Critical Studies in Mass Communication* 6, no. 2 (1989); Kevin Carragee, "Interpretive Media Study and Interpretive Social Science," *Critical Studies in Mass Communication* 7, no. 2 (June 1990); and John Corner, "Meaning, Genre, and Context," in *Mass Media and Society*, eds. John Curran and Michael Gurevitch, 267–84 (London and New York: Arnold, 1991).

37 Robert McChesney, "The Internet and U.S. Communication Policy-Making in Historical and Critical Perspective," *Journal of Communication* 46, no. 1 (1996).

38 David Morley, "Unanswered Questions in Audience Research," *The Communication Review* 9 (2006): 103.

39 Fiske, *Television Culture*, 318.

40 Fiske, *Television Culture*, 326.

41 Philo, *Seeing Is Believing.*

42 Mirca Madianou, "Shifting Identities," in *Discursive Constructions of Identity in European Politics*, ed. Richard Mole (Basingstoke and New York: Palgrave MacMillan, 2007), 114.

43 Bird, "Seeking the Audience for News."

44 Morley, *Television, Audiences, and Cultural Studies.*

45 Neuman, *Digital Difference.*

46 Marion Just et al., took this approach in *Crosstalk* (Chicago, IL: University of Chicago Press, 1996).

47 For more on focus groups and interview methods, see Anders Hansen et al., *Mass Communication Research Methods* (New York: NYU Press, 1998); Robert Merton et al., *The Focused Interview* (New York: Free Press, 1990); Grant McCracken, *The Long Interview* (Newbury Park, CA: Sage, 1988).

48 I recruited the first set of informants by inviting students in two "media and society" classes to participate in the project, with the incentive of extra credit in the course. Everyone over age 18 enrolled in the course was welcome to join the discussion groups, regardless of gender or ethnicity; about half of them chose to do so.

49 The fact that they displayed little political interest or knowledge doesn't necessarily mean that they possessed little; it could mean that to some extent they didn't seek to demonstrate these characteristics to their peers.

50 I also used snowball sampling methods to identify some preexisting audience communities—as Radway and Gray both did Janice Radway, *Reading the Romance* (Philadelphia: University of Pennsylvania Press, 1991); Ann Gray, *Video Playtime* (London: Routledge, 1992).

51 Ninety percent of the 24 activists who joined the study were white, 90 percent were college-educated, 68 percent were under the age of 30, and 55 percent were male.

52 For instance, the nonprofit group Fairness and Accuracy in Reporting (FAIR) publishes newsletters and magazines documenting incidents of media bias and censorship, while researchers at Project Censored publicize an annual list of politically sensitive stories they found to be ignored or underreported by mainstream news.

53 Tony Harcup, *Alternative Journalism, Alternative Voices* (Abingdon, UK, and New York: Routledge, 2013).

54 Nick Couldry, *Why Voice Matters: Culture and Politics After Neoliberalism* (Thousand Oaks, CA: Sage, 2010), 1.

55 Sonia Livingstone, "Giving People a Voice," *Communication, Culture, and Critique* 3 (2010); Tony Harcup, "Asking the Readers," *Journalism Practice* 10, no. 6 (2016).

56 Abercrombie and Longhurst, *Audiences*, 121.

57 John Downing, "Audiences and Readers of Alternative Media," 625.

58 Henry Jenkins, *Textual Poachers: Television Fans and Participatory Culture* (New York: Routledge, 1992).

59 Fiske, *Television Culture*, 9.

3

PARSING DIVERGENT RESPONSES TO MAINSTREAM NEWS

A spokesman for the American Association of Retired Persons said it would help senior citizens.

A Democratic senator said it would treat seniors like guinea pigs and destroy Medicare as we know it.

One academic expert said it would increase the cost of traditional Medicare, while another said most of its funds would go directly to drug-company profits.

"It" was the prescription-drug legislation, intended to cover 40 million senior citizens and disabled people, that was wending its way through Congress when I watched *ABC World News Tonight* with groups of students and alternative-media users. This healthcare reform effort was the lead story in the newscast, which also featured international and national news on a variety of political events and social issues: the war in Iraq; military families' struggles; the granting of prison leave to a would-be assassin; the release of a new birth control pill; the death penalty verdict for a domestic terrorist; and security concerns for a London visit by a U.S. president.

ABC News long used the slogan "More Americans get their news from ABC News than from any other source."[1] Yet the media environment has undoubtedly become more fragmented and audiences more segmented in the 21st century.[2] Ratings for evening news programs like *ABC World News Tonight* declined by almost half in four decades, from 36 percent of the U.S. population in 1970 to 19 percent in 2009.[3] Nonetheless, around 5.2 million Americans still watch the evening news on ABC, CBS, or NBC, in addition to 1.2 million who view CNN, Fox News, or MSNBC during prime time.[4] According to the Pew Research Center, more U.S. adults say TV is their favorite news platform (44 percent), compared with 34 percent who prefer the web, 14 percent who prefer radio, and 7 percent who prefer print. In sum, a plurality of Americans still prefer watching the news on television.

On the night in question, ABC News devoted three minutes to "Rx for Seniors" in an in-depth segment called "A Closer Look." Producers included sound bites or on-camera interviews for the sources listed previously (a lobbyist, a senator, and two experts), along with footage of Congressional Republicans meeting with the U.S. president, of doctors talking to the elderly and helping them into wheelchairs, of senior citizens taking pills and pulling money from their wallets. A series of graphics—accompanied by images of white tablets tumbling out of dispensers, of red pills falling into hands—summarized the benefits, charges, deductibles, maximums, co-payments, means tests, private-competition clauses, and other intricacies of the proposed drug plan.

When I got together with people to talk about the news, we started off by watching the program that featured this Medicare story.[5] Viewing this material together helped engender conversation about mainstream media that was anchored in a concrete, shared experience. The newscast stimulated vigorous discussions in which both students and alternative-media admirers consistently cited the prescription-drug law as one of the most newsworthy items of the day and one of the topics most relevant to their own lives. The legislation seemed so meaningful to both groups that almost all of the 48 participants offered some input to the Medicare discussion, which accounted for nearly a quarter of the total time we spent talking about the news.

In parsing this discourse, I took cues from Kim Christian Schrøder's multidimensional model of news reception.[6] There were three steps in this analysis. First, I compared the degree to which these audience groups were able to understand the information presented in this news story, a dimension that Schrøder calls "comprehension." Next, I compared the degree to which both groups displayed awareness that the news story was not a transparent representation of reality but rather that it was "socially constructed"—the outcome of production processes and choices made by news personnel.[7] This dimension, which takes the form of a continuum from immersion to critical distance, is called "discrimination." Third, I compared the degree to which the two groups appeared to perceive the story as taking a stance on Medicare, a *position* with which they could agree or disagree. (These dimensions do not occur in sequential order, according to Schrøder; they may occur simultaneously, or near simultaneously, and can only be separated analytically.) My analysis reveals substantial differences—and some similarities—between how students and alternative-media enthusiasts made meaning from this news story about Medicare reform.

First, the student groups. In terms of comprehension, students indicated that *they didn't get anything out of it, they got lost, it was too much information at once, the story went over their heads, they were confused, the story didn't make any sense,* and *they had no idea what it meant* (in their words). In terms of discrimination, students discussed socially constructed elements of the program such as time constraints, visual biases, the narrative demands of news, and the storytellers' desire to evoke emotions.[8] In terms of position, students did not perceive the story (or its producers) as taking a position for or against Medicare reform; they deemed the news story *pretty close to fair*. Thus, students did not express any subjective experience of taking a position in agreement or disagreement with the story's perspective.

By comparison, the alternative-media users reported little difficulty comprehending the information in ABC News' coverage of Medicare reform. Like students, alternative viewers discerned time constraints, visual biases, and tendencies toward sensationalism. Both groups interpreted the newscast in terms of professional practices through which journalists socially construct the news. Yet only the alternative group linked the story's shortcomings to the political-economic motives of media producers beholden to a corporate-commercial business model. They compared the news story to *a press release, photo ops*, and *propaganda*, as well as *a game, a video for children*. While alternative viewers recognized producers' attempts to portray a balanced point of view, they nonetheless interpreted the story as favoring the legislation, a stance they opposed.

This chapter shares detailed passages from my conversations with student and alternative news audiences that represent their interpretations of the Medicare story in their own words. We'll look first at how they articulated their comprehension of the news, followed by their interpretive discrimination and positioning vis-à-vis the text. Delving deeper into this discourse will illustrate patterns of variation in the audiences' understandings of the news story, in their awareness of the journalistic processes and constraints influencing the story's construction, and in their ability to oppose the story's perceived position on Medicare reform.

"They're Going to Help Senior Citizens"

Medicare reform might not have ranked as the day's top news story, by virtue of having aired in the middle of the program, but it could be considered the program's main story. Clocking in at three minutes, the report was substantially longer and more comprehensive than any other segment in the half-hour program. Yet comprehensiveness did not equal comprehension in this instance. Despite the producers' apparent intention to cover the subject in depth, most of the students who discussed this news item with me said they could not make much sense of it. Mike, a junior, said, "I got nothing out of that [Medicare story].[9] All I heard was a bunch of statistics, but I have no idea what it means." Jim, a senior, commented, "The story doesn't make any sense." Freshman Adam and sophomore Brandon concurred:

ADAM: The Medicare story is the one that would affect me the most [compared to others in this broadcast], but it's also one of the stories that I understood the least because it went *fwick* [making a noise and gesture signaling "over his head"].

BRANDON: I think it was just too much information, all at one time. They had charts and graphs, and they had little bullets about years and how much it's going to go up and down, and so on and so forth. I got lost after a few seconds.

Ashley, a sophomore, remarked that drug companies would be primary beneficiaries of the plan—an assertion that was reported at several points in the story. First-year student Sharon asked about the private-competition provision, which she didn't understand and wished the program had explained better. The students did not know how to interpret conflicting claims about who will benefit, and how, from the passage of the prescription-drug act. Our conversations indicated that this audience understood the meaning of this story as essentially being about "helping the elderly":

MATT: At first they were talking about how they're going to help senior citizens. And then right at the end they say the people who are going to benefit most are people who do the prescription drugs and the healthcare providers. Yeah, I was confused over the whole thing.

BRANDON: When I first saw it, I thought it was good, that they're trying to help out the elderly. I kind of felt sorry for them, that they didn't have any money to get drugs. It sounded like the government wants to help them, but at the end I was kind of confused. I didn't know whether they were trying to help them or screw them over or what.

Students demonstrated some cynicism toward the political processes featured in the newscast but generally didn't question the prescription-drug plan's stated purpose. For instance, Drayton wondered aloud whether Democrats genuinely opposed the plan or wanted to prevent Republicans from taking credit for it but maintained that the goal of this legislation was helping old people get better access to prescription drugs. "I thought it was interesting how Medicare, all these health issues with the elderly, it seems like the Democrats and Republicans are still going at each other," the junior said. "People are more concerned about politics than about giving the elderly help."

Discussion among the students, who acted confused about the Medicare story, suggested they had few resources outside of this newscast to help them understand the issue. Fauve, a third-year student, said:

I just find it interesting—everyone's been saying social issues like Medicare and prescription pills are the most important and relevant issues to us, to a lot of people in society today—that it's weird because they're not really covered a lot [in the news].

When asked if they've read or watched anything else about this issue, only two students noted having prior exposure to it: a pre-med student who had read some articles for class and a criminal-justice major who had discussed it with a relative who worked for a drug company.

In sum, student discussions of this news coverage hinged on the bill's anticipated outcome of improving senior citizens' access to drugs. This perceived theme reflected the visual and verbal content of the program, which prominently featured images of elderly people needing help and an interview with an AARP spokesperson who said, "We've got millions of people who can't wait for *perfect*. They need help *now*."

Yet this viewpoint represented only one possible interpretation of information provided in the news segment, which featured three other interviews with a Democratic politician and two public-health scholars—all of them skeptical of the proposed law's ability to deliver on its promise. It was those doubtful viewpoints that dominated the alternative interpretation. Viewers in the alternative groups homed in on that criticism, giving the arguments espoused by the Democratic senator and two professors more emphasis in their discussion.

"This Is Definitely *for* the Pharmaceutical Companies"

Unlike the seemingly confused students, alternative-media users acted confident in their comprehension of the news report. Whereas students named Medicare the least informative (though most important) story in the broadcast, the alternative groups deemed it one of the most informative. They not only professed to understand the details of the issue presented in the story but also referred to extratextual information. When asked what the story about prescription drugs was about, both Joe, a legal observer for protests, and Beki, a democratic-globalization activist, contemplated instead what the story *wasn't* about:

JOE: They don't go into the history of how this new legislation was developed: who developed it, who's in favor of it, who's against it. They did manage to say that one big winner is the drug companies, which I thought was good—I mean, I'm happy when I hear a statement like that on the evening news. But if that newscast were all I heard about the new Medicare plan, I wouldn't feel that I knew very much at all about it.

BEKI: Right, there's a complete lack of detail. They had that one thing where they showed [the senator] just saying, "We're using our senior citizens as guinea pigs," but what does that mean? When they brought up the [Senator Ted] Kennedy thing, they showed him as *angry*. It almost seems like they put it in to show "Oh, well, there *is* an opposition, but we don't really know what they're talking about or why they're opposed to anything."

This exchange demonstrated some of the assumptions that underlie the alternative evaluation of news content: that giving audiences an oversimplified or emotional perspective on the world is bad, while providing them with balance, context, and economic analyses is good. Beki's last statement here also showed an interpretive technique, which proved to be common among the alternative news readers, of voicing thoughts attributed to producers, an imagined "they."

The alternative-media users contrasted the claims of people who supported and opposed the Medicare bill in ways that the students did not. For instance, graphic designer Jodi criticized the program for offering a prominent platform for the AARP spokesman to make his case while presenting a Democratic senator's perspective in a five-second sound bite that ignored the substance of his argument. She believed that providing perspectives critical of corporations was essential to creating "balanced" news:

JODI: In comparison to the one little brief clip that I could barely hear of [the senator] shouting, this other guy was like, "People can't wait for perfect." They're not even taking the time to look at the fine print in all this. . . . Still, [the news producers] did preface [the story] in a way that "this is definitely *for* the pharmaceutical companies." I remember that in this segment, and I felt that this segment was more balanced in that way.

After Jodi pointed out the story's acknowledgment of how prescription-drug companies would benefit from the law, environmental-action organizer Jason suggested that the segment nonetheless overlooked the economic interests of private health insurers in Medicare reform. His interpretation stressed again concerns about journalistic balance and about what's missing in the news:

JASON: That's a piece that's been completely removed from the debate about healthcare in this country for several years now. It's extremely complex and it's just unfortunate when I see a piece like that, because I do feel they threw in several different elements that, like Jodi said, make it the more balanced of any we saw. It's the light version because there is so much to that issue, you could read a book about that issue. . . . So much gets left out.

These alternative-media users believed that from watching only this evening newscast, the *soi-disant* "A Closer Look," they would not understand the issue of prescription-drug reform well enough to form a useful evaluation—as, indeed, the students did not.

Because the students' comprehension of the Medicare story depended upon information internal to this newscast, they were not able to construct a clear meaning beyond the simplistic message "helping old people get drugs," which was strongly supported on-screen (especially through images). On the other hand, the alternative group's comprehension of "what the Medicare story means" relied on their conscious recognition of journalism's deficiencies, which compelled them to refer to interpretive resources actually and potentially available through sources external to the program. This broader context led them to construe the news story (and the new law) as favoring drug companies and endorsing Medicare privatization, despite the program's face-value effort to represent opposition.

As this dialogue makes clear, the student viewers were unable to make much sense of the newscast and their interpretations diverged dramatically from those of the alternative viewers. Having examined the comprehension dimension of audience responses to news, let's now turn our attention to discrimination.

"Let's Have Some Guy Get Really Angry"

To view news as socially constructed means recognizing that media content is created by people who work under intense time constraints with high productivity expectations and rely on standardized routines to improve efficiency and meet deadlines. That news producers are members of a profession with ideologies and cultural norms (including objectivity, sourcing routines, a competitive ethos), which often take precedence over the personal ideologies or norms of individuals within the profession. That news is an economic commodity and an industrial product, manufactured in an organizational structure subject to acute financial pressures. That news contains mythic elements and narrative qualities, as well as facts; that it demands telling stories to entertain and engage audiences, as well as to inform them.

Did alternative and student audiences acknowledge, in our discussions, the social constructedness of this ABC News segment about Medicare reform? Did they show an understanding of how the story was produced by people within a system of political, economic, organizational, and other processes that effectively constrained the form and content of that story? To what degree did these groups immerse themselves in or critically distance themselves from the program?

Students and alternative-media users alike talked about how producers assembled the news with a motive of attracting viewers' attention. They mentioned that journalists were in the business of telling stories and that television does so through compelling imagery, close-ups, color, movement, and emotion. Both groups talked about visual bias and sensationalism as routine features of TV news, sometimes due to choices made by producers. One student posed a question that stimulated discussion illustrating this conception:

ADAM: Did anybody think that quote from the . . . I don't remember who said it, but it seemed really out of place: "These seniors are just guinea pigs!" I was just taking my notes and watching and then suddenly. . .

[Several students: Yeah.]

ADAM: It seemed like this excuse to have this attention-getter.

MIKE: It was . . . the congressman from Massachusetts, who's a Democrat. He said, "This is just a test about something and our senior citizens are guinea pigs."

MARISSA: Oh, yeah. I didn't even understand that.

ADAM: Do they really address that, that quote?

[All speak at once.]

MARISSA: No. It's just to make the story negative.

ADAM: It was like, "This is a dry story. . . . Let's have some guy get really angry."

In this dialogue, the students displayed a critical stance by recognizing that news producers chose story elements based on desires to get viewers' attention and to dramatize a dull story, even if those elements did not provide much information. They were constructivists, but in a different way from activists.

The alternative audience echoed the students' view that the newscast aimed not solely to inform but also to entice people to watch and keep watching. They similarly perceived the "angry" clip as fulfilling a sensational function. Jen, who worked with an anarchist collective and prison reading program, and Monique, who volunteered with human-rights organizations, likened the image-driven news program to a game and a children's video, respectively:

JEN: There were a whole couple of minutes where they just showed people's faces, having words coming out of their faces. I thought that was funny. I know there's a lot of emphasis on doing close-ups with people, and interviews with random people. . . . But seeing the words come across the screen it was like, "Is this a game?"

MONIQUE: The pictures tell you all. . . . To me, it seems like a little video for children, when you're watching news, because everything is explained by a picture. The old lady goes to the pharmacy, you see prescription drugs, you see the woman counting the pills. It's so simplistic to me.

Like Monique, Janice thought visuals dumbed down or oversimplified the reporting; nonetheless, she said the only thing she remembered about the story was

the pretty little pills falling down the chute. They didn't really explain how much it affects the seniors and how much more money they will pay for their prescriptions than they do for their lights [electricity], but boy, I sure do remember seeing those pretty little pills falling out of the bottle.

The alternative viewers were not immune to news imagery's emotional power. Liz, for one, said she was saddened by pictures of an old woman buying a gelatin dessert mix and an old man getting helped into a wheelchair. Yet they recognized the segment's use of visuals as a technique to generate negative emotions such as sorrow and fear (along with positive ones, like unintentional humor) that serve sensationalism rather than understanding, much as the students understood its purpose as merely making the story "negative." The following exchange between the legal observer Cody and the peace activist Nick was representative of the group's response to emotional contrivance they saw in the news:

CODY: There was that line where they had [the senator] saying. . . .

NICK: Yeah . . . for 15 seconds, that "it's a social experiment". . .

CODY: Because they have to have something it seems, that's like, "Be afraid of this! Be afraid of this!" in every single story. If they can't say something that you can be afraid of, they show a picture of something that you should be afraid of.

Thus, both the alternative-media users and students said journalists used sensationalism to heighten the dramatic, emotional, and visual appeal of news programs in order to persuade audiences to pay attention. But the alternative group linked these dramatic motives to an aspect of television programming that no student mentioned: the drive for ratings and advertisers.

"Now You Need a Sleeping Pill"

Hearty discussions of the corporate structure of news took place in all the alternative groups, nearly eclipsing other aspects of their responses to the program. While the students discerned some sensational tendencies, they did not discuss connections between the producers' desire to tell compelling stories and the demands of news media's commercial structure: to appeal to large audiences, promote consumerism, satisfy advertisers, and maximize profits.[10] One student, Adam, mentioned that the Medicare segment was "brought to you by [sleeping-pill brand]," referring to a sponsorship graphic unintentionally left on the videotape after I edited out the commercials. He was the only student who commented on the ad, and he did so as an afterthought to our discussion, on his way out the door.

That advertisement for sleep medication did not escape the alternative audience's notice to a similar extent. They built a collective interpretation of that ad based on their belief that in journalism, corporate and commercial motives overshadow partisan and educational ones. Political activist Sarah imagined what thoughts might have passed through the ABC producers' minds when they inserted the ad in the program. She wondered aloud whether they "didn't deliberately put that 'sponsored-by' [graphic] right before the story, just to sort of make clear that 'We know, we know, their money pays for us.'" She thus perceived both TV journalists and their viewers as consciously acknowledging the tension between news and commerce.

Some alternative-media users considered the broadcasters to be in devious collusion with advertisers. When anti-globalization protester Liz called attention to the Medicare story's commercial sponsor, her like-minded friends Ami and Chris found humor in the conflict and congruence of news and advertising interests:

LIZ: As far as how the newscast was being presented, I liked how they advertised for [sleeping-pill brand] in the prescription-drug segment of the newscast.
[Everyone laughs.]

AMI: "Now you need a sleeping pill!" Which is why I thought that was funny.
CHRIS: Yeah. Is this show on late at night? 'Cause if you watch late-night TV sometimes, there are a lot of [sleeping-pill] commercials. You're up late at night, you're like, "Shit, I'm awake!"
LIZ: They use it for anxiety, too. Which is related: you can't sleep 'cause you're anxious. They give you all this bad news, then "Just take a pill, it'll be alright!"
CHRIS: "Just take some [sleep-medication brand]."

To this alternative-media audience, the newscast included an imperative to consume sponsors' products. They could imagine, with an air of jest, that producers selected bad news to foster viewer anxiety and directly addressed audiences in commands: Just take a pill, just take some sleep medication.

Other alternative viewers found the combination of a news story about prescription-drug access with an ad for anti-anxiety pills more troubling than amusing. Both Nick and Fred, an advocate for local currency movements, initially laughed when Cody mentioned the sponsorship, but their conversation quickly turned to how advertising undermined this newscast's credibility in the Medicare story as well as in another segment about the release of a new birth control pill:

FRED: I mean, how critical is the reporting going to be of [a new contraceptive pill], when [a sleeping-pill manufacturer] is one of their sponsors?
CODY: You don't know, maybe it is, but either way it's going to lead me to say, "Well, what *is* that?" Even if it *was* critical, I don't know that I would trust anything that they were saying when one of their advertisers is a drug company.

The commercial model's negative influence on news cropped up again and again in alternative news audience discussions. In talking about prescription-drug coverage, for instance, Jodi went beyond the Medicare segment to suggest that most news and commercials were "the same" because they're both "advertising a lifestyle, or a way of being," in her words. Their structural critique of corporate media drove discussions of how drug-manufacturer sponsorship compromised news portrayals of healthcare insurance and prescription drugs—as well as other items in this broadcast specifically and the prevailing information environment generally.

"They Said It in Tricky Wording"

Students, who took the news story about prescription drugs at close to face value, accepted the position that the reform legislation would achieve its purported goal of improving senior citizens' access to drugs. For example, junior Marissa noted that no one had been helping seniors get prescription drugs and that "now they're doing something about it." Her peer Tom found it encouraging that "they know it's not perfect, but they support it"—referring to the AARP spokesperson, who was the lone voice of support in this newscast— "because something needs to be done right away." Their discourse offered no indication that they consciously recognized agreement between the program's stance and their own viewpoint.

On the other hand, the alternative viewers indicated their knowing rejection of the program's ostensible position when they turned the conversation toward information external to the news segment. Joe judged the report negligent of historical actors and their actions, as already shown. Such critical positioning was also evident when Beki bemoaned the story's lack of detail, when Jason pointed out a piece missing from its debate, and when Jodi suggested it ignored the fine print and that she wouldn't necessarily trust its claims.

Liz, a 21-year-old student, resembled the younger audience grouping in terms of age and occupation. Yet her reflections on the Medicare story aligned closely with the other alternative viewers in her group. She described the position she saw in this newscast—that the legislation was good news for seniors— and contrasted it with her own evaluation of the issue, drawing on knowledge not available within the program:

LIZ: They were showing pictures of senior citizens and really making a connection with the people that are watching this newscast like, "And the Democrats find something *wrong* with it." They weren't saying *what* the Democrats find wrong with it. I know I didn't get it! I was getting good news, good news flashing up about the plan, that "Oh, seniors are going to get this." It wasn't until you thought to yourself: they're privatizing the companies, that means the [private-insurance] guys are going to make more. They mentioned in passing that it'll be direct profits, but they said it in tricky wording that you wouldn't have caught, if you didn't know the vocabulary.

Here, Liz perceived the journalists as taking a position in support of the Republican-backed legislation. She implied that news producers intended to mislead or misinform audiences, because they mentioned this crucial point quickly and in "tricky wording." She suggested that viewers should not rely on what news producers show or say but rather should think to (and for) themselves—a critical act of interpretation in which she and other alternative-media fans found pleasure. Yet a question remains: what is the vocabulary, and how did she acquire it?

Similarly, other alternative viewers recognized and rejected a range of perceived textual stances. According to Nathaniel, the news segment subtly demonized sources who disapproved of the Medicare bill, portraying them as troublemakers trying to "stop seniors from getting their prescription drug benefits. Anyone who has this critical analysis is . . . somehow impeding progress." Beki, too, thought the story took an overly upbeat position toward the legislation. "Some people are acknowledging it might not be perfect, but it's better than nothing so we should accept it," she commented. "That's the gist of it: People who disagree with the plan are just disrupting senior citizens from getting their drugs."

In an analogous vein, Smithy and Ryan both saw and disagreed with a positive spin in the news report. They attributed their ability to reject this position to having consumed information external to the program itself. Smithy, who said he knew from other sources that the AARP was "sold out" on this bill, thought *other* viewers might not be informed enough to interpret the newscast wisely:

SMITHY: From the segment I thought it was built up as a good thing, with a few crumbs thrown in for the appearance of a balanced story. If someone were totally gullible and totally manipulable by media, it would have been a good thing. That's all they were hearing about it for maybe the first 30 seconds.

Smithy seemed to assume that mass, mainstream audiences were indeed gullible and manipulable—an interpretation widespread among these alternative-media admirers.

"It Was a Subtle Propagandistic Presentation"

Media critics of various political leanings often respond to news stories by discriminating between what they consider to be liberal and conservative viewpoints. A notable surprise in these conversations about the Medicare story was the relatively low level of attention paid to political factors, including partisan bias, among possible constraints on this news report.

Students commented on the partisan maneuvering involved with passing prescription-drug legislation as well as the possible political implications of the bill, but they did not identify partisan bias in the news coverage or ascribe political motivations to journalists. Marissa said news producers seem to "feel sorry for Democrats, that they're getting put in a corner. They know they're in a losing situation"; apart from this ambivalent statement, which didn't necessarily suggest an interpretation of political favoritism, discussions of partisanship were virtually absent. Asked whether the segment takes a point of view, junior Anthony replied that no, it is "pretty close to fair. It kind of puts out both ideas on the issue but they don't really support the plan because they say it had these problems."

A couple of the alternative viewers, who seemed like outliers in these group discussions, showed a tendency to interpret this news coverage through the lens of political bias. Nathaniel, for one, compared the report to White House talking points:

NATHANIEL: The prescription-drug story, that was like the press release that the Bush Administration and the Republican Congress sent to ABC News. They were just taking the talking points right from the press release, putting them into the story, showing the photo ops that, again, were clearly staged.

Likewise, pro-choice activist Smithy characterized the news story as a "subtle propagandistic presentation" that merely sought the appearance of partisan balance:

SMITHY: The words that made it propaganda were "that will make it easier for seniors to get care". . . . It was presented as "Well, our beloved president has now done something great for seniors." They threw in [a Democratic senator] later, but I thought the opposition was painted as kind of "these silly, predictable, little fringe people on the sidelines who would dare oppose this." [in a mocking tone]

It's difficult to discern from these comments, though, whether they believed journalists propagandize intentionally (guided by partisan bias) or unwittingly (i.e., manipulated by skillful politicians or perhaps out of sheer laziness). But Smithy's response shows, once more, how the alternative viewers put words into the mouths of journalists as they interpret the news.

Considering this group's commitment to a range of liberal causes—including some explicitly partisan activities, such as volunteering for Democratic political candidates—I was somewhat surprised that only two people pointed to conservative biases in this program. Most of the alternative-media users, like the students, did not portray partisanship as the prevailing influence on this news segment. Even Ryan, a presidential campaign volunteer, opined that the news was not

necessarily unfair or inaccurate. It's just a lack of depth. In the 22 minutes they have, take away the commercials, you can't get deeply involved in five or six different things that they covered. . . . It just barely glanced the surface of that issue.

The alternative-media audience based their opposition to the "position" in news less on their perception of political motives among journalists than on commercial goals among media corporations.

"Opposing Forces Are at Work"

These conversations show how two different audience groupings converged and diverged in their interpretations of a mainstream news story. The student group professed not to understand much in the news segment, while the alternative group claimed that its meaning was clear. To the extent that students understood the Medicare story, they interpreted it as meaning that politicians were helping old people get pills. Alternative-media users, on the other hand, largely saw the story as favoring the healthcare insurance industry. To arrive at these interpretations, both groups critically detached themselves from the story and discerned it as socially constructed by news producers who opted to dramatize the story, emphasize visual imagery, and insert strong emotions in the hope of getting and keeping viewers' attention—namely, to sensationalize. However, only the alternative-media users acknowledged corporate owners and commercial sponsors as agents participating in the social construction of news. This understanding of "how news media work" heightened critical distance and helped the alternative group to ascribe a position to the news story that conflicted with their own stances on healthcare reform.

It is in this third dimension of media reception, *position*, that the possibility of *opposition* rests. The student and alternative groups both constructed active and aware readings, but only the latter perceived a rhetorical grain in the news story, which enabled them to go against that grain. Resistant interpretations only occur when people are consciously aware of a difference between the meaning they create and the meaning they believe was intended by producers. As Schrøder said, "[Opposition] necessarily occurs in the face of a position that one acknowledges and then rejects."[11] Or, as John Fiske proposed, "The power of making one's own meaning can exist only in recognition that opposing . . . forces are at work in the text."[12] Audiences that do not see opposing forces in a news story cannot resist those forces.

This finding of resistant interpretations in an alternative-media audience recalls those identified by other research. These alternative viewers attributed manipulative motives to producers, as Corner and Richardson's had. My informants assumed that other people lacked adequate extratextual resources to help them interpret the news "correctly," in line with the theory of displaced readings. One intriguing study comparable to mine is Mirca Madianou's interviews with Greek news viewers who showed shifting identities and asymmetrical patterns of interpretation.[13] Many of her discussants described the news as sensationalized, commercial, and ratings focused. Their criticism of journalism was often based on an awareness of social construction, generic conventions, and how economics affect the content and agenda of TV news. Yet she found differences between those who used alternative sources such as foreign-language media and those who were more dependent on mainstream, domestic news.

Also notable here is Andy Ruddock, whose critical approach to news audience research showed how ambiguous the distinction between resistant and nonresistant interpretations can be. In one study, he assembled focus groups of church-going viewers to watch and discuss the U.S. news program *Nightline*.[14] His audience, which demonstrated some knowledge of media literacy that helped them question claims made by the news, did not quite fit the profile of cultural dupes. These viewers brought information, experiences, and perspectives to bear that were not provided in the newscast—but there were also "moments where their reactions appeared to be constrained by the information provided." Ruddock concluded:[15]

> Media audiences can duck and dive on the ropes like a canny but outclassed boxer, but they end up losing the decision. Ideology might miss a few blows, but it lands a fair few into the bargain, and this is enough to get the job done. . . . Alternative scripts were available, but the general ideological milieu of the audience did not allow them to breathe, to become fully fledged political positions capable of overturning the text's parameters.

This research showed how the abilities of an audience—even a fairly knowledgeable and media literate one—to interpret news in resistant ways were constrained. The fact that audiences are able to "routinely deflect ideological arrows," he said, does not outweigh the fact that they "are situated in cultures that heavily prefer some meanings over others."

In some ways, Ruddock's viewers demonstrated frustration and cynicism more so than opposition or resistance—as my student viewers did. They sensed the absence of information that would help them reach an informed opinion and felt that "there was something that the show was not telling them."[16] Similarly, my student viewers were frustrated by the news program, whose deficiencies restricted their ability to comprehend the news story, yet alone to interpret it oppositionally. Rather than characterizing these students as cultural dopes, I follow Justin Lewis in noting that the narrative structure of television news is too ambiguous, too simplistic for a complex genre of mediated messages that is almost incoherent by nature. (Let's remember: the interpretations reported here respond to a three-minute story called "A Closer Look"; the typical news segment is even shorter and more superficial.) I believe that rather than rejecting the meanings of mainstream news by consuming and interpreting it in oppositional ways, students have "resisted the news" by simply not attending to it much.

Structural Influences on Interpretive Differences

The responses of these two audience groups to this news story show some central tendencies as well as some variations. What are some factors that might account for those differences? There are several possible explanations for why the alternative audience's interpretation of news was more aware and more resistant than the student audience's interpretation.

One factor that somewhat influenced their interpretations, I believe, was age. People who participated in the alternative news groups were overall a bit older, more educated, and more experienced than those in the student groups. (Though not excessively so, two-thirds of the alternative viewers were under 22, as were all of the students. The other third of the alternative group averaged age 44.) Personal involvement with social movements and protest actions was another distinguishing factor, which gave some of the activists firsthand experience in attracting and receiving press attention, in working with journalists as news sources, and in witnessing disparities between real-world events and mediated representations. This lived experience likely influenced alternative-media users' understanding of "the way media work."

A factor that more significantly influenced their interpretation of this news story was *motivation*. This is a fourth dimension of Schrøder's reception model, which he describes as both cognitive and affective processes through which people decide whether a media message is "worth their while." Motivation extends beyond a given media text into the whole situation surrounding its consumption. I posit that the alternative-media users were, as activists, more invested in the newscast and our conversation than the students were. They also were likely more motivated to display their knowledge of public affairs, news production, and national politics than were students—a peer group in which acting smart about current events is not always socially desirable or beneficial. Some might have understood more about the story than they let on but preferred to "play dumb," declining to engage deeply with the newscast and discussions about it. Some students might have been uninterested in the story, deemed it irrelevant to their lives, or apathetic about interpreting it or performing their interpretation for a researcher. Their rejection of a media message could be attributed to a refusal to engage with message, not only to a lack of comprehension or an oppositional interpretation.

A fourth extratextual factor, and most important to this discussion, that fosters or constrains interpretive resistance is consumption of a wide range of news sources—especially a preponderance of alternative media. Activist and student informants had different contextual resources upon which to draw in interpreting news stories, as an analysis of diary data will establish in Chapter 7. The activists paid at least as much attention to MSM as other people, students a bit less. Activists paid much more attention to alternative media than other people, students almost none. The student viewers, who relied on mainstream sources, discussed only information internal to the program to interpret its meaning. The alternative viewers used frequent extratextual references to invoke broader lay theories about structural features of mainstream news—especially its corporate, commercial model—which they contrasted with alternative media. A reader's level of experience with competing narratives is one of many factors that enable and constrain interpretation. People with more, and a wider range of, media texts to take into account when interpreting a news message will construct richer meanings. The conclusion that viewers who rejected a mainstream news story had more access to alternative sources and that people dependent on mainstream sources found it more difficult to challenge the news is supported by studies from Greg Philo, Mirca Madianou, and other audience researchers.[17]

Additional evidence for this view is offered by the conversations I had with alternative-media users. Ryan, for one, extended the discussion of this Medicare story to *all* mainstream coverage of healthcare reform, saying he found it "fairly obvious that industry conglomerates, pharmaceutical industry conglomerates were going to reap great rewards from this bill. . . . I didn't see a whole lot of discussion in mainstream media regarding that." He said he had seen or heard such alternative positions reported in NPR programming, *Mother Jones*, and *American Prospect*. Like others, he claimed that alternative media was an important interpretive resource that nurtured the ability to, among other things, catch "tricky wording." Through abundant intertextual and extratextual references, the alternative audience indicated that their experiences with diverse media such as public broadcasting, niche magazines, books on media criticism, and independent online reporting provided essential interpretive resources that helped them recognize, evaluate, and reject the positions in mainstream news. This audience's "social knowledge of what might be true"—and might not be true—was influenced by their exposure to alternative media.

As I had hypothesized, the alternative viewers' discussion focused on details absent from the newscast, on *how much gets left out*, in their words. However, the alternative context that they valued so highly seemed to offer not just facts and information missing from mainstream news but also critical perspectives, frameworks, and schemata that guide their interpretations. Put differently, alternative sources might have helped them make sense of news not only by giving them information but also by giving them frameworks to organize that information. In this book, I propose that people familiar with left-of-center alternative media have access to lay theories about "how the news works" that many other people do not. More precisely, they have several theories: about news professionals' motives and attitudes toward audiences; about the influence of the political-economic structure of commercial, corporate media on production of mainstream news; and about mainstream audiences' attitudes toward the news.

Notes

1 More Americans still get their news from television, though no longer from ABC News specifically—as was perhaps the case in 2004 when this study was conducted. Local networks were the most popular news sources (46 percent) in 2018 compared to cable (31 percent) and national network (30 percent). Fox News Channel became the most-watched among cable news networks for the first time in 2016, attracting around 2.4 million primetime viewers. Pew Research Center, "Americans Still Prefer Watching to Reading the News—and Mostly Still through Television," Dec. 3, 2018.

2 W. Russell Neuman, *The Future of the Mass Audience* (New York: Cambridge University Press, 1991); and Joseph Turow, *Breaking Up America* (Chicago, IL: University of Chicago Press, 1997).

3 Jonathan Ladd, *Why Americans Hate the Media and How It Matters* (Princeton, NJ: Princeton University Press, 2012).

4 Pew Research Center, "Americans Still Prefer Watching."

5 The interviews were loosely structured to provide consistency across groups. Participants were encouraged to digress from open-ended questions and discuss other topics that arose. I used focus groups simulating everyday talk with the hope that they would offer more spontaneity, require less direction, and make an appealing research experience for activists, who received a modest sum for participating in these sessions. The groups were relatively homogeneous and small enough (four to six people each) that I felt confident of drawing responses from everyone. Robert Merton et al., *The Focused Interview: A Manual of Problems and Procedures* (New York: Free Press, 1990).

6 Kim Christian Schrøder, "Making Sense of Audience Discourses," *European Journal of Cultural Studies* 3, no. 2 (2000).

7 A large body of scholarship from a variety of perspectives has described myriad factors involved in the social construction of reality. For an overview, see William Gamson et al., "Media Images and the Social Construction of Reality," *Annual Review of Sociology* 18 (1992).

8 Many scholars have revealed the narrative and mythic elements of journalism, whose practitioners often try to tell "good stories" more so than to shape public opinion or policy—and who often draw on wider cultural formulas in doing so. An analysis of how these activist and student audiences perceived storytelling in mainstream news would make a fruitful analysis, though beyond the scope of this project. See S. Elizabeth Bird and Robert Dardenne, "Rethinking News and Myth as Storytelling," in *The Handbook of Journalism Studies*, eds. Karin Wahl-Jorgensen and Thomas Hanitzsch (London: Routledge, 2008); and Jack Lule, *Daily News, Eternal Stories* (New York: Guilford Press, 2001).

9 I use discussants' real names here with their permission, except for Cody and Smithy, who asked to be identified by pseudonyms.

10 Young people are becoming less critical of tabloid-style news narratives, according to S. Elizabeth Bird. She believes that while dramatic news plays a valuable role in everyday life, the replacement of rational, serious journalism with disconnected highly personal narratives of talk shows and reality programming nonetheless poses a threat to public discourse. Bird, "News We Can Use," *Javnost—The Public* 5, no. 3 (1998).

11 Schrøder, "Making Sense."

12 John Fiske, *Understanding Popular Culture* (Winchester, MA: Unwin Hyman, 1989), 71.

13 Mirca Madianou, "Shifting Identities," in *Discursive Constructions of Identity in European Politics*, ed. Richard Mole (Basingstoke and New York: Palgrave MacMillan, 2007).

14 Andy Ruddock, "Scientific Criticism?" *Atlantic Journal of Communication* 6, no. 1 (1998).
15 Ruddock, "Scientific Criticism?" 77.
16 Ruddock, "Scientific Criticism?" 75.
17 Greg Philo, *Seeing Is Believing* (London: Routledge, 1990), and Madianou, "Shifting Identities," 114.

4

LAY THEORIES OF THE MASS AUDIENCE FOR NEWS

"How did this program make you feel about the news, your life, the world?" That's what I asked groups of college students and alternative-media users after we watched the evening news together.

The first story: the death penalty looked certain for sniper John Moham- med, whom a jury had found guilty of first-degree murder and terrorism. Sec- ond, Ronald Reagan's family challenged a psychiatrist's recommendation that failed assassin John Hinckley, Jr., be granted unsupervised leaves from prison. Next up: the latest from Iraq, where civilians wept at their losses as U.S. gener- als promised to kill or imprison insurgents. Then, reporters visited a military base in Kentucky to interview families lamenting loved ones lost in war overseas. Briefs on suicide bombings in Turkey and security precautions for a presidential visit to London rounded out the first half of the program.

It escaped no one's notice that the top stories of the day were all *bad* news. When I posed the aforementioned question to students, they said they felt "depressed" as well as "scared," "helpless," "pissed off," "furious," sad, frus- trated, and unhappy after watching this newscast. In the alternative-media groups, people similarly reported being "touched" by stories, feeling "bad" for victims, finding the news "troubling" or "disappointing," being angry about what's happening in the world as well as how journalists reported those events. Both groups assumed that producers had crammed the program with bad news, strong emotions, and spectacular visuals because sensational content appealed to viewers.

This chapter examines the interpretive strategies through which alternative- media users perceived and tried to resist the sensational power they perceived in a news program. Building on earlier discussion of how participants achieved critical distance from this newscast, I describe how they contrasted their own interpretive skills with those of an imaginary mainstream audience that they characterized as gullible, manipulable, apathetic, inattentive, and uninformed. They denied that sensational content appealed to them personally—evidence of what communication scholars call the "third-person effect" (TPE), the widespread tendency for people to feel that they are smarter or more knowledgeable than others and thus less susceptible to media influence. In mass-communication theory, the term "third-person effect" refers to the expectation that a media message will have its greatest influence on "them" (the grammatical third person) rather than on "me" or "you."[1] We will see not only *that* people evoke the third-person effect—a well-established research finding—but *how* these alternative-media users do so, in their own words.[2]

Unlike quantitative methods that tend to reinforce analytical distinctions between participants and others, my qualitative research design offered a naturalistic context with nondirectional questions where people could express multiple and shifting identities, change their minds, even contradict themselves. And these respondents did all of these things. As I was intrigued to discover, the alternative-media users played games of interpretation in which they alternately took on the identities of both journalists and theoretical viewers. They invented dialogue for this absent audience of fictional others and posed hypothetical statements about how they would respond to the newscast *if* they were those other people. The discussion that follows will share discursive evidence of how this alternative-media audience articulated interpretations of mainstream news in ways that were both resistant *and* displaced—in other words, that they contrasted their own understandings with both the rhetorical grain they perceived in the text *and* the rhetoric that they assumed other viewers would accept at face value.[3]

I had designed the study to provide a control group of sorts: an audience of students with more or less typical media habits and levels of engagement with news, whose responses I could contrast with those of alternative-media users. Perhaps I needn't have bothered constructing a comparison group: these conversations demonstrate that alternative viewers had brought along their own typical audience, as they spontaneously compared themselves to hypothetical other people when interpreting the news. Yet they also displayed first-person and second-person effects, as well as third-person ones: tendencies to feel that *I* or *you* are susceptible to media influence too. As you will see, they described themselves as alternately invulnerable and susceptible to the effects of mainstream media. Their conceptions of their own critical abilities and allegiances were not quite as self-assured as they might have appeared.

"It's Supposed to Stir Emotion"

One of the first things that struck viewers about the newscast was the prominence of guns. "The first three stories were all stuff that involved guns," Sarah said. Rich noticed this too:

There was this one point where they kept on showing rapid clips of police officers running around, with their guns drawn, creating panic, and giving you almost a sense of ADD, attention deficit disorder, because they kept repeatedly flashing all these different scenes.

Smithy saw these images as simulating threats to audiences: "They show a gun, pointing at the screen like 'Look, there's a gun pointing at *you!*'" (emphasis theirs).

The producers' intention in using so many guns in the newsreel was to stimulate feelings, said Henrik, who remarked upon the strong emotional content of these reports on terrorism, war, and murder. "Especially the story about the sniper shootings," he says. "It looks like it was created like a music video. I counted over 10 cuts in a very short time, the switching of pictures. . . . These things they use to create emotions." According to Cody, the sniper story exemplified how TV news both reflects audiences' feelings toward world events and cultivates those feelings:

CODY: When you see visuals of this in a repeated way—if you are in front of the TV, you probably hear something about it almost every day—it just makes it so much bigger than it really is. To me, that's just instilling fear so that people are more likely to depend upon the authorities or the government to work, to suppress them for their safety and freedom. Just how they say the word "*Guilty!*" with a red background . . . or how Mohammed looks, his head down and the lines on his face accentuated with the lighting . . . [the voiceover says] "no remorse," "absence of emotion" . . . so his absence of emotion is supposed to stir more emotion in us.

She suggested that visual and verbal techniques in the news tended to distort *other* viewers' perspectives—not her own, presumably—regarding the nature of criminals and their victims as well as the pervasiveness of criminality and victimization in our society. This interpretation echoes the argument of luminary media scholar George Gerbner that the symbolic culture of TV violence produces a "Mean World Syndrome," in which heavy viewers think social reality is more malevolent than light viewers do and concomitantly support conservative leaders who promise to address their fear and mistrust.[4] (Let's note that Gerbner considered the notions that audiences are powerful and enjoy a diverse range of media choices to be "fairy tales." And he dubbed the process through which heavy TV viewers developed this shared fear *mainstreaming*.)

Drawing comparisons between programs in the United States and his native Germany, Henrik suggested that Americans were "a little more emotional than European people. . . . We are not coldhearted, but here they seem a little more *susceptible?* [questioning tone] for dealing with all these emotional pictures." He checked the word in his German-English dictionary, as the rest of the group chimed in the correct pronunciation. Sarah countered that people everywhere were susceptible, Americans no more or less than others. Henrik defended his observation, explaining that German news about Iraq never featured interviews with "sharp emotional statements" from citizens or soldier's family members. While Henrik's attempt to distinguish between susceptible and unsusceptible audiences by using the categories *American* and *European* did not elicit much group support, some activists did perceive differences between the information systems available to audiences in different nations. Joni wondered whether TV news showed patriotic, status-quo stories because "that's what Americans want." Jen suggested that the "average American citizen" might be repulsed by Indymedia websites featuring "weird pictures about SOA [School of the Americas] protests and things. That's not really news to most people." In this exchange, some speakers alternately classified themselves as activists, Americans, and human beings—underscoring their conflicting individual identities and mobile group memberships.[5]

Participants agreed that emotions dominated this broadcast. They observed that a narrow range of human responses was invoked: ones serving as "a motivation to watch the show," especially sorrow and fear. They described the program's focus on feelings as sensationalism, which they linked to commercialism, and distinguished these emotional stories from "real" news. For instance, Chuck responded that one interview, with a man whose son had just been killed in Iraq, "wasn't even really part of the news":

CHUCK: I mean, what do you expect? His kid's dead, he's not going to be jumping for joy over it. That's one of the ways that I find some news people kind of like jackals. They don't really care about the person, they just want to catch the emotional shot.

Other exchanges focused on interviews with military wives. Jodi, like Chuck, wondered what the point of such segments was, because they didn't give any new information. Her voice radiated sarcasm:

It's not like anyone is watching that and saying, "Wow, they're *sad* that their husbands might be going to Iraq? Well, I didn't know that. . . . Thank you for the *news*!" That's not really the definition of "news" to me (emphases hers).

This response is a superb example of what Erving Goffman called an overlayed "keying," a spoken statement that uses vocal cues to indicate that it is not intended to be interpreted straight but rather understood as sarcasm, irony, words from someone else's mouth, and the like.[6] Though these alternative-media fans seemed sincerely engaged in the mainstream newscast, they frequently expressed an ironic stance. My analysis will show some ways in which their interpretative behavior was characteristic of ironic readings. As Kim Christian Schrøder's news reception model predicted, these resistant viewers' responses commuted between immersion in and distance from the newscast, between vulnerability and invulnerability to the persuasive power they perceived therein.

"I Watch With Detached Amusement"

Several viewers said the segment evoked their sympathy while others distanced themselves from that emotion by qualifying it as "the illusion of sympathy" or as "orchestrated sympathy,"—that is, a manipulation by news producers. Nick characterized the news staple of sticking a microphone in someone's face and asking how it feels to lose a loved one as "pandering" to audiences (an assumption that viewers wanted to see such emotionally exploitative scenes) and creating "the illusion of sympathy with the gratification of enjoying their pain" (an assumption that the public did derive satisfaction from viewing this). In Smithy's view, only people who supported the troops were shown in this sympathetic light:

SMITHY: That is *orchestrated* sympathy, because even though on a human level all people's deaths matter, all human suffering matters, in my view, it was still manipulated because it was like, "We are sensitized to this guy because we're looking at him, and what's omitted is the suffering of all the people who are lumped as the collective bogeymen, and we're already emotional because we started off by watching the sniper, you know, and the criminals of the month." (emphasis his)

Because many of these alternative-media users thought mainstream newscasts tried to exploit their feelings, they took pleasure in denying producers this supposed satisfaction by refusing to respond in an "obedient" way. When asked if any of the stories emotionally engaged them, Chris replied, "I don't know. . . . I get a little angry when I watch the news, but mostly I just watch it devoid of all emotion." In another group, a 24-year-old activist named Janice hinted at such detachment with a sense of irony—as well as, perhaps, a touch of compassion fatigue:

> It sucks in Iraq, okay. It sucks in a town where people are sending their children to Iraq, okay. It sucks to be old and on Medicare, okay. And it sucks to be a menstruating woman. They didn't really say anything new!

Some of her peers expressed their critical disengagement more directly, as this exchange illustrated:

JONI: I watch the news with *detached amusement.*

[Everyone else nods.]

INTERVIEWER: Yeah?

JONI: To a point. Seeing it like that, on the front page or in the mass media, I don't always feel like it's directed at me *per se*, because of where I place myself in society. So I feel like I'm always kind of *looking at it sideways*. And therefore, *I'm not going to get what they want me to get.*

JODI: Yeah. With the sniper thing, I was like, "Oh gosh, here it goes again. . . ." There are 10 million other things in the world that they can cover, yet they're choosing to focus on this. And, I got tired of it. Often I watch CNN. . . . They're notorious for just all day focusing on one topic, and it's really annoying, and I feel less emotion. (emphases added)

Here, Jodi noted that she often watched CNN, although elsewhere she tried to downplay her use of corporate media. This snippet of dialogue conveys the ironic responses that a mainstream newscast elicited from these alternative-media fans: sarcasm, detached amusement, emotionlessness. They "looked at the news sideways" because of "where they place themselves in society." They resisted the sensational overtures that they perceived in the mass media while also distancing themselves from the audiences for whom mainstream news was presumably intended. This detachment, which connected the meanings they constructed from news texts with the social identities that they had built for themselves, showed audience agency at work and in play. Yet, as we shall see, they tended to imply that other people lacked this creative power.

"What Would Someone Else Be Thinking?"

The alternative-media audience actively acknowledged the polysemous nature of this newscast, talking emphatically about the multiple meanings they perceived. By contrast, the student audience did not; indeed, their interpretive frustration might have arisen partly from efforts to arrive at a single fixed meaning that appeared inaccessible to them. The student viewers said journalists interpreted the world but did not seem to recognize also that audiences interpreted the news. The alternative viewers described both phenomena. Some examples:

Henrik pointed out that we all saw the same news, the same episode, and got different interpretations.

Jodi described the newscast as a "picture book that you have to interpret," which frustrated her because she's "just watching pictures without knowing any of the context."

Nick said he tried to enter into the point of view of people he saw in the news, wondering what their communicative goals were and what resources they brought to bear. "I sort of write the news and ads in my own head, in anticipation," he commented. "I sort of look at the world as if I were writing it as a story, and anticipate where it's going."

Monique, a native of France, said she "played a game" while watching the newscast: she pretended she could not speak English and didn't understand the narration. Calling upon her knowledge of photography, she tried to interpret the news through its visual aspects, rather than its verbal ones.

Liz discussed how a story about "rounding up suspects in Iraq" enabled audiences to interpret the report in different ways:

LIZ: How much are they suspecting these people of? Why are they rounding them up? They show this [Iraqi] woman who's saying "What do they want from us?" but they didn't define the "they." They left it open, so you could take that either way. If I was a supporter of the war sitting there watching it, I'd be like, "Yeah, what does *Saddam* want from us?" I tried to watch the newscast almost like, "What would someone [else] be thinking if they're watching this?" (emphasis hers)

Liz thus asserted that the meaning of texts was "open" and could be "taken either way." She considered the ambiguous "they" from the position of a person who supported the war, in opposition to her own anti-war viewpoint (in which "they" means Americans). She pretended to respond to the text as another person, by voicing an imaginary interpretation that differed from her own.

This passage exemplifies several ways in which these alternative-media users played polysemous games of interpretation as they watched the news. They role-played, invented dialogue, described their vision of "ordinary" viewers, and posed hypothetical statements. These games, which recurred in all the alternative viewer groups, reveal high levels of creativity as well as empathy. Hypothetical statements require the *I* to put oneself in the shoes of *you* or *them*—pronouns that indicate grammatical and social positions relative to the mass audience. Pronoun usage played a key role in this interaction, as the alternative-media enthusiasts signaled a range of shifting personal identities and collective boundaries. Assuming alternate pronominal roles as both *us* and *them* was one of their central interpretive strategies.

Alternating Pronouns: *Us* and *Them*

Pronoun usage is creative, complex, and ambiguous. In everyday conversation, we use pronouns to conjure both closeness and distance between ourselves and other categories of people. For example, I can use the first-person plural *we* in this book in multiple ways: to signify more exclusive groups or more inclusive ones—just me and you (a single reader), me and everyone reading this book, or me and broader categories of people such as academics specifically or intellectuals generally or all humans. Like so many other elements of communication, pronouns are polysemous.

In the discourse of these news viewers, who are *we*? Who are *you*? Who are *they*? The first-person singular pronoun *I* often refers to oneself—but often it does not. Sometimes we use *I* as a piece of mimicry, as part of a quote in which we are voicing the words of another speaker or playing the role of devil's advocate. The first-person plural pronoun *we* often expresses collective identities, when people refer to themselves as members of a group. The second-person pronoun *you* can also be used instead of *we* in a collective way to mean something similar: *people like us*. In addition, *you* can be used instead of *them* to make generalizations, in more personal terms, about unspecified people.

As you can see, people systematically shift pronominal referents. Conversational language constantly alternates between *I, we, you,* and *they* to denote individual and group identities, which reflects the social reality that these identities are multiple and mutable. Pronouns thus have referents only in an interactional situation where listeners can make sense of such shifts in "footing."[7] Interpreting these referential shifts requires listeners' to have access to and understand the speakers' sociological and grammatical contexts, which surveys and experiments rarely provide.

The third-person plural pronoun *they*, however, is qualitatively distinct from the first- and second-person plural pronouns *we* and *you*. It's more impersonal, more abstract. Pronouns like *I, we,* and *you* connect us with other people through talk, whereas *he, she,* and *they* separate us from other people. These latter pronouns refer to people being talked about, rather than talked to. Third-person references, as Martin Malone explained, "point to who we are not. They are powerful metaphors for 'other'."[8] The pronoun *they* and phrases like *those people* imply a comparison between ourselves and others that often conveys a moral judgment. The grammatical third person is also key to the third-person effect: the perception that a mediated message will have its greatest influence on *them* rather than *me* or *you*.

Discussants' use of *we* frequently communicated their identities as both alternative-media consumers and activists, whereas *they* revealed disparities and similarities that informants perceived between in-group members (*we, alternative-media users, activists*) and out-group members (*they, other people who don't use alternative media, non-activists*). Though our discussions nominally focused on the TV program we had just watched together, they often interpreted the news by reference to their personal experiences as activists, in which they interacted with a wide range of people. Being an activist often entails assuming dual perspectives and learning to think of oneself as both *us* and *them*. Many contrasted their own interpretations of the newscast with responses they had heard from specific other people: husbands, uncles, sisters, mothers-in-law, neighbors. One discussant referred to older people she knew who "trust the news so much":

MONIQUE: I'm talking to a woman, she's 70-something, trying to educate her about politics. But when I talk about the lies, about the war, *"Oh, Monique, don't talk like that! The president wouldn't do that! And if it was true, how come the TV doesn't talk about it!"* That's what I hear. *They* really believe what they hear is true.

INTERVIEWER: Why don't you?

MONIQUE: Because *I* know better. Because *I'm* smarter. Because *I* don't listen to the TV. (emphases added)

Her comment illustrates how these viewers used the third-person pronoun *they* to refer to an absent audience of "others" whom they consider more vulnerable to media messages than themselves.[9] (Indeed, one wonders how many audience members—if any—consider themselves to be mainstream or ordinary targets of news messages.) This activist isn't unique in believing that she's smarter and knows better than other people: this is a common attitudinal phenomenon called the "third-person effect."

"That's the Way People Are"

These conversations exemplify the robust research finding that people tend to envision media content—TV commercials, newscasts, fictional programs—having greater influence on the grammatical third-person *them* than on *me* or *you*.[10] First articulated in 1983, this theory proposes that people assume mediated messages will affect how others both think and act more than it affects their own thoughts and actions. In this view, "other people" presumably trust the representations of reality that they see in television news and believe that, say, the real world *is* mean.

The desirability and genre of a media message can influence its perceived effects on self and others. These alternative-media enthusiasts considered mainstream media a compromised genre, while they view alternative news sources as desirable. It's not surprising, then, that they perceived themselves as able to see through the version of reality proffered in mainstream news while other people "fell" for it—that is, interpreted its content uncritically.[11] They described other people as more impressionable and susceptible to televised spectacle—especially to sensational appeals and visual persuasion. The comment that "people are actually duped into" believing what they saw on television is an extreme version of this attitude. Other participants similarly described "other people" as lacking critical distance and reacting to news programs in a manner akin to audiences at pro-wrestling events:

JODI: When *they* hear something *they* like, *they* cheer. If *they* hear something *they* don't like, *they* boo.

JOE: It's a sound bite or a catchphrase society. [The president] will stand at the podium . . . and *people* see that image and they hear 10 seconds of a speech and that's enough for *them*.

LIZ: *They're* so dumb that *they're* not going to question at all what *they're* seeing. (emphases added)

These alternative-media enthusiasts frequently compared their own interpretations to those of a generic audience for mainstream media. Throughout
our discussions, they referred to "most people," "the ordinary" viewer, "people
generally," "other people," "an average citizen," the American people, "the vast
majority of people," and similar constructions. Sometimes they simply distinguished themselves from *people* or *them*.

By contrast, these alternative-media users saw themselves as usually, though
not uniformly, skeptical and jaded about the news. When one person commented
that he did not "get what they want me to get" from watching the news but that
other people did, another jumped in to elaborate upon the us–them distinction:

JANICE: I think *other people*, they're not going to be as educated on issues. I
think activists are more passionate about the news, which is why we don't
normally watch ABC News. The *average person* wouldn't even pay any
attention to the news. That's the way *people* are. My uncle would never,
ever watch the news. He just so doesn't care.

JONI: Judge Judy! *They'd* rather watch "Judge Judy."

JANICE: But there's no point being like, "Well, it's us against *them*, and *they're*
never going to get it." It's easy to say "Oh, *people* are uneducated," but as
much as I believe it sometimes, I don't want to believe it. . . . But yeah, *people* don't take the time to research. I wish *they* would go back and research
more, try to get the facts about the story, not just take it as it's presented and
say "This is the truth, they said it on TV."(emphases added)

These comments suggest that Janice considered average viewers more susceptible to media messages, more ignorant about current events, more apathetic
toward the news, and more disengaged from civic life. Other alternative-media
users indicated the same. "Most people watching that newscast are going to
assume that what [the president's son] said is completely accurate, and it probably isn't," Cody said. "I would think it's probably not, but who knows, I'll
never know from *that* newscast" (emphasis theirs).

These viewers saw connections between the public's gullibility and its disin-
terest, disengagement, and lack of knowledge—placing the blame on audiences
as often as they did on news producers. "*The general people* don't pay attention.
They lose interest very easily," one said. "If TV news was going to actually be in
depth, it'd have to be a two-hour-long program. That's not what *people* want,"
another said. "Generally, *people* just aren't going to watch it at all. *They're* going
to tune it out," a third said. A fourth person shared this sentiment but went
further, suggesting a solution to the problem of an inattentive public:

LIZ: The *American people*, specifically, need convenience and *they* need it right
now. I don't know what's better: For *them* to stop sensationalizing the news

so that *people* will get the correct news or if they sensationalize the news so more *people* watch it. (emphases added)

This statement echoes an oft-made assumption during these discussions: that ordinary viewers enjoy sensationalism and seek to be entertained rather than informed by the news. Thus, these alternative-media fans made intellectual and moral judgments about the hypothetical mass audience, whom they imagined having an inferior relationship with and understanding of news media. They also asserted what I call their sense of "media superiority"—which includes both intellectual and moral components—that correspondingly contributed to and resulted from their invulnerability.[12]

"We Might as Well Watch TV and Let It Rule Over Us"

In guiding these discussions, I continually asked participants what "struck" them most about the newscast. Later, in listening to dozens of hours of audiotape and reading hundreds pages of interview transcripts, the thing that struck *me* most was how often the alternative-media users spoke in invisible quotation marks, expressing the thoughts they envisaged running through the minds of other people. Sometimes the role they played was that of newscasters or newsmakers, and sometimes it was other news viewers. I clearly heard their tones of voice change, as they shifted from their own perspectives to those of hypothetical others. A statement including the phrases *They're like . . .* or *They go . . .* followed by an exclamation such as *Oh, Well,* or *Okay* often signaled that the alternative viewer was assuming the role of imagined journalists or audiences whose viewpoints differed from his or her own.

Journalist Role-Play

On several occasions, people invented dialogue in which journalists told viewers what to think or how to feel. One discussant did so when she commented:[13]

JODI: First they go with the sniper thing, then the war stuff, then it's like, *"Feel good for the patriotism, he believes in the country, he's a good man."* Then one of the last shots was this big American flag over a highway of cars, it was like, *"Support the troops! Support oil!"* (emphases added)

Here, she assumed the role of producers, voicing their supposed intentions to promote patriotic sentiment among viewers—and the presumed power of news rhetoric to have a strong effect upon the mass audience. This dialogue exemplifies how this person translated the ulterior messages of the newscast using the imperative form: feel good! Support the troops![14]

Rich used an analogous interpretive strategy as he expressed the thoughts he imagined journalists having as they went to a military base: "When they go to this town and show this community in mourning, it's kind of like, *'Well, if you're against the war then you're against these people as well. Look at these crying people. They have yellow ribbons.'"* He found the video footage of a big flag above the highway and people driving SUVs "really funny," however—an ironic response that contradicted the goals he attributed to producers. "I felt like, 'Yeah, that *is* America,'" he said (emphases his). "And I thought maybe they should have done a story on why there are so many cars." His own reaction challenged the dominant ideology he perceived.

Numerous discussants discerned status-quo intentions in this newscast. For example, one person invented dialogue to describe the report on prescription-drug legislation, which he called a "subtle propagandistic presentation":

SMITHY: It was presented as, *"Well, our beloved president has now done something great for seniors."* . . . I thought the opposition was painted as these silly, predictable, little fringe people on the sidelines who would dare to oppose this. It was built up as a good thing and then it's like, *"Okay, throw a few crumbs in another direction for the appearance of a balanced story."* I think that if someone was totally gullible and totally manipulable by media, it would have already been a good thing. (emphases added)

Cody related a comparable observation about the military families story, proposing that journalists were

like, *"Well, we don't want to tell you what's going on in Iraq, and how this is affecting everything, so it's much easier to just say, we're going to be sympathetic for the soldiers. We'll just put up a soldier's wife and have her say how she feels. Nobody argue with her."* (emphasis added)

In a similar way, Beki imagined producers' perspectives when she explained her observation that journalists chose formulaic stories. But she remained ambivalent regarding whether status-quo messages were deliberate:

BEKI: Maybe they're not sitting down and actually being like, *"Okay, let's do a story that upholds sexism and let's do a story that's going to invoke fear in people's lives, and let's do a story that upholds racism"* or whatever. Maybe it's not like their actual purposeful intentions, but that's how it comes across to me. (emphases added)

Beki thus recognized that she was constructing an interpretation in her own mind, rather than assuming that she could divine the de facto goals of news producers.

In these acts of inventing dialogue, alternative-media users described the effects that they thought news producers wished to have upon audiences, whether it was fostering support for military activities overseas, upholding sexism and racism, or instilling exaggerated social fears. Their comments indicated a belief that the news had limited effects on them personally but that other audiences were more susceptible to such messages.

Audience Role-Play

My discussants frequently imagined how other viewers would respond to the newscast. For example, one participant played a game of interpretation by adopting an elderly acquaintance's perspective. "Let's pretend I didn't know anything about [the Medicare legislation], and I were an old lady," she said:

MONIQUE: I'd probably be scared because it did mention that 60 percent of the money for the plan would actually go to the pharmaceutical companies. If you really listen and pay attention—not a lot of people really listen to the words, you know?—*if* that was the first time I heard about it, it would be pretty scary. (emphasis added)

This passage indicates that Monique contrasted her own interpretive acts (listening to the words, paying attention) with those of a specific other who resembled the generic public ("a lot of people"), whom she imagined didn't know anything about the issue. Unlike her, they believed what they saw on TV to be true and were hearing this news for the first time. She described a hypothetical situation in which the news affected other people in stronger ways than it affected her.

In an earlier anecdote about discussing politics with a septuagenarian, Monique ascribed dialogue to the woman (*"Don't talk like that!"*). In a similar vein, Jodi invented dialogue when I asked her how she felt about the world and her life after watching this news show. She replied sarcastically, *"Yeah, the world is weak and we can't do much about it, so we might as well watch TV and let it rule over us."* This statement diverged from the empowered stance she typically exhibited toward social affairs, so the response was clearly the voice of an imaginary viewer whom she perceived to be dominated by television's *weltanschauung*.

On several occasions, viewers invented dialogue in which journalists stated a proposition that they imagined a mass audience accepting. Cody talked about how she perceived producers using a combination of empathy and fear to motivate audiences to pay attention to the news. She thought journalists were encouraging viewers to see themselves as victims and that audiences would think, *"This could happen to me, therefore I should pay attention to this newscast."* Cody interpreted the interaction thus: "It was, 'A new birth control for women that could be helpful but may be a risk!' But they didn't go into the risk; it was just enough to get people to go, *'Oh, there might be risks? Let's watch.'*" She believed that rather than reaching their own conclusions about an issue such as the new contraceptive reported here, a lot of people want to be told. *"Just tell me what's the right thing. I don't have time to hear about all these different facts and opinions. I don't want to hear about the study of the pill, and what's good and what's bad."*

Cody thus perceived "a lot of people" as lacking motivation to interpret the news as creatively and energetically as she did.

"If I Didn't Know What I Know"

These alternative-media fans believed other people's perceptions of social reality were distorted by using mainstream, commercial sources. Nick thought such media skewed people's fear of crime and noted that his sister, who read mainstream papers, believed "there's a crime happening at every street corner here in [Philadelphia] and I should never step out of my house." Janice said she watched ABC News or Fox News so she could understand her mother-in-law's and neighbors' worldview, because "it's shaped by their media." Such statements resonate with Gerbner's Mean World Syndrome as well as his Cultivation Theory, which proposed that watching television gradually inculcates viewers into believing that reality corresponds closely to mediated depictions. With the pronoun *their* modifying *media*, Janice distanced herself from people who watched network news, drawing another boundary between herself and third persons. These alternative-media users viewed *them* as passively receiving inadequate, inferior news while they themselves actively sought out more information from credible sources. I have described the alternative-media audience's attitude toward mass audiences elsewhere as a sense of "media superiority" over people who do not consume news from diverse and noncommercial sources.[15] Interestingly, many alternative fans assumed themselves to be less exposed and the average person more exposed to mainstream media, when the opposite is true.

The connection between decreased susceptibility and alternative-media use was demonstrated in a third game of interpretation that these viewers played. When I asked how the program made them feel, some replied by posing questions to qualify their responses. "You mean, *if* I didn't know what I know about it? How would it make me feel *if* this were all I knew?" Joe asked. He used the conditional tense: "*If* you don't have the insight to see beyond it, to question the source of the story or to understand the rhetorical strategies that are being employed . . ." (emphases added). He believed he had become less naïve about media by talking to friends and reading books, including media criticism by the likes of Noam Chomsky, an important influence on left-wing media criticism.

Monique similarly contrasted her interpretation of the news with how she imagined a senior citizen might interpret it: "*if* that was the first time I heard about." She played a game of putting herself in the position of people using news sources different to her own: "I always wonder when I see people on the street, what do they know? I wonder what they're thinking. Are they reading the paper?" When I asked her why she didn't believe everything she saw in the news, she initially replied that she "knows better." Then, she switched from *I* to *we*, a shift in footing that reflects a sense of shared perspective within this group:

> Because I don't listen to the TV. Because we do research, because we listen, because we have access to news from overseas. I get information, I make my own decisions, I see the facts, and I compare them with overseas things that I hear.[16]

The plural pronoun *we* referred to her status as a member of a group, identifying herself with an activist collectivity.[17]

Examining these conditionals-contrary-to-fact shows how alternative-media users create boundaries between themselves and third persons. This third-person effect has a behavioral component, as well as a perceptual one.[18] Differences in real-world action result from differences in news interpretation. At least three people opined that this newscast's sensationalism had the effect, intended or unintended, of supporting the existing power structure. As Joni commented:

JONI: It's like, *"Here are people crying! And here's somebody else crying! And here's a picture of somebody that died!"* And like boom-boom-boom-boom-boom. I don't think it really provides a viewpoint per se; it's more, very, just status-quo oriented. The writers are like, "What does America want to hear? America wants to hear some sad news, America wants to see some something about these murderers. . . ." (emphases added)

Once again, these alternative viewers assumed that the general public craves news that incites negative emotions and that journalists are just giving people what they want. They suggested that people manipulable by media would support the policies purportedly promoted by the newscast and that such audiences were behaving passively toward media as well as toward life.

Yet the alternative-media fans expressed hope that other audiences were only partially susceptible to sensational media manipulation—while recognizing themselves as partially susceptible too.

Simultaneously Vulnerable and Invulnerable

The alternative-media fans considered themselves to be not immune but more resistant to the supposed power of mainstream news than other people, thanks to their participation in a counter-public sphere semi-detached from corporate, commercial interests. At first glance, their high regard for their own news interpretations might seem arrogant or elitist. However, their sense of media superiority is mitigated by the shifting identities that they related in these conversations. Systematic alternation between first-person plural and third-person plural pronouns was one conversational cue that they identified with multiple groups.[19] There were many moments when participants used *we* and *us* to identify themselves as ordinary viewers and to signal their own vulnerability.

One person called himself a "formerly naïve consumer of network news" and noted that his reactions used to be more "emotional." By acknowledging that he used to be more gullible and once belonged to the out-group, he smudged the line between *us* and *them*. Another commented that "the main thing advertising does is make *us* feel inadequate," suggesting that he was susceptible, that media influenced the first person as well as the third person. A third person blatantly announced her own vulnerability to televised spectacle: "I'm very gullible, so I'm like, 'There are visuals!'" A fourth noted that the newscast's emotional content "was something that the *common person* could connect to. You know, a crying woman is something that *we* can relate to," alternating between third and first persons. A fifth included herself among "people" by saying,

> We get educated in a certain way that we don't want to hear [critical] things. We want to live in the illusion of "we're free" because that's what we're taught our whole lives. Not too many people want to shatter that comfort zone.

In a discussion about how TV news influences civic engagement, some of these viewers further acknowledged their own susceptibility to news messages:

JOE: I think [the news] renders *me* kind of passive. And powerless.

NATHANIEL: It's disempowering either way, as a quote-unquote *"normal"* person and as a quote-unquote "activist". As the *normal person*, it's disempowering because *you're* just getting fed this information, there's no way to tie it into something broader. It's assumed that *you're* going to take it at its face value. And as an activist, it's disempowering because it makes *me* realize again and again what *we're* actually up against.

BEKI: People in my family and *other people* I know who watch the news are really angry about life and what's going on in the world. . . . *They're* constantly reminded every time *they* turn on the TV that "*I* don't have control over my life". Watching the news scares *me* since I'm like, "This is what *people* are watching. And this is what *they're* focusing on." It reminds me of what *we're* fighting, how powerful a mechanism it is.

NATHANIEL: It cultivates this "can't fight city hall" mentality. "What can *I* do?" (emphases added)

This excerpt illuminates additional discursive complexities linked to first-person and second-person effects. Alternative-media fans acknowledged that mainstream news did exert some influence over them. Their use of an indefinite *you* rather than *they* when referring to "the normal person" suggests that these viewers not feel entirely distinct from the so-called mass audience; such usage evokes pronominal ambiguity and systemic alternation.[20] Although this might appear to be a contradiction, it's probable that most of us oscillate between being active interpreters and passive dupes of media texts.

Their interchangeable use of first- and third-person grammar, of the pronouns *they* and *we*, implies a sense of doubleness, that these alternative-media fans identified themselves as both part of and apart from the general public. The ability to migrate mentally between different social identities serves a crucial purpose to activism. They used games of interpretation not just to separate themselves from the supposedly gullible public but also to envision how it feels to be upset about what's going in the world and to have no control over one's life. Interpretive roleplaying is a means of empathizing with other people, not merely feeling superior to them.

Ambivalent Views of Audience Agency

Listening to alternative news fan's interpretations of this newscast illustrates what they disliked about mainstream media, both within and beyond the program. They disapproved of many elements of visual and verbal rhetoric they perceived in the news, such as an authoritative tone that they translated into imperatives, a focus on people as actual or potential victims, and a disempowering portrayal of current events. Outside of the program, they criticized mainstream news for seeking profit, relying on commercial support, and catering to advertisers—a political-economic perspective entailing certain extratextual knowledge, lay theories, and cultural resources. Sensationalism served as a bridge linking journalistic texts to their contexts of production. These discussions also hinted at some qualities, such as public "empowerment," that they associated with alternative media.

These alternative-media users shared many understandings of social reality, intersubjective meanings, and strategies for decoding news that marked them as an interpretive community. They found power and pleasure in playful strategies like role-playing, inventing dialogue, and posing "if" statements through which they pretended to respond to the news in the voices of other people. Some of their power and pleasure derived from a sense of detached amusement or critical distance, which is characteristic of contemporary bourgeois aesthetics that distrust affective immediacy and the loss of rational control, according to Henry Jenkins. Detachment "bestows a certain degree of freedom from the ideological [complicity] demanded by the text," he said. "Distance empowers, proximity dominates."[21] Paradoxically, the alternative-media fans appeared to be passionate about, proximate to, and engaged in the news program while also dispassionate about, distanced, and disengaged from its sensational qualities.

Such signs of creative resistance to semiotic power of mainstream news suggest that many audiences have a high degree of interpretive freedom. A paradox remains: these resistant respondents believed that, by and large, ordinary viewers lacked the critical distance and rational control that they themselves exercised. This is not unusual, as Manuel Castells observed; people who struggle for social change commonly view others as "passive receptacles of ideological manipulation."[22] Alternative-media users considered people who did not seek out such diverse sources—whether through apathy, ignorance or naivety—to be more receptive to hegemonic messages in mainstream news, more likely to accept elite perspectives on society. These empowered viewers imagined that "negative" emotions like sorrow and fear *do* motivate other people to watch TV news—that the average American does seek emotionally exploitative scenes, does enjoy watching other humans suffer, and does judge personal safety on the basis of violent media images. They suggested that mainstream news simultaneously had limited effects on themselves and powerful effects on people who were presumably dependent on mainstream news for their understanding of the world. These alternative-media fans offered a view of audience agency that's equal parts optimistic and pessimistic.

These alternative-media fans clearly had lay theories about "how news audiences work" as well as "how news professionals work" and "how news professionals think that news audiences work." The interpretation that I offer here is a reflection of a reflection of a reflection. My earlier description of these viewers putting themselves inside the minds of news professionals hinted at some audience assumptions about what "they" are "trying to do." These liberal activists thought journalists had conscious or unconscious motives for telling the public how to feel, whom to sympathize with, whom to support and to not support. The thing is: this audience imagined reporters being nearly as powerless in making the news as audiences were in interpreting stories. So, in their view, who really *does* have control over mainstream journalism?

Notes

1 For comprehensive overviews of this theory, see W. Phillips Davison, "The Third-Person Effect in Communication," *Public Opinion Quarterly* 47, no. 1 (1983); Albert Gunther and J.D. Storey, "The Influence of Presumed Influence," *Journal of Communication* 53 (2003); and Richard M. Perloff, "The Third-Person Effect," in *Media Effects*, ed. Jennings Bryant and Dorf Zillman (Mahwah, NJ: Erlbaum, 2002).

2 Using the constant comparative approach advocated by Barney Glaser and Anselm Strauss, I evaluated discourse by seeking thematic connections throughout the body of data, using computers to code and organize dialogue. First, transcripts were dissected according to the sender–message–receiver model, distilling from participants' discourse their viewpoints on these broad phases of mass communication. That initial examination suggested that something akin to TPE was happening, as activists constantly distinguished between their own reception of media messages and other people's. I was somewhat surprised at first by this finding, since the study's original intentions did not involve third-person perceptions or behaviors. Glaser

and Strauss, *The Discovery of Grounded Theory: Strategies for Qualitative Research* (Chicago, IL: Aldine Publishing, 1967).

3 During the analysis and writing phases of this study, I consulted discussants by sending them my tentative findings and asking for feedback. While this kind of "member check" can boost research validity, I also considered it an ethical responsibility and a personal pleasure. I enjoyed sharing my research with them and hoped the benefits would be mutual. Six activists who participated in the study offered insights. Some said they appreciated my literature review, "objective eye," or interpretation; others wrote several pages detailing points on which they found my discussion ambiguous or my focus too narrow. One discussant thought I had presented the student interpretations as too dumb or naïve; in response, I've characterized students here as more sophisticated than I previously had. It was gratifying when a discussant thanked me for "doing something practical rather than merely academic."

4 For more on Gerbner's work and influence, see Gerbner et al., "Growing Up with Television," in *Media Effects*, eds. Jennings Bryan and Dorf Zillmann (Mahwah, NJ: Erlbaum, 2002).

5 One study participant, Nick, explained to me that he "vacillated between identities" and felt "like a sort of hybrid." When he was with activists, he prodded them to learn about the intellectual background, history, and gnosis of activism, and when he was with professors, he urged them to get out of their classrooms and take a position in the world.

6 Erving Goffman, *Forms of Talk* (Philadelphia: University of Pennsylvania Press, 1981), 174.

7 Goffman, *Forms of Talk*, 174.

8 Martin Malone, *Worlds of Talk: The Presentation of Self in Everyday Conversation* (Malden, MA: Polity, 1997), 73.

9 All italics in quotations are added by me, to emphasize participants' use of pronouns, imaginary dialogue, and other words or phrases significant to this analysis.

10 One meta-analysis suggests that TPE findings are less robust among nonrandom, noncollege samples than often assumed; see Bryant Paul et al., "The Third-Person Effect," *Mass Communication and Society* 3, no. 1 (2000).

11 Perloff, "The Third-Person Effect."

12 For more on media superiority and additional analysis of pronominal usage in this audience discourse, see Jennifer Rauch, "Superiority and Susceptibility," *Discourse and Communication* 4, no. 3 (2010).

13 In this section, the dialogue that activists appear to have invented for role-playing purposes is presented in an italicized font style for clarity and emphasis.

14 A 2004 study by the University of Maryland found that the *more* Americans consumed commercial TV news (especially Fox News) coverage of the war in Iraq, the *less* they knew about the subject and the more likely they were to support the Bush Administration. As Robert McChesney observed, "A more damning comment on the U.S. news media would be difficult to imagine, as it goes directly against what a free press is supposed to do in a democratic society"; see *The Problem of the Media* (New York: Monthly Review, 2004), 123.

15 Rauch, "Superiority and Susceptibility."

16 Goffman, *Forms of Talk*, cited in Malone, *Worlds of Talk*, 46.

17 Malone, *Worlds of Talk*.

18 Davison, "The Third-Person Effect."

19 Malone, *Worlds of Talk*.

20 Malone, *Worlds of Talk*.

21 Henry Jenkins, *Textual Poachers* (New York: Routledge, 1992), 61; see also Pierre Bourdieu, "The Aristocracy of Culture," *Media, Culture, and Society* 2, no. 3 (1980).

22 Manuel Castells, *The Rise of the Network Society* (Oxford: Blackwell, 1996), 5.

5

LAY THEORIES OF THE POLITICAL ECONOMY OF NEWS

They're trying to get the most sensational stories and spin them in the most sensational ways so they can compete for viewers, so they can compete for ratings, so they can compete for money from advertisers. It's not information for the purpose of information. It's information for the purpose of creating a sensational story that's going to make money for the parent company that's controlling the broadcast.

—*Nathaniel, 24, environmental activist*

Alternative-media fans who discussed the news with me saw several distinct and somewhat devious motives driving the production of mainstream TV journalism. "They're trying to get below the level of what's conscious, the intellectual process, the judgment," one said. "They're trying to deliberately expand the notion of terrorism. They're trying to take the anger people feel over 9–11 and . . . stretch it out," another said. "They're trying to get the viewer to see themselves as the victim, that *'this could happen to me, therefore I should pay attention to this newscast,'*" a third said. In other words, "they" are trying to create sensational stories and compete for advertising revenue, as Nathaniel explained previously, in two terse sentences using the words "sensational" and "compete" three times each. In essence, these liberal activists perceived journalism as a chain of processes for converting audience emotions into corporate profits.

Tabloid-style coverage and elite criticism of mainstream media—more so than rising political partisanship—are primary contributors to Americans' increasing dislike and mistrust of journalism.[1] If elite criticism is an important source of negative attitudes toward institutional media, as Jonathan Ladd observed, then "one place we should see their influence is in the effects of consuming news from alternative-media outlets." He postulated that political blogs and other alternative news sites have become important means through which criticism of "lamestream" media by politicians, political activists, opinion columnists, and other elites reaches the public.

In this chapter, you will see how alternative-media consumers think and talk about tabloid-style news, focusing on their structural critique of news and their lay theory that sensationalism is not an end in itself but a means of earning profit. By sensationalism, I mean approaches to news presentation that heighten the importance or urgency of a topic by conveying strong emotions and provoking visceral reactions through language, sounds, and images. Sensationalism plays an important role in promoting news consumption; it is, at least partly, a strategy through which media organizations do propaganda on their own behalf.[2] An obsession with economic biases, which outweighed political ones, distinguished the interpretations of mainstream news shared by liberal alternative-media users from the evaluations offered by less engaged students as well as by conservative alternative-media users (as a future chapter will explore).

Discussants in the student and alternative groups alike talked about the news program in terms of what various people were "trying" to do. In the first case, students frequently interpreted news in relation to the motives of the social actors featured in the program. Iraqi civilians were trying to defend themselves, Rush Limbaugh was trying to make people feel sorry for him, and Congressional leaders were trying to help the elderly. Only three comments suggested that the students thought "they" were journalists rather than social actors. "They were trying to capture your attention," Jim said. "They were trying to get both sides of the story," Marissa said. "The news was trying to create an idea in people's heads," Mike said. And none of the student viewers used third-person plural pronouns in reference to corporate owners or advertisers, as the alternative viewers were wont to do.

As I will recount, these alternative-media enthusiasts ascribed ultimate control over TV news to corporate owners, advertisers and, to some extent, powerful sources—with journalists, viewers, grassroots sources, and the public playing minor roles. This chapter further examines their view of journalism as socially constructed, including through sourcing routines that prioritize elite perspectives and marginalize citizens. We will explore some interpretive strategies through which resistant readers tried to defuse the manipulative power that they saw in sensational news. And, we will take stock of extratextual resources and cultural schemata that they drew upon when interpreting the newscast— namely, their experiences as activists and their uses of alternative media, in which media criticism and political-economic theory from public intellectuals like Noam Chomsky, Edward Herman, and Robert McChesney featured prominently.

Before diving further into the implications of this perspective, let's take a close look at the journalistic agendas captured in the introductory quotes from liberal news viewers. Who are *they*? What are *they* trying to do? What do *they* want? How and why do *they* do it? Their discussions used the pronoun *they* in several ways: what *people* featured in this program were trying to do, what *activists* in the world were trying to do, and what *viewers* were trying to do as they watched the news (read graphics, for instance, or listen to voice-overs). But their most telling application of *they* referred to media personnel, which, you might be surprised to learn, rarely included news reporters.[3]

Was It News or an Advertisement?

When I asked a group of alternative-media users what stood out in their minds about a mainstream newscast we had just watched together, three of them launched into a conversation about the business of media. "The last one, I wondered if it was news or an advertisement," Fred said, referring to a segment reporting on a new contraceptive pill:

FRED: There was a woman who said, "Gee, my period is so inconvenient." That little bit seems very much like, *"Oh boy, you should take this pill 'cause your period's so inconvenient."* It seems so much like a canned thing from a TV commercial, "Oh, my period was so blah-blah," or "My teeth were so yellow, then I took. . . ." (emphasis added)

Likewise, Cody noted that a news report about a prescription drug was placed after a story about prescription-drug legislation—a segment that had been sponsored by a prescription-drug company. She perceived a conflict of interest here between news values and commercial ones. Others in the group criticized the link between production decisions and economic imperatives, too:

CODY: Mainstream media is all about ratings and everything's driven by ratings . . . and money. The tag-lines for each of the segments were talking about terrorism. I think it's because the word itself just brings in people's sense of fear, and people will continue to come back and watch the news. Even with the birth-control pill, what was the tagline on that? It was, *"A new birth control for women that could be helpful . . . but may be a risk! Now, a commercial . . ."* (emphasis added)

[*Nick and Fred laugh*]

NICK: You're exactly right that they're driven by ratings. Ratings are how they get the advertisers. And who's going to advertise on them? It's also the media conglomerates . . . ABC is owned by Disney and someone from ABC News is interviewing the head of Disney. How do you interview your boss? How critical can you be of the entertainment industry?

This exchange, which took place in my first discussion with alternative-media enthusiasts, brought up a multitude of themes related to the market model of media that were reprised in all of the discussions. From their perspective, the traditional wall between media organizations' news and advertising functions has been battered by profit demands. Mainstream news is now created to advance the economic interests of corporate owners and commercial sponsors, not to educate the public. The subjugation of informational motives to political-economic ones undermines the credibility of news. In order to satisfy owners and advertisers, news producers pursue stories predictably attractive to the largest possible audience and downplay topics potentially offensive to powerful people. Corporate commercialism thus yields sensationalism as well as self-censorship.

These liberal viewers blamed the predominance of tabloid-style journalism on corporate imperatives of ratings, advertising, and profit. To them, the commercial demand for ratings debased news standards, including through the trivialization of substantial issues and the sensationalization of inconsequential matters. For example, Ryan avowed that profit motives were detrimental to the spread of political information:

RYAN: At the end of the day, television is an expensive medium and they need to sell advertising, so they need to get people watching the shows and watching the advertisements. Whatever they need to do to tweak the show to get more people watching, is what they will do, and the interest of the bottom line is not always in the interest of in-depth, fair, accurate reporting.

Whereas in Sarah's pragmatic view, the bottom line with the news was, well, the bottom line:

SARAH: Businesses exist to make money. I'm not saying they don't sometimes exist to do good. . . . I am sure that there have been people in TV journalism who really wanted to use the medium to make the world a better place. However, they can't make the world a better place if their show gets yanked off the air because it's bleeding cash.

Such hearty observations about the corporate, commercial structure of news dominated the collective interpretation of alternative-media users. This differed markedly from discussions with students, who commented on the same newscast with scant attention to its commercial or corporate aspects. Students sometimes alluded to audience expectations for sensational elements such as emotion, entertainment, and humor in television news. They did not remark upon a relationship between the producers' desire to tell compelling stories and the systemic demands of news media: to attract large audiences, satisfy advertisers, promote consumerism, squelch corporate criticism, and maximize profits.

One student, Adam, mentioned that the Medicare segment was "brought to you by [sleeping-pill brand]," referring to a sponsor graphic in the newscast.

He was the only student who commented on the ad, and he did so as an afterthought to our discussion, on his way out the door. That advertisement did not similarly escape the alternative viewers' notice. Projecting thoughts into the minds of news producers, Sarah wondered aloud whether they "didn't deliberately put that 'sponsored by' [sleeping-pill brand graphic] right before the story, just to sort of make clear that *'We know, we know, their money pays for us.'*" She thus theorized that TV journalists consciously acknowledged the tension between news and commerce, as she and her peers did.

Who Are They?

In order to streamline discussion and concentrate on news content, I had edited all of the commercials out of the recorded program used in these focus groups. However, the alternative news audience detected the presence of advertisers despite this absence. They insisted that news derives much of its meaning from its interplay with commercials. Jason said he appreciated my intentions in cutting the ads but that it was "significant what a difference it would make with the commercials there." Jodi seconded the motion and noted that the line between genres was fuzzy: "It's all a blur: commercials, news, action movies, sci-fi movies. . . . All that kind of blends into each other."

This comparison of news to advertising, this blurring of genres and motives, represented a strong theme in my conversations with liberal media users. Fred wondered "if it was news or an advertisement." Chuck said, "The news becomes sort of an advertisement." To Monique, news producers had "one goal in mind: to sell the advertisement." Jason said, "As long as mainstream media are funded and paid for by huge corporations, the news is treated like entertainment that's kind of sugarcoating these advertisements that people are trying to get across." Rich believed that broadcasters' dependence on ad revenue made the anchorperson "just a salesperson." "The stories they report build fear, and you don't consciously see the advertisements," he said, suggesting that TV news portrayed public places as unfit for anything but shopping. "[The message is] *Just stay inside your place, but it's okay to go outside to buy these products',*" he said. As these quotes demonstrate, discussants perceived the profit orientation of journalism as having dire consequences for not only news portrayals but also public attitudes and real-world behaviors.

When these fans of left-wing alternative media talked about what "they" were trying to do in the news, the pronoun almost always referred to advertisers and owners. Reporters were largely absent from their critique of mainstream journalism, as were government officials and regulators. Liz remarked, "The people who own the media are actually controlling the news stories"—*not* the people who produce the news stories. In these discussions, they seldom referred to journalists, who were usually seen as doing the bidding of their bosses. To wit, Sarah wrapped up a group session with this conversational gambit:

"Anybody here think that the makers of that news program truly did the best job they felt they could, to present the news that day?" Her question was met with silence from the others. After a few seconds, she continued her train of thought:

SARAH: It makes you wonder at the people who were dying their whole lives to go into journalism, who worked on the high-school or college paper, who fought with editors about what should and shouldn't be included. This just doesn't seem like what the people I knew who were journalism majors went into journalism to do.

SEAN: That's the nature of the beast. If you're going to change society, they just weed you out by not giving you the job.

The nature of the beast. Here, the mainstream media system was a beast beyond challenge, whose flaws were naturalized. Sean's belief that mission-oriented journalists are "weeded out" resonates with Todd Gitlin's view that structural routines help "clamp" negative frames onto reporting of movements through "the ways journalists are socialized, trained, recruited, assigned, edited, rewarded, and promoted on the job."[4] These liberal viewers believed that mainstream news producers would not "make waves, question the status quo in any profound way," as Joe put it, as long as doing so might pose a threat to their employer's economic interests. Thus were individual writers, reporters, editors, and producers dismissed as impotent against structural forces.

These discussants invoked what Herbert Gans calls the "journalistic disempowerment" caused by conglomeration in the news media industry, where profit pressures and editorial cutbacks reduce professionals' control over the news and their autonomy in shaping it.[5] Many journalists have experienced downward professional mobility, Gans wrote, in which audiences participate primarily by disappearing and disapproving—that is, through declining interest in and rising dissatisfaction with the news.[6] If that is so, then advertisers and owners are not solely to blame for deficiencies in corporate news: mainstream audiences themselves are implicated too. As one person proposed earlier, sensationalism presumably succeeds in making money for media owners by "getting more people watching" the news while "in-depth, fair, accurate reporting" does not.

What Are They Trying to Do?

In the minds of these alternative-media fans, for-profit journalism resembled advertising and, to a lesser extent, public relations and propaganda, because it was more concerned with persuading audiences than informing them. Their interpretation of news producers' agenda went something like this: tap into viewers' subconscious. Trigger negative emotions. Make audiences afraid and insecure. Scare people into watching the news and staying attentive. Avoid criticizing media owners and advertisers. Get ratings and make money. Guided by the beacon of profit, mainstream news organizations were seen as trying to promote their content, commercial sponsors, and a culture amenable to their sponsors and themselves. Per these discussants, protecting the interests of corporate owners and commercial advertisers sometimes entailed self-censorship. They saw mainstream news producers as trying to frame, filter, and censor stories to make content align with elite interests.

To cite some examples: Chuck opined that journalists censored themselves to avoid criticizing media owners:

CHUCK: You'll never see negative stuff. . . . If there's a problem with [a media corporation], you won't see the fact that they committed fraud or something, that won't show up on their TV stations. And they make news segments that are very thinly veiled advertisements for their other TV shows and stuff.

Joe said viewers must take the context of media owners and advertisers into account when evaluating news content:

JOE: What's the commercial network that's being produced by it? What's the ownership structure that's putting this thing out? What are their commercial interests and are they going to make waves, to question the status quo in any profound way? That would pose a threat to their own existence.

Cody thought that, in effect, the news was "run by advertisers":

CODY: Now the news is like any other show. We all know that corporations own the media, and this affects how much the news stations can put on. If they say too much in one direction or another, even if it's factually true, someone's going to pull their advertising. They don't have to prove that what someone is said is untrue. The popular notion, the fantasy of what news used to be, is that all you have to be able to do is back up what you're saying with facts. That's not true anymore. If the advertisers don't like it, you don't have a show.

These viewers "all knew" that news organizations routinely declined to report on problems of their corporate owners as well as, more broadly, to criticize corporations and corporatism. "The big corporate moguls" did not want a spotlight on their own activities, Jodi remarked. News corporations like General Electric or Disney were only able to represent a certain view of society, Sean said. They believed that sensational coverage of violent interpersonal crimes dominated the news because it served the profit interests of Big Media. And, they suggested that a dearth of attention to institutional violence and corporate crime resulted from media owners' sympathies with big business. "Obviously they are [sympathetic to corporate and military interests]," Rich said, because ABC was owned by Walt Disney and NBC was owned by GE, which manufactures missiles. These discussants viewed commercialization and self-censorship together yielding a form of cooperation, collaboration, or collusion, if not quite a conspiracy, that effectively filtered content.

A vigorous conversation erupted among Ami, Chris, and Liz on the topic of how to make the news more informative and more useful. When Chris said mainstream media "would probably have to divorce themselves of all their sponsors in order to do it," Ami and Liz enthusiastically assented. Feeling encouraged, Chris gave a passionate oration:

CHRIS: There can't be a free media if the people who own it have vested interests in all the same things that they don't want you to know about. Reporting has to be from the standpoint where you're going to uncover a story . . . you're going to find out that your backwater is being poisoned by this corporation, and that corporation owns the media that they're not going to let you know that. Or you're going to find out that we're using daisy-cutters in Afghanistan, which is a bomb that is specifically only meant to kill human beings. But you're not going to find that out because GE makes daisy-cutters and they own the media. You know what I mean.

One can detect here a resonance with Edward Herman and Noam Chomsky's "propaganda model" that describes news coverage being filtered through the interests of people who control and finance media. According to their widely read book *Manufacturing Consent: The Political Economy of the Mass Media*, structural pressures compel mainstream journalists to self-censor, thereby constraining the free circulation of information without overt government censorship.[7] One of these "filters," or structural constraints, is the enormous size, concentrated ownership, and profit orientation of dominant news organizations. A second is news media's reliance on advertising as a primary source of income, including an internalization of advertisers' lust for affluent audiences. A third is symbiosis between reporters and elite sources, officials, and "experts"—a relationship rooted in media organizations' imperatives to maintain access and to produce news cheaply.[8] In this classic critique of mass media, which harkens to the Frankfurt School and other theories of social legitimation, Herman and Chomsky stressed the industry's mutual interests with government sources, the corporate sector, and advertisers. As a result of these filters, they conclude, the mass media fail to provide the kind of information that people need to make sense of the world.

Echoing these scholars, my liberal discussants argued that mainstream journalism propagandizes on behalf of the powerful, forsaking its responsibilities to the public. They criticized the news for offering audiences a particular version of reality espoused by powerful political-economic actors. To many of these alternative-media fans, economic motives were a dominant influence on mainstream news content, more so than political ones. However, some viewers more explicitly linked their interpretations of this newscast to propaganda, a form of political persuasion, than to advertising, a form of economic persuasion. Yet political-economic is hyphenated for a reason; it is difficult to untangle the political and economic interests in the media sphere. According to the prolific public intellectual McChesney, who built on the work of Herman and Chomsky, advertising *is* corporate propaganda.[9]

Several people used the term "propaganda," including Smithy, Sean, Beki, and Nathaniel. Smithy, for one, thought the program was a "subtle propagandistic presentation." Sean said all corporate news amounts to "propaganda" because it reflects elite rather than majority views of society. Beki and Nathaniel saw the media and government working together in a "whole system, a propaganda machine" or a "propaganda mechanism" that creates a "farce of democracy" and an "illusion of information." Nathaniel said that the public needs journalists to interpret current events and that those interlocutors have an agenda: "What are they trying to do? To me it's so sophisticated. It is! It's propaganda."

These alternative viewers offered other provocative interpretations of what "their" motives were and how "they" pursued those agendas: through sensational language, emotions, drama, visuals, and victimization (in their words: *by getting below the conscious level; by expanding the notion of terrorism; by creating an image; by making viewers see themselves as victims; by enhancing people's anger; by using Sept. 11 as leverage; by hitting you over the head with drama*) as well as through brevity and feigned objectivity (*by boiling it down to a 30-second piece; by avoiding taking an overt position*). Some means of persuasion that they identified in the newscast were rhetoric, framing, and sourcing patterns—ideas that further hint at the direct or indirect influence of critics like Gitlin, Herman, and Chomsky on their interpretations.

How Are They Trying to Do It?

Rhetorical language played an essential role in news persuasion, according to discussants. When Nathaniel suggested that the vocabulary in the newscast resembled talking points from a Republican press release, Beki agreed. "I think if you were to sit down and compare the two, they'd be very similar," she said. "And if you watch different news sources, all of them are using the same rhetoric and the same phrases." Like others in her group, she thought the program content obeyed a certain political-economic logic. "There's obviously an agenda that they're trying to portray in the news. They have an agenda, they want reactions from people, they want support." Some words they strongly associated with propagandistic rhetoric—that they saw as ideologically loaded—were *terrorism, convenience,* and *victim.*

Some discussants referred to this process as "framing," a term that Gitlin and other critical media scholars have used. Framing is a narrative device that suggests a particular interpretation for a news story by emphasizing certain themes and downplaying other information—which makes news more dramatic while often oversimplifying issues and focusing on personalities. In his seminal book *The Whole World Is Watching*, Gitlin analyzed frames through which journalists covered the 1960s student movement. Like Herman and Chomsky, he proposed that when journalists make decisions about what to cover and how, they tend to (perhaps unconsciously) serve the interests of political and economic elites.[10] Unlike them, he described news coverage as driven not as much by deliberate political-economic goals as by the routine conventions of everyday reporting.

These alternative viewers linked framing to rhetorical choices and images as well as sourcing patterns and attempts at formal balance. "You have to frame the issues some way, you have to use language," Nick said. "The degree of inflammatory language [varies between] Fox News versus ABC versus NPR. But they're all framing issues. That's inescapable. You have to." Fred agreed with this assessment, and Jodi elaborated on it. In discussing the program's balance and sourcing, she replaced Nick's and Fred's vocabulary of *framing* with the paradoxical *unbiased slant*:

JODI: It's interesting because I think they try to show and act like they have an unbiased slant on things, or to show both sides. But with certain issues they never show both sides, like with the death penalty issue. They always show the family members who are in favor of the death penalty. . . .

NICK: Uh-huh [agreeing].

JODI: . . . but you never see the family members who aren't. And that's one way, where I always notice that. It's always one-sided with that issue.

These liberal activists perceived professional norms as squeezing ideology between the lines of the news text, subtly shading the words and sources that journalists included and excluded. When we talked about a news clip depicting victims of a U.S. bombing campaign, one viewer saw persuasive intent in a combination of words and images. "I feel like I got another taste of how propagandizing the news is implemented," Smithy remarked, explaining how he thought the newscast defused potential sympathy for victims of U.S. aggression:

SMITHY: By the time you see the woman crying outside the Iraqi town of Tikrit, you have already been desensitized to her, if you're totally manipulated by the corporate media, to the plight of the people in that town, because it is A) a *"stronghold"* [laughing] and B) a *"hotbed of insurgency."* (emphases theirs)

They took issue with the persistent presence of victims among news sources in this program. When people who were neither experts nor officials were interviewed, they said, those people were often victims or members of victims' families—cast as passive, helpless, and vengeful. Cody thought there was "always a *victim* speaking" (emphasis theirs):

CODY: Whether it's a wife of a soldier that's [been killed in action] or whether it's somebody who's fearful of the sniper or whatever. In my opinion, it's a way of trying to get the viewer to see themselves as the victim, that *"This could happen to me, therefore I should pay attention to this newscast."*

Once again, this discussant voiced an imaginary response to news by an absent viewer. Many of these alternative-media users believed that journalists overrepresented victims of crime to compel audiences to pay attention—a result of the sensationalism they see permeating the mainstream news landscape.

In many regards, this is the kind of rhetorical analysis that Herman and Chomsky performed. They noted that words like *genocide* were frequently used to describe victimization by states that are U.S. enemies and rarely applied to U.S.-sponsored actions that could qualify as genocidal. Their study found that "worthy" victims in countries allied with the United States received more news coverage (by a factor of 10) than "unworthy" victims in non-allied countries, for instance.[11] Their propaganda model suggests that mainstream news disproportionately features terrorism "experts" (quotation marks in the original) who are government officials, journalists, or spokespeople for conservative think tanks, to the exclusion of voices critical of an escalated "war on terror."[12] Indeed, the use of "experts" who support the official slant of news and advance dominant ideologies is at the heart of a process they call "manufacturing consent." The term is borrowed from 1920s press critic Walter Lippmann, who thought it both necessary and good for journalists to manipulate public opinion.

Akin to my respondents' claims about the news, Chomsky and Herman's propaganda model describes how mainstream media prevents the public from fully understanding political realities—not so much by suppressing certain facts (though that does happen) but more often by selectively presenting, emphasizing, and contextualizing facts. This echoes Gitlin's explanation of framing as "principles of selection, emphasis, and presentation composed of little tacit theories about what exists, what happens, and what matters."[13] These analysts agreed that journalistic omission of facts was a minor concern relative to the problems of whether facts are presented with appropriate emphasis, tone, and contextualization. Neither propagandistic nor framing processes require powerful people to directly control news content or intervene in news production; they take place without journalists' deliberate participation, so the resulting news bears little relation to reporters' personal beliefs or motives.

My discussants acknowledged many such structural influences on news production. They noted that it was easier for journalists to assemble the news when they could get information from official sources who were readily available.

(This observation resonates with research showing that journalistic routines rely on access to public officials, which gives such sources great influence over news agendas and frames.)[14] As Joe explained:

JOE: They have the big soap-box, so it's just so easy to interview someone from the military when you're investigating a recent military operation. It costs a lot of money and it's difficult to talk to all the people whose lives are impacted by that military action. And really to investigate and find out what the real impact of it was. . . . Who exactly is it that [U.S. soldiers in Iraq] killed and arrested, who are these people? From a practical perspective, it's a lot easier to just quote the official sources.

They observed that the "experts" upon whom journalists depend typically represent organizations trying to influence public policy that have an agenda. They believed that much of the persuasion in news derives not from explicit propaganda attempts but from factors like sensationalism, dramatization, and personalization that are, apparently, just responding to popular demand.[15]

What Do They Want?

Despite their conviction that news circulates in a market manipulated by corporations—not by an invisible hand—these informants suggested that mainstream media were essentially responding to public appetites. (In this respect, these activists resembled the students, who believed that TV news simply gave audiences what they wanted. The students attributed journalism's emphasis on bad news, violence, and fear to media's desire to attract and excite viewers. "It kind of just shows you what our society as a whole wants to see," Brandon theorized. "People just want to be entertained, in general, so it's just entertaining," Anthony said, echoing the group's theory that news was more desirable for recreation than for information.) In other words, the alternative-media fans assumed that TV journalists chose sensational stories because they were popular with audiences. They saw news producers as valuing human interest, which supposedly translated into higher ratings, over public interest, which supposedly did not. This interpretation tended to reduce other people to pawns, re-iterating the lay theories shared in a previous chapter about powerful media and vulnerable publics.

A few illustrative examples: Sarah said producers featured a story about a public official's sex scandal because it was "what they expect people to be interested in":

SARAH: They do have to get ratings, they have to pay their bills. Therefore, whatever's going on with [the sex scandal], they're going to report it. Even if it's really not news. I mean, it's a fun story and they're in business, and the public seems to like fun stories.

Likewise, Ryan said, "Whatever they need to do to tweak the show to get more people watching, is what they will do, and the interest of the bottom line is not always in the interest of in-depth, fair, accurate reporting." His reply, like others recounted here, assumed that mainstream viewers craved entertainment and rejected news that was in-depth, fair, and accurate. Chris similarly assumed that few audiences wanted to watch investigative news:

CHRIS: And the point about "giving the people what they want," well, I just don't think that that's the media's job. The media's job is investigative reporting. They're supposed to give people the truth, not necessarily what they want.

At the same time, he believed that news had a duty to deliver such goods to the public, regardless of whether the market demanded them.

Discussants tied the "mass" audience's alleged preference for sensational news to cultural factors. In one lively discussion, Liz and Amy said people needed to be interested in order to watch the news and that producers aired short news clips because viewers lost interest very easily. Chris said he thought people preferred snippets because they were conditioned to have short attention spans "by the way that we are visually socialized. A long time ago people used to sit and listen to a radio for an hour." Then, Liz elaborated on a paradox that she called "a problem with our system," not just a problem with the media:

LIZ: I don't know what's better, for them to stop sensationalizing the news so that people will get the correct news or if they sensationalize the news so more people watch it. There's a paradox there. What do you do? There is a problem with people being misinformed. It's a very real problem, but how do you fix it?

Several assumptions about the nature of news and the nature of its audiences— for instance, that sensationalism appealed to most people, and that sensationalism misinformed people—undergird such statements, which were common among these viewers. The problems of news, they said, essentially resulted from the facts that mainstream media had to earn profits through advertising and that mainstream audiences wanted sensationalism, so that media "naturally" had no choice but to give audiences what they presumably demanded.

Experiences With Media Criticism

How did these liberal activists acquire and develop their interpretive frameworks regarding the political-economic influences on journalism production? A response from Liz offered some clues:

LIZ: It's so interwoven: there are corporations who own the media, who own corporations. . . . Capitalism is supposed to be guided by invisible market forces that are going to keep everything egalitarian across the board. It doesn't happen that way. There's a monopoly on the media and until that's broken up and broken down, we can't change [the system].

She distinguished here between market forces and corporate power, identifying capitalist media as a case of market *failure*, rather than success. She referred to a *media monopoly*, a critical concept that places news content in an ownership framework where a half-dozen corporations control the vast majority of U.S. newspapers, magazines, radio, and television stations, book publishers, and movie companies.[16]

According to Eric Alterman, the eminent media critic, "No book on the media has proved as influential to our understanding of the dangers of corporate consolidation to democracy and the marketplace of ideas" as *The New Media Monopoly* by Ben Bagdikian, a Pulitzer-Prize-winning journalist and devotee of both left- and right-wing alternative media. Analysts such as Bagdikian, Chomsky, Herman, and McChesney have argued forcefully for decades that enormous, for-profit news organizations dominate the global media system and transmit messages favorable to the governmental and corporate elite (to which mainstream journalists are often presumed to belong), rather than pursuing the wider public interest.[17] This domination results not from crude conspiratorial interventions but from cooperation and internalization of management priorities, which results in media companies avoiding certain kinds of competition and offering a narrow range of highly duplicative content. Just as these public intellectuals might do, Liz refuted the alleged invisible hand of the market and proposed that media corporations sought monopoly (or, more accurately, oligopoly) power in order to subvert the market.

These activist, alternative viewers reported having been exposed to the ideas of many high-profile media critics. Liz, for one, had taken a college course with Daniel Chomsky, Noam's nephew, a political scientist who shares his family's interest in how mainstream media supports elite views. Some activists displayed familiarity with other critical media analysts, such as Neil Postman, author of best-selling books like *Amusing Ourselves to Death: Public Discourse in the Age of Show Business*. Participants' media diaries indicated that more than half of them regularly access the *Nation*, the alternative publication to which Alterman, McChesney, and Naomi Klein have consistently contributed. The conceptions of corporate media power articulated in alternative news outlets like the *Nation, Progressive, Democracy Now!, Z Magazine*, Indymedia, and *Adbusters* have deeply shaped activists' worldviews.[18]

Postman, Klein, and McChesney have played important roles in popularizing this strand of media analysis. In *Amusing Ourselves to Death*, Postman argued that the blurring of TV news with advertising posed a grave threat to public discourse. "Television serves us most ill when it co-opts serious modes of discourse—news, politics, science, education, commerce, religion—and turns them into entertainment packages," he wrote. "*The A-Team* and *Cheers* are no threat to our public health. *60 Minutes, Eyewitness News*, and *Sesame Street* are."[19] In *How to Watch TV News*, he explained to readers that news is made, not gathered; that news is a commercial enterprise guided by money, management, and viewer demographics; and that images have a bias toward motion, violence, excitement, brevity, and drama that fosters sensationalism while precluding complexity.[20] Journalist and activist Naomi Klein has written for the *Globe and Mail, Guardian,* and *Harper's* as well as the *Nation.* In her international best-seller *No Logo,* she scrutinized the growing influence of multinational corporations, sponsors, and advertisers in countless dimensions of cultural life. Klein singled out corporate censorship by media giants ABC-Disney and Viacom over media properties like ABC News and CBS News for special scorn. Her book has been called a "bible" of the anti-corporate movement.[21] In more than a dozen books, McChesney has argued that media corporations concentrate power, influence policy, and commercialize journalism—undermining the quality of news available to the public.[22] He co-founded the nonprofit group Free Press (with another *Nation* contributor, John Nichols) to advocate for independent ownership of media platforms and journalism that holds the powerful accountable.

I base my claim that these discussants derived interpretive resources from their experiences with alternative media also on the fact that they themselves said this was so. They believed that having access to alternative media—another model of journalism, another mode of communication—equipped them to better understand, analyze, criticize, and resist the power of mainstream news.[23] They said that alternative news sources gave them the insight to question sources, to understand rhetorical strategies, to see beyond mainstream coverage.

The Price of Living in a Free Society?

These conversations with alternative-media users offered considerable evidence that they perceived an overwhelming—perhaps over-determining—influence of media's corporate and commercial structure on the selection and presentation of news. A wide range of research supports such contentions that journalism, due to industrial practices and structural pressures, represents and reinforces elite frameworks for understanding the world.[24] Analysts agree that mainstream news takes the form it does due to a combination of factors, including the economic realities of the business, the dependence of journalists on sources who control information, and routine industrial, organizational, and professional practices of news gathering.[25] These latter two factors attracted less comment in our discussions than the former one did, perhaps due to the conspicuousness of corporate criticism among liberal audiences.

This audience's concerns about sensationalism, and especially about sympathetic heroes and victims, parallels findings that news stories tend to *personalize* (downplaying bigger social, economic, and political issues in favor of trivial individual trials and tragedies), *dramatize* (featuring human-interest stories rather than analytical or scientific formats and relying on visuals, sometimes as cheap emotional devices), and *fragment* (isolating individual events and social actors from larger contexts). Together, such narrative tendencies in journalism make it hard for audiences to see causes of chronic social problems, historical patterns, the workings of institutions, and connections across issues.[26] My point in this section is not to assess whether this audience's understandings of "how news media work" are right or wrong, but to highlight some similarities and differences between their lay theories and academic ones.

This alternative-media audience's perception of news as dominated by political-economic forces coincides with those of social-movement actors studied elsewhere. For instance, Patrick McCurdy's analysis of activists' discourse concluded that they predominantly viewed news media through a political-economic lens. Participants in a G-8 protest in Scotland collectively agreed that media organizations selected news to maximize sales while de-emphasizing or ignoring news stories that might jeopardize advertising accounts or criticize the capitalist system.[27] They said mainstream media overwhelmingly quoted powerful officials and leaders, used its power to promote values preferred by the corporate world, and neglected the needs of many groups throughout society. McCurdy concluded that his respondents' theories about news media bore a strong resemblance to those of radical critics popular in the global justice movement such as Chomsky, Klein, and McChesney—much as I conclude about mine.

These interpretations of mainstream news are perhaps not unique to activists. Research by Mirca Madianou mentioned earlier found that Greek viewers (who may or may not have been activists) were generally critical of news content and practices. Those discussants also used the pronoun *they* to convey their perceptions of what journalists, media owners, and politicians were trying to do with the news. As Madianou reported, someone named Haris said, "*They* show incidents like these to fill up the duration of the program." To which Lena replied, "*They* have to make up something. That's what it comes to. But we should not fool ourselves, we should not think that those working in the media are socially altruistic." Spyros interjected, "*They* are companies." Responded Lena, "Exactly. And companies have to have profits. Otherwise what's the point? They'll shut down. This is what we need to remember. In order to make profits they will do anything, even illegal things." Dafne said, "*They* show these incidents because *they* want to distract our attention from other matters." Fotis added, "*They* want us to be in constant tension with Turkey." Giota concluded, "*They* are misleading us." These six cynical viewers suspected that news production was guided by political-economic goals, not informative or pro-social ones. The perspectives of Madianou's discussants and mine might differ in degree but not in kind.

Activists and alternative-media fans—groups that often intersect—see a difference between a free, open market for news and one dominated by giant firms. These audience members theorized that media corporations did not obey the logic of the market but, rather, sought monopoly power in order to subvert the market. However, my study suggests some possible shortcomings in lay knowledge of news economics. (Which doesn't mean discussants were not aware of these aspects of news economics; they might have had additional knowledge and theories about media that did not arise in these conversations.) Some viewers pointed out that the public chooses from a limited range of news programming, but they didn't elaborate on what those limiting factors might be. They assumed that organizations program particular kinds of news (say, sensational stories) because it is popular with audiences. By eliding corporate news with corporate media, the group's structural analyses overlooked how a newscast is, in fact, *not* like any other show.

These lay theories of news economics are partly true, and they are incomplete. My focus groups did not address how news as a commodity is distinct from other media commodities, how media are different from other corporate products (for instance, due to high first-copy costs and low additional costs per copy), and how the media business is dissimilar from other industries. This alternative news audience expressed strong theories about corporate power over media representations but talked very little about corporate influence on government policies toward media or advertiser influence over target audience demographics and hence content. You could say they have internalized a Chomskyite critique of the news media system to a greater degree than a McChesneyite one.

As McChesney has richly articulated, news broadcasters lobby fervently to maintain and expand government-granted privileges, such as the lucrative licenses over public airwaves given to for-profit corporations. News organizations get tax deductions for their advertising expenses, which is effectively a government subsidy for commercials. News programmers make decisions based on costs as well as the ability to attract affluent consumers with disposable income sought by advertisers; this is why journalism often ignores poor and working-class audiences. According to McChesney, the commercial media system is not set up to create good journalism or even to just make money. It is set up to generate *maximum* returns for its investors—and has been successful at doing that. Criticizing media owners for such choices is misguided when they are behaving rationally according to the current media structure. A better solution would be to "change the nature of the system so that it is no longer rational to produce what passes for journalism today," McChesney said.[28] This would require the public—including activists and alternative-media advocates—to shift attention from criticizing news content to reforming the news media system.

This chapter provided evidence that some audiences recognized and rejected the market model of news that regards audiences as consumers and neglects public goods such as an informed citizenry as externalities, even though they thought most audiences were basically getting what they wanted. My discussants espoused a public-service model that addresses people as citizens—a model they associated with alternative media. They didn't quite say so, but the basis of their economic thought about news media seemed to a vision of journalism as a public utility. They talked about huge corporations perverting the market, but it's unlikely that they wanted a different kind of commercial system. What these alternative-media fans preferred was not to improve the market system for commercial media so that it functions more freely, but to build a nonmarket, noncommercial system.

The next few chapters will disentangle some of the factors that might influence such critical interpretations of mainstream news. What cultural resources contribute to this audience's developing theories about the attitudes and behaviors of audiences, journalists, and news organizations? Why does this audience imagine it can resist the power of news better than other groups of people can? First, however, we will consider their identity as activists with firsthand experience participating in protest actions and journalism processes.

Notes

1 Jonathan Ladd, *Why Americans Hate the Media and How It Matters* (Princeton, NJ: Princeton University Press, 2012).
2 Michael Schudson, *Discovering the News* (New York: Basic Books, 1978).
3 Although it was occasionally difficult to interpret which category of media-related personnel—journalists themselves, corporate owners, advertisers, and so forth—discussants were referring to with the pronoun *they*, it was clear that this group perceived sensationalism as a driving force.
4 Todd Gitlin, *The Whole World is Watching* (Berkeley: University of California Press, 1980), 11.
5 Herbert Gans, *Democracy and the News* (New York: Oxford University Press, 2003), 24.
6 Gans, *Democracy and the News.*
7 Nearly half of journalists surveyed by Pew said they had sometimes consciously engaged in self-censorship to serve the commercial interests of their employers or advertisers. Only a quarter of respondents stated this had never happened, to their knowledge. Pew Research Center, "Self-Censorship," April 30, 2000.
8 Edward Herman and Noam Chomsky, *Manufacturing Consent* (New York: Pantheon, 2002), xi.
9 Robert McChesney, *Digital Disconnect* (Boston, MA: The New Press, 2014).
10 Other foundational works on framing theory and analysis include Robert Entman, "Framing: Toward Clarification of a Fractured Paradigm," *Journal of Communication* 43, no. 4 (1993); William Gamson and Andre Modigliani, "Media Discourse and Public Opinion on Nuclear Power," *American Journal of Sociology* 95 (1989); Erving Goffman, *Frame Analysis: An Essay on the Organization of Experience* (Cambridge, MA: Harvard University Press, 1974); Shanto Iyengar, *Is Anyone Responsible?* (Chicago, IL: University of Chicago Press, 1991); and Gaye Tuchman, *Making News* (New York: The Free Press, 1978).

11 Herman and Chomsky, *Manufacturing Consent*, 39–40.

12 They analyzed PBS Newshour as an example of a news source that is politically centrist. See Herman and Chomsky, *Manufacturing Consent*, 25.

13 Gitlin, *Whole World Is Watching*, 12.

14 For more on sourcing routines, see Phyllis Kaniss, *Making Local News* (Chicago, IL: University of Chicago Press, 1991); and Pamela Shoemaker and Stephen Reese, *Mediating the Message* (White Plains, NY: Longman, 1996).

15 For more discussion of nonideological biases like sensationalism, dramatization, and personalization, see W. Lance Bennett, *News: The Politics of Illusion* (Chicago, IL: The University of Chicago Press, 2016).

16 Ben Bagdikian, *The New Media Monopoly* (Boston, MA: Beacon Press, 2004).

17 Joshua Atkinson discusses relationships among globalization critics, activism, and alternative media in "Conceptualizing Global Justice Audiences of Alternative Media," *The Communication Review* 8 (2005).

18 Joshua Atkinson, *Alternative Media and Politics of Resistance* (New York: Peter Lang, 2010); Joshua Atkinson and Debbie S. Dougherty, "Alternative Media and Social Justice Movements," *Western Journal of Communication* 70, no. 1 (2006); John Downing, "Audiences and Readers of Alternative Media," *Media, Culture, and Society* 25, no. 5 (2003): 626. Some alternative news projects, like *The Mule* in Manchester, UK, are consciously informed by Herman and Chomsky's propaganda model. See Tony Harcup, "News with a Kick," *Communication, Culture, and Critique* 7, no. 4 (2014).

19 See Postman, *Amusing Ourselves to Death* (New York: Penguin, 1985).

20 See Neil Postman, *How to Watch TV News* (New York: Penguin, 1992).

21 Naomi Klein, *No Logo: Taking Aim at the Brand Bullies* (New York: Picador USA, 1999).

22 McChesney, *Problem of the Media*; *Rich Media, Poor Democracy*; *Digital Disconnect*; and *People Get Ready*. Critical researchers are not alone to scrutinize the growing influence of corporatization on the press; professional journalists similarly lament these trends in publications such as *Columbia Journalism Review*.

23 Although my student-informants didn't analyze the discursive power of language or sources of this news program in any meaningful way, one might say that they "resisted" its messages nonetheless—by preferring not to watch the news, as Marissa and Adam and Fauve and Ashley said they did, and as their media diaries (reported in Chapter 8) confirm.

24 For an overview of scholarship on the influence of political economy and journalistic routines on media content, see Bennett, *News: The Politics of Illusion*, in addition to Chomsky, Gitlin, Herman, McChesney, and Tuchman.

25 Bennett, *News: The Politics of Illusion*, 130.

26 Bennett, *News: The Politics of Illusion*.

27 Patrick McCurdy, "Mediation, Practice, and Lay Theories of Media," in *Mediation and Protest Movements*, eds. Bart Cammaerts, Alice Mattoni, and Patrick McCurdy (Bristol, UK, and Chicago, IL: Intellect Ltd., 2013).

28 Robert McChesney, *The Problem of the Media* (New York: Monthly Review, 2004), 97.

6

ACTIVIST INTERACTIONS WITH MAINSTREAM JOURNALISM

When you are an activist, you know that things do not simply happen on their own, in a natural process. You are more passionate about the news, which is why you do not normally watch mainstream news; it makes you realize again and again what you are actually up against. You look at the news not just to see what is going on but also how it is being described. You want to have some kind of influence on society. And you think that creating your own media, and creating community, is more important than just criticizing stuff. This is a small, paraphrased sample of some ways in which alternative-media users described their identities as activists to me, as we discussed mainstream news.

Activists comprise an interpretive community that shares understandings of social reality, intersubjective meanings, and strategies for decoding media texts. Some interlocking factors that influence these activists' communal interpretations are their experiences with alternative media, their experiences with social-movement actions, and the liberal/progressive political orientation of these experiences. Future chapters will address discussants' use of alternative media and their liberal perspectives in greater detail. Here, let's take a close look at the extent to which their views of journalism are intertwined with their positions as social activists. You will see how their personal involvement in a leftist, activist cultural context endowed them with a particular set of discursive resources that informed and shaped how they thought about news.

As social-movement actors, these alternative-media users have a "reflexive awareness of the logic of news" stemming not only from their "bifurcated position" as both *audiences for* and *actors in* the news, as Patrick McCurdy noted.[1] I propose further that liberal activism creates a subcultural environment that shapes people's understandings of TV programs and other news messages in ways that are not only idiosyncratic but also resistant (and in ways that conservative activism does not—a point to which we will return). McCurdy's research underscored two interrelated features of activists' lay theories of news. The first was their criticism of the influence of corporate-libertarian media on public culture and, in particular, the power of advertising over journalism, which I discussed earlier. The second was their criticism of news representations of social movements and social protests that spurred concerns about interacting with mainstream media.

While "activists" and "alternative-media users" are not entirely equivocal groups, they substantially overlap. Activists routinely use independent, alternative, grassroots, community, and radical media as avenues for making sense of their political and cultural terrain. Many social-movement actors—who feel that corporate, commercial news media are hostile toward them—rely on alternative outlets to frame collective issues and events, communicate within and across movements, and speak directly to current or potential participants. People who participate in protests and other political actions are "more prone to rely on alternative media" than on mainstream sources.[2] Some experts consider alternative media to be largely "synonymous with activism," because they are such an integral component in building activist networks, worldviews, and protest events.[3] Alternative media are valuable resources in movement activity that rank among the news sources most trusted by social-movement participants.

This chapter focuses on activists' understanding of the pressures and processes involved in journalism production, their frustrated pursuit of sympathetic news coverage, and their experience with alternative models of news that empirically diverge from mainstream media. Along the way, we will delve into their communal perceptions of how power operates in and through the news. I pay special attention to the phenomenon of "framing," following Todd Gitlin and other influential scholars, who consider such processes central to understanding social movements. To activists' minds, the discursive choices made by journalists have the effect of "disempowering" audiences, a term from leftist cultural politics whose use indicates that these viewers brought information and analytical skills from elsewhere to their news interpretations.

A segment in the newscast that provoked particularly strong responses was a report on protests in London against an upcoming visit from the U.S. president. One discussant, Jodi, commented upon the image of an upside-down American flag in the story, which to this audience meant journalists were trivializing the British demonstration: "Wow, that's typically the case from everything I've ever seen in terms of any coverage of popular protests," Jason generalized:

JASON: It's always about, *"Well, there was an upside-down flag"* or *"There were this many people"* or *"[There were] this many confrontations with the police,"* [instead of being about] *"These are the substantive coverage of why people protests, what their issues were and what they had to say."* I see that again and again in the coverage of mass protest.

His comment elicited a chorus of "Right, right" from fellow viewers. To which Nathaniel added, "[The newscaster said,] *'There are going to be large protests,'* and they emphasized that word *disruption.* There's going to be *disruption.* I noticed that."

Members of this group said they avidly followed protest coverage in the media. "That's actually one of the few times I'll actually tune into mainstream media, when I've been part of an event and I want to see what kind of coverage it got," Nathaniel said, minimizing the attention he routinely pays to traditional news sources. "I'll flick it on and see what they have to say." Liz and Amy interjected their own perceptions of inadequate protest coverage, along with firsthand experience being consulted by journalists as a news source:

LIZ: Even when protests were happening every day, it would be maybe a 10-second clip. That's probably even being generous. . . . You could find numbers [about the size of the protest] in the mainstream newspaper, but they always underestimate. Always.

AMI: You can also look at the police numbers, and then double or triple them accordingly!

[Everyone laughs.]

LIZ: [A TV reporter called me] after a protest. And he was like, "Are the pro-testers actually doing anything?" or something like that. [The reporter] agreed with me 100 percent and said, "I'm not supposed to say this, but I agree with you. And I'm going to try to get you on. I'm going to put all sorts of stars and checks next to your name." But every caller [to the newscast] was like, "[Activists are] stupid! And they make me late for work! And they make me late getting home! And they cause traffic jams!"

She further recounted being interviewed by a reporter who had said he wanted to let her activist group tell their side of the story:

LIZ: When the article came out, our entire interview was basically chopped apart and made me sound like the biggest idiot. And I know that happens frequently. . . . They made us just sound like we were students without a clue, that we were blocking traffic for no reason, that we had no motive going into it, that we come from broken families; there was all sorts of stuff. It was not a very flattering article.

For activists, such interactions highlight the distance between real-world events and mediated versions of events—along with the processes through which journalists transform reality into selective, flawed reconstructions. First-hand experience of the disjuncture between social-movement activities and media representations significantly influenced their awareness of framing, their interpretations of news coverage, and their trust in journalism.

"You Have to Frame the Issues Some Way"

The Whole World Is Watching: Mass Media in the Making and Unmaking of the
New Left.
The Sixties: Years of Hope, Days of Rage.
Media Unlimited: How the Torrent of Images and Sounds Overwhelms Our Lives.

These three books represent a fraction of the commentary published by Todd
Gitlin, the journalist and sociologist who entered public life in the 1960s as an
activist and leader of Students for a Democratic Society.[4] Over a half century,
his insights on interactions between activists and news media have circulated
widely in the mainstream and alternative press.[5] A professor at several U.S.
universities, Gitlin has also taught globally at institutions in Paris, Berlin, Oslo,
Toronto, Shanghai, Cairo, British Colombia, Tunisia, Switzerland, Italy, and
elsewhere. Having served on the boards of Greenpeace USA and *Dissent* magazine, his worldview is firmly planted in leftist activism and media criticism.

We have encountered already the tendency of activists and alternative-media
users to interpret news stories in light of how they saw journalists framing
social issues and events. They thought news frames often served ideological
or propagandistic purposes. They perceived mainstream reporters representing
protest as a form of disruption, violence, terrorism. To them, news producers
used language and images to portray soldiers as heroes, Iraqi resisters as insurgents, victims as vengeful, viewers as victims-in-waiting, activists as stunted
children. They detected many themes being excluded from or downplayed in
news frames—to wit, the vast majority of protests, people opposing the death
penalty, and more.

Gitlin has significantly influenced lay thinking about frames, which he
described as persistent, patterned principles of cognition, interpretation, and
presentation by which symbol-handlers routinely organize discourse.[6] He likened frames to assumptions and "little tacit theories" about what exists, what
happens, what matters, and what does not. "At each moment the world is rife
with events," Gitlin noted. "Even within a given event there is an infinity
of noticeable details" that requires journalists to select, emphasize, downplay,
reject, and exclude material. News frames are not windows flung open to let in
reality; rather, they are screened portals that obstruct much of the view.

Countless scholars have theorized framing in myriad ways, upon which
I'll touch just a few here—those relevant to the goal of illuminating activist interpretations of mainstream news. (By necessity, I am vastly abridging
discussion the scholarship on framing theory, which could fill a chapter of its
own.) Frames have been analogized to storylines, narratives, schemata, and
structures. Gitlin, notably, drew upon the work of Erving Goffman, Herbert
Gans, and Gaye Tuchman as he articulated his conception of framing in the
classic *The Whole World Is Watching*, which focused on news representations

of social protest.[7] You can envision frames as coming from both inside news organizations (news-gathering routines, journalists' choices, inertia, social construction, the nature of events) and outside them (powerful sources, economic factors, audience expectations, the dominant culture).

Framing is unavoidable and unacknowledged, according to Gitlin. Journalists necessarily adopt certain news frames to help them organize social reality, process large amounts of information quickly, and package it efficiently for relay to their audiences. This routinized approach leads journalists to report on "the event, not the condition; the conflict, not the consensus; the fact that 'advances the story,' not the one that explains it."[8] As a result, the underlying causes of protests are often not misrepresented or distorted but simply omitted. Frames matter because, to an important degree, they affect whether and how audiences who rely on news reports take action on social issues.

Many reporters treat the social world as an aggregation of objective *things* that they witness and convey to audiences. By contrast, many of the activists with whom I spoke considered social reality as a series of *processes* in which subjective humans participate. This suggests a fundamental difference in epistemology between activists and journalists, who seem to think about reality quite differently. Activists said news media do not reflect the world but, in important ways, constitute it—a claim that many journalists would deny. Thanks to deep collective and individual histories of direct and indirect experiences with journalists, activists have a particular set of knowledge about reporting conventions and values—about what it takes to "make the news."[9] They recognize news as a complex, mutually dependent social process in which activists and reporters often negotiate with each other over what shape the final story will take.

While activists tend to criticize and reject news portrayals of social-movement events and issues, Gitlin said, audiences with less direct experience of the situations are likely to accept uncritically the media version of the story.[10] One of his main concerns was that news audiences were vulnerable to the ways in which journalists routinely framed political protests—echoing the activists' concerns about being portrayed as trivial, disruptive, and ineffectual. Indeed, the deepest effects of media framing might come from coverage that is relatively consistent and repeated over a long time. Ultimately, framing (and propaganda, for that matter) would not matter much if it failed to influence audiences and manufacture consent.

News framing has real-world implications. Frames influence public opinion by making certain aspects of a story more salient, which can activate specific thoughts and ideas for readers. Experiments show that audiences who experience protest coverage supportive of the status quo, instead of social change, are more critical of activists and less critical of police.[11] They are less likely to identify with activists, to support protesters' free-speech rights, to consider protests an effective means of social action, and to deem protests newsworthy. News frames also influence how readers understand issues and whether they attribute responsibility for public problems to government officials, to victims, or to broader societal forces.[12] Journalists' use of loaded terms like *war* and *terrorism*—language to which these activists were sensitive—evoked emotional public responses following the Sept. 11 attacks that helped enable enactment of policies compromising American civil liberties.[13]

However, news frames do not have a uniform influence on all audiences. Different people interpret the same frames in divergent ways, according to individual factors such as differing levels of political sophistication, critical reading abilities, and experiences with cultural resources beyond those reflected in mainstream media.[14] Theories of news framing balance structure and agency while bridging cognition and culture, according to William Gamson and his coauthors. Most people know or intuit that news reports pre-organize the world and do not come to us in raw form. But "we are active processors and however encoded our received reality, we may decode it in different ways," said Gamson's team. "The very vulnerability of the framing process makes it a locus of potential struggle, not a leaden reality to which we all inevitably must yield."[15]

"We Are More Passionate About the News"

Before continuing the analysis of activists' discourse about mainstream news, let's acknowledge that they are obsessed with news in ways that the general public is not. Earlier I referred to them as news fans, junkies, enthusiasts, aficionados. Social-movement actors such as these are preoccupied with news media for a multitude of reasons. On a consumption level, they are in a near-constant state of media surveillance. They follow the news closely to stay informed about public affairs and to monitor what the less-active public might be reading, watching, or listening to—which helps guide their strategies and tactics. Movement participants use news to gauge what opportunities and challenges exist, who their enemies and allies are, and what kind of actions might be most effective. On a production level, activists frequently participate in mainstream news as sources interviewed and consulted by journalists, as Liz mentioned earlier. This is the bifurcated position of which McCurdy spoke.

In part, their intense attention to news coverage is motivated by instrumental purposes like educating the public about activist causes, building support for issues and events, and spurring audiences to join the pursuit of social change. To this end, some activists receive training in how to interact effectively with media personnel, further adding to their knowledge of and opinions about journalism. In part, their fixation on news coverage, even when it is unfavorable, also serves symbolic purposes resonating with the ritual mode of communication. Getting media attention animates activists and increases their morale. As Gitlin noted, press coverage gives activists some psychological compensation for hard work, some gratification that what they do matters in the world.[16]

Social-movement actors are alternately energized by, ambivalent toward, and frustrated with their endeavors to secure favorable mainstream publicity.

Many activists who struggle to get social-change issues and events covered wind up disappointed. They think mainstream journalists too often ignore their efforts and portray them in negative ways.[17] Research reliably confirms such perceptions about the quantity and quality of news coverage of social movements and protest events. Scholars have found, sometimes by comparing press coverage with police records of protests that occurred, that only a small percent of protest events are covered by major news organizations.[18] Sarah Sobieraj's work suggests that as little as 0.04 percent of voluntary associations who sought publicity had their events covered by journalists in a meaningful way.[19] When activists do manage to attract media attention for their causes, the coverage is unlikely to be substantive, serious, or sympathetic.[20]

Protest actions, in particular, are routinely characterized as disorderly, violent, and pointless. Such tendencies, which were evident in many news representations of Black Lives Matter events in 2020, have been widespread for more than half a century. One pioneering study showed that news coverage framed a 1970 London demonstration as potentially violent for weeks before it even started.[21] A pair of Hong Kong scholars identified a "protest paradigm": the press's tendency to show low tolerance for social conflict and high concern for social order by advocating suppressive measures to end protest, supporting government policies, and criticizing protesters harshly.[22] Studies have routinely shown that corporate reporters emphasize activists' deviance and disruption while downplaying their social critique and political efficacy.[23] My own research found *New York Times* reporters following the protest paradigm in coverage of demonstrations against the World Trade Organizations. Journalists used delegitimizing language to describe activists and framed the events as confrontations, spectacles, and riots—what my colleagues and I called the "tabloidization of protest."[24] Other scholars have identified a hierarchy according to the nature of the protest. Anti-racism rallies were most likely to be framed as riots whereas protests related to healthcare, immigration, and the environment were more likely to be portrayed as legitimate; the dominant frame, across a gamut of protest issues, was spectacle.[25] Such news coverage not only discourages public support for protest movements, it impedes change and exacerbates conflict.

Correspondingly, social-movement actors often plan their activities with an eye toward satisfying journalistic agendas and routines. This can amount to a kind of pandering that dilutes, contorts, redirects, or overwhelms their activities.[26] Instead of the movement becoming the media, the media risks becoming the movement. Sobieraj has persuasively argued that the "rampant media-centrism" of 21st-century social movements is counterproductive, that activists are losing the publicity game. Nonetheless, ongoing attempts to intervene in the mainstream news sphere have helped many activists to understand how corporate, commercial media works. Many activists who become cynical toward journalism gravitate toward alternative news producers who treat social movements better. They are also motivated to expose the flaws of for-profit media and to foster independent channels of communication, in order to promote their viewpoints and mobilize the public.[27] *Mobilization* or lack thereof is key to their worldview. As my conversations with activists demonstrate, they perceive mainstream media as deactivating the public and alternative media as offering potential activation.

"It Renders You Passive"

The binary terms *empowerment* and *disempowerment* figured conspicuously in activist interpretations of mainstream news. The dichotomy is rooted in 1960s student movement groups and community organizing campaigns. Empowerment conveys the sense of a subordinate, aggrieved group "taking power away from powers-that-be," while disempowerment connotes the opposite: elites who maintain power over subaltern groups.[28] In our conversations, activists repeatedly described elements of news discourse in terms of disempowerment and empowerment (which suggests processes) as well as *power* and *powerlessness* (which suggest objective states of being). To them, a mainstream newscast both reflected and sustained unequal power relations between elite groups and mass audiences.

"Mainstream media is part of the powers—that-be," Joe said.

Watching the news, Beki said, reminded her "what a powerful mechanism it is."

Jason said that if he got his news from mainstream media, he imagined it would make him feel "fear, powerlessness, alienation."

What specific elements of this newscast reinforced elite power or depleted public vigor, in the activists' view? Their discussion focused mainly on grammatical choices, rhetorical strategies, and language practices. For instance, they perceived an authoritative tone permeating these news stories, in part through frequent use of declarative statements. They thought non-elite people were inordinately represented as victims in the news, rather than as captains of their own fates. They perceived journalists as disproportionately favoring "experts" as sources by contrasting with ordinary citizens—a view that can be linked to these activists' personal experiences as spokespeople for their causes.

Fred explicitly tied disempowerment to the discursive authority of journalists and sources, as he interpreted the newscast's messages in the form of verbal imperatives:

FRED: It ends up, you're very disempowered. In the previews, they say *"We're going to talk about [a new contraceptive pill] after the break."* It's like, *"It will impact women's lives* [laughs]. *There's nothing you can do about it."* All that implies, *"We're the authorities and you're powerless."* [The news seems to say] *"Rely on the figures that we present."* "Doctor Jones says, *'This is wrong,'*" and these authoritative figures say, *"The economy is doing well."* (emphases added)

Fred and the other activists rendered the content of this program into simplistic, commanding statements such as: "Rely on our figures," "He can target any one of you," "Here is the important stuff," "It will impact women's lives," "They are the bogeymen," "It will make it easier," "You can't fight City Hall," and "Go to ABCNews.com."

From their perspective, news sourcing patterns had powerful effects upon audiences as citizens. They thought journalism's reliance on expert testimony conveyed messages about power to viewers. Rich agreed with Fred, explaining how the newscast's authoritative tone affected him, as a viewer:

RICH: [It makes me think], "Okay. My opinions don't count because I'm not an authority on this topic." A lot of stories just don't encourage people to do things on our own. It relies heavily on authorities on TV, paid authorities, people who have so many degrees, they know so much about this. You think, "I'm the one who's being affected by it directly, but what the hell do I know?" To me, it's sad, to think that people can't depend on themselves or that they [supposedly lack] the capacity or aren't encouraged to do so.

Rich and his fellow activists thus identified the presence of expert sources in the newscast as undermining or denying viewers' own experiences. "They're like, *'We conducted a survey, and 90 percent of Americans are happy working 28 extra hours a week for free,'*" he said. "Well, *I'm* not happy, but I better start being happy because everyone else is, because the experts say so" (emphases added). To this, Monique replied, "You're right. Where do they get their estimates from? Did they ever ask you? They didn't ask *me*" (emphases theirs). She recognized the authority exercised in such sourcing patterns, but responded by opposing that power rather than accepting it uncritically.

"It Pacifies You, Definitely"

Despite their bountiful critical resources, these activists said they were unable to entirely disarm the power in news discourse. When I asked a group how this program made them feel about things going on in the world, Nathaniel and Beki explained that even though they knew better, they still felt "disempowered." They worried that the news potentially diminished everyone's potency, both in interpreting the news and acting in the wider world:

NATHANIEL: I think it's disempowering either way, as a quote-unquote "normal" person and as a quote-unquote "activist." I would say as, the normal person it's disempowering because you're just getting fed this information, there's no way to tie it into something broader. This is thrown at you and it's assumed that you're going to take it *at its face value.* And as an activist I think it's disempowering because it makes me realize again and again and again what we're actually up against.

BEKI: Yeah. I think it cultivates a sense of negative anger. I see that in people in my family and other people I know who watch the news and who are really angry about life and about what's going on in the world. I think a lot of people are disempowered by watching the news. They're constantly reminded every time they turn on the TV, *"I don't have control over my life."* (emphases added)

In this passage, Nathaniel suggested that "normal" people (contrasted with activists) tended to take the news at face value and Beki distanced herself from "other" people who, she believed, felt disempowered by the news. They also indicated that powerlessness made people feel frustrated and angry. Similarly, when Cody said, "It pacifies you, definitely," Fred followed up by saying, "You're very disempowered." Then Nick jumped in to elaborate on how he perceived journalists' routines of objectivity disempowering viewers, using more imperatives and declaratives:

NICK: We can look at this and be entertained by it, and watch it, and then what difference does it make? And if it's all just going to happen anyway. . . . [The message is], *"We can sit around and talk about it all we want, but this is what's going to happen. Get ready for it, try to lie down and enjoy it, you can't fight back."* (emphases added)

In these and other observations, the activists consistently problematized how citizenship and public opinion are portrayed in television news, detecting an absence of images of ordinary people substantively engaged in politics. Alternative media have often been cited as a source of empowerment.[29] Some people use *empowerment* to convey a personal commitment, a public commitment, or to link the two. Here, these activists were affirming a desire for collective empowerment as a guiding principle for both media and activism.[30] This moral vocabulary of empowerment encouraged people to think and act in a public-spirited way, to see social responsibilities as more meaningful than an individual duty to express oneself.[31]

This view of collective empowerment raises some questions: to what extent is media a meaningful force in bestowing or withholding power from people—by comparison to government forces, or the business sphere, or even individuals themselves? Empowerment means different things to different people. For urban environmental activists, it can mean standing out angrily, yelling into a mic; for suburban activists, it can be associated with quieter, personal development. In varying groups of activists and volunteers, Paul Lichterman and Nina Eliasoph found some people interpreting individualist language to mean community involvement, as making community involvement possible.[32] The language of empowerment in my focus groups similarly blended the personal and collective spheres, just as they elided the pronouns *I* and *we*. Activists expressed a perception that media, especially corporate-commercial ones, sapped people of power but that people could resist that usurpation or reclaim that power—a potential unequally realized.

In talking about discursive power in journalism, these activists articulated how they saw people—even themselves, though less so—being pacified by mainstream news. They believed viewers were disempowered not just by world events as represented in news programming, but also by a media system that posed journalism as the sole source of knowledge and that relegated citizens to the role of spectators. This audience wanted, instead, for people to be *activated* by the news. They wanted not for journalists to talk at (or down to) audiences but for journalists and audiences to engage in public discourse as equals. They subscribed to a Habermasian notion of communicative rationality, in which detached audiences participate discursively in the democratic process. These activists shared with Jürgen Habermas a belief that corporate and government forces had colonized the "public sphere," the standard translation of *Öffentlichkeit*, which implies an ability not just to speak but also to be seen and heard by everyone.[33] While his earlier work was criticized for proposing a unitary and homogeneous sphere, Habermas later tauted alternative media's role in promoting civic participation.[34] Independent news sources are essential components of the public sphere because they provide "unpolluted" information that citizens need to exercise sovereignty over the state.[35] The public sphere is also a cultural space "in which collective identities and solidarities essential for the functioning of differentiated societies are forged," according to Alexander and Jacobs, who lauded the ritual role of television in political communication. "Underpinning the working of civil society are shared beliefs, a feeling of mutuality and a common cultural framework" that ritual communication helps sustain.

My discussants' vision of news as dialogue arose in the very first activist meeting, when Nick lamented that "you cannot get an honest person-to-person conversation" in mainstream media. He linked that shortcoming to the instrumental, persuasive, and profit motives he perceived in journalism. For example, he said that news was produced to shape people's impressions and that journalists presumed holding "direct control" over viewers. In idealizing news as a springboard for public conversation, Nick and the other activists argued that the power of journalism should be harnessed for dialogical and deliberative purposes rather than the propagandistic or manipulative ones they found in this newscast.

While ordinary audiences were presumably unprepared to resist the elite power and journalistic authority exercised through news, so were reporters themselves. As we saw in a previous chapter, these alternative viewers regarded journalists as having been disempowered by corporate and commercial overlords. In a somewhat incongruous move for activists—who value the ability of the common person to affect social change—they saw news workers having negligible agency. This viewpoint risks reducing journalists to the role of "stenographers to power," to borrow a leftist phrase, rather than autonomous professionals. It overlooks ways in which the press, such as through investigative journalism, can serve as agents of social change. This perception of quasi-powerless journalists and audiences contrasts markedly with their otherwise robust democratic idealism, their belief in a system controlled by the citizenry. If wider audiences parallel activists' perception that for-profit journalists lack autonomy vis-à-vis elite powers, it's little wonder that mainstream news enjoys low credibility with its audiences.

Despite all these forces of domination, these activists had seemingly managed to take back some power themselves. What factors contributed to that achievement, in their eyes?

You Need "Insight to See Beyond It"

In these discussions, activists constructed, deconstructed, and challenged the discursive power of mainstream journalism. Instead of taking the news text at face value, they evaluated its framing strategies by reference to a wider context from which certain words and sources were chosen over others. Calling himself a "formerly naïve consumer of network news," Joe explained that he had not always been as informed as he now considered himself:

JOE; I can remember watching news and you know, your reactions are formed by what you see. If you don't have the insight to see beyond it, to question the source of the story or to understand the rhetorical strategies that are being employed, it does inform your reactions to it. You're thinking about your emotional reactions.

He asserted that if *this* news were all he knew, it would "render me kind of passive, and powerless." The activists' interpretation drew upon not only watching the content of this program but also from having the "insight to see beyond it." They believed that homogeneous news from a narrow range of sources encouraged indoctrination, whereas access to journalism representing diverse viewpoints, norms, and practices helped people to resist the influence of mainstream news.

Activist conversations revealed experiential knowledge of how news media work that they gained and shared through multiple routes, including firsthand conversations, second-hand sources, and personal observations. These activists were largely middle class and university educated, which endowed them with certain discursive resources. They were familiar with critical content, thoughts, and theories from movement intellectuals as well as a range of forms and models, frames and frameworks. In addition to Gitlin, we have noted that Chomsky is arguably this generation's most influential critic of mainstream media. His name inevitably comes up when you talk with activists about media. Signs of Chomsky's enduring popularity include lectures to standing-room-only audiences, numerous appearances in documentary films, and prolific writing in books as well as articles for alternative news outlets. He has repeatedly described the U.S. news system as propaganda—a view of elite media power that resounded among the activists with whom I spoke.[36]

Like many activists, these discussants believed that alternative media used different practices, offered supportive frames of social movements, and were more empowering of the citizenry than mainstream news. Scholarship largely supports such perceptions with evidence that alternative news practices are empirically different from mainstream ones.[37] Alternative journalists often practice native reporting and counter-elite sourcing that prefers ordinary citizens to elite actors, giving grassroots sources a platform to speak directly to audiences.[38] Scholars have found clear differences in professional norms and language choices that distinguish independent news outlets and activist communication genres than traditional media.[39] Alternative news sites that emphasize citizen voices and views rely less on the protest paradigm than do mainstream news organizations like the *New York Times*.[40]

Alternative media often treat their audiences as active participants in social and political change. Sometimes this takes the form of directives and grammatical references to audiences that give agency to participants, according to Amoshaun Toft.[41] In his analysis, the inclusive naming of participants (*we*) and their active role in clauses (*marching peacefully, not going to back up*) were prevalent in the alternative news program *Democracy Now!* Toft proposes that such discursive strategies in alternative media help build collective identities for social movements, connect dispersed activists, and contribute to making social change happen.

Much research beyond my own suggests that such audiences see a difference between alternative and mainstream approaches to news. Extant qualitative studies of alternative-media users have found, for example, that listeners to Australian community radio felt "empowered" by the amateur broadcasters, who tried to engage audiences in a public conversation.[42] Readers of a British alternative paper said it did more than inform them, it activated them—in part by engendering solidarity and helping them network with like-minded people.[43] Readers of the *Leeds Citizen* said this alternative paper had inspired them to take specific actions such as organizing public debates and sending comments to public officials. They said the news site helped demystify the way public decisions are made and provided a better understanding of how city government worked, which better equipped people for democratic engagement.[44]

By contrast, traditional journalism routines and practices tend to present the world as existing "out there" somewhere under the influence of elites and officials, not average citizens.[45] It represents the public as passive and infrequently calls upon audiences to get involved with civic life, which contributes to producing a disengaged citizenry.[46] Mainstream news stories emphasize "continual defeat" of social activism and provide "a rationale for residents to opt out of the political process altogether," which can create a "sense of powerlessness" and lead citizens to believe "they cannot change society."[47] Mainstream media "promote apathy, cynicism, and quiescence rather than active citizenship and participation," as William Gamson and his coauthors concluded. Nonetheless, they were optimistic about the possibility that social-movement actors who read polysemous media images (more so than facts or information) in oppositional ways would offer competing constructions of reality, find support from other audiences, and to go beyond imagery.[48]

Alternative media habitually feature specific calls to action that contribute to building *collective action frames.*[49] These are "action-oriented sets of beliefs and meanings that inspire and legitimate the activities and campaigns" of social movements that are "not merely aggregations of individual attitudes and perceptions but also the outcome of negotiating shared meaning."[50] Collective action frames are constructed through a process wherein activists reach a mutual understanding of a social problem, decide who or what is to blame, propose a solution, articulate strategies for affecting change, and urge others to act in concert. This final step is the "agency" component of collective action frames, which provides a public "call to arms" and motivation for joining activist efforts.

In essence, the activists in these focus groups criticized mainstream news for not explicitly calling upon audiences to participate in processes of social and political change, as they believe alternative media do. While mainstream news might have the power to tell stories, attract audiences, and make money, they said, it ultimately failed in an instrumental goal they valued: coaxing ordinary people into public life and responsible citizenship.

Activists Are an Interpretive Community

Activist interpretations of mainstream news reveal perceptions shared by idealistic audiences regarding the implications of media messages for public participation and popular power-building. The findings reported here reaffirm other research on activists' attitudes toward the media, which has uncovered remarkable cynicism toward the news production process among social-movement actors. This analysis helps to unpack skepticism about how the mainstream news environment functions, as McCurdy proposed doing.[51] The study of lay theories helps us to better understand how activist movements contest prevalent frames, offer counter-frames, and represent themselves to journalists and ultimately the public. These lay theories of news media might not be exhaustive or necessarily correct, but they guide action nonetheless.[52] Media experiences inform activism and, recursively, activism informs their media experiences.

One vital purpose of this book is to shed light on discursive, symbolic, and ritual communication processes through which activists use alternative media as a resource for creating identities both individual and collective. Research on political communication, journalism, and social movements has told us a lot about how activists produce media to organize, publicize, and frame their issues and events—following the transmission model. Ritual approaches to alternative media and activist communication are less common. A landmark study by Douglas McLeod and James Hertog hinted at some symbolic meanings of alternative press coverage.[53] They found significant differences between mainstream and alternative media framing of anarchist marches; the former stigmatized demonstrators and characterized protests as failures, while the latter conveyed the theme "we are not alone." Independent and alternative media help foster feelings of community, political affinity, emotional attachment, and belonging between and across movements.[54]

Scholarship on activist media use has typically focused on individual or organizational efforts to influence public attitudes and behaviors—in other words, on moments of transmission. Many studies have looked at how activists produce and circulate messages through alternative media and—especially—how they employ digital networks and social media to promote their causes, recruit supporters, and organize events.[55] We have learned much about the instrumental effectiveness of activist communication: how it influenced public opinion on nuclear power, helped the women's movement build a public identity, and how it educated a large audience about a labor strike.[56] It has also examined how producers of alternative journalism attempt to reach, maximize, engage, and mobilize their audiences.[57] This transmission emphasis results partly from the relative ease with which one can examine social-movement ideas and actions via websites, spokespeople, and/or participants in, say, Occupy Wall Street or Arab Spring or Black Lives Matter. Members of activist groups that are trying to "get their message out" have innate incentives to cooperate with research that propagates their ideas and publicizes their work.

By contrast with such instrumental approaches, I address the dynamic, symbolic communication that takes place among activist audiences, a conversation to be continued anon. This book depicts strategies through which social-movement actors interpret the news and negotiate shared meanings about mediated experience and social life. Activism has become an increasingly important identity resource in era where traditional markers of identification are increasingly unstable. Yet we should avoid conceiving of this identity as an activist/nonactivist binary and think of it, instead, as a continuum. Many attributes of the media criticism that I've ascribed here to activists are also pertinent to broader alternative audiences, itself a hybrid category, as the next chapter will discuss.

Notes

1 Patrick McCurdy, "Mediation, Practice, and Lay Theories of Media," in *Mediation and Protest Movements*, eds. Bart Cammaerts, Alice Mattoni and Patrick McCurdy (Bristol, UK, and Chicago, IL: Intellect Ltd., 2013).

2 Michael Boyle and Mike Schmierbach, "Media Use and Protest," *Communication Quarterly* 57, no. 1 (2009); and Cinzia Padovani, "Citizens' Communication and the 2009 G8 Summit in L'Aquila, Italy," *International Journal of Communication* 4 (2010).

3 Joshua Atkinson and Linda Jean Kenix, *Alternative Meets Mainstream Media* (Lanham, MD: Rowman and Littlefield, 2019).

4 A few of his other dozen books include *Occupy Nation; The Twilight of Common Dreams; Inside Prime Time; The Bulldozer and the Big Tent; The Intellectuals and the Flag; Letters to a Young Activist; Watching Television;* and *Campfires of the Resistance*.

5 To give an indicator of the broad reach of Gitlin's ideas: mainstream news sources in which his writings or interviews have appeared include ABC, CBS, CNN, the *New York Times, Los Angeles Times, Washington Post, San Francisco Chronicle, San Francisco Examiner, Boston Globe, NY Observer, LA Review of Books,* and *Newsday.* Alternative news sources include PBS, National Public Radio, *The New Republic,* the *Nation, Wilson Quarterly, Harper's,* the *American Prospect,* the *Occupied Wall Street Journal, Washington Spectator, San Francisco Express Times,* OpenDemocracy.net, and BillMoyers.com.

6 Todd Gitlin, *The Whole World Is Watching* (Berkeley: University of California Press, 1980).

7 See Erving Goffman, *Frame Analysis* (Cambridge, MA: Harvard University Press, 1974); and Gaye Tuchman, *Making the News* (New York: The Free Press, 1978).

8 Gitlin, *Whole World Is Watching*, 98.

9 This knowledge has been disseminated widely in activist guides that address media coverage such as Charlotte Ryan, *Prime-Time Activism* (Boston, MA: South End Press, 1991); Jason Salzman, *Making the News* (Cambridge, MA: Westview Press, 2003); Aidan Ricketts, *The Activist's Handbook* (London: Zed, 2012); and Randy Shaw, *The Activist's Handbook*, 2nd ed. (Oakland: University of California Press, 2013).

10 Gitlin, *Whole World Is Watching*, 245.

11 Douglas McLeod and Benjamin Detenber, "Framing Effects of TV News Coverage of Social Protest," *Journal of Communication* 49, no. 3 (1999).

12 Shanto Iyengar and Donald Kinder, *News that Matters* (Chicago, IL: University of Chicago Press, 1987).

13 Douglas McLeod and Dhavan Shah, *News Frames and National Security* (New York: Cambridge University Press, 2015).

14 Shanto Iyengar, *Is Anyone Responsible?* (Chicago, IL: University of Chicago Press, 1991).

15 William Gamson et al., "Media Images and the Social Construction of Reality," *Annual Review of Sociology* 18 (1992): 384.

16 Gitlin, *Whole World Is Watching*.

17 Gitlin, *Whole World Is Watching*; Sarah Sobieraj, *Soundbitten* (New York: NYU Press, 2011); Susan Herbst, *Reading Public Opinion* (Chicago, IL: University of Chicago Press, 1998).

18 For example, Olivier Fillieule, "'Plus Ça Change, Moins Ça Change'," in *Acts of Dissent,* eds. Dieter Rucht et al. (Lanham, MD: Rowman and Littlefield, 1999); and Peter Hocke, "Determining the Selection Bias in Local and National Newspaper Reports of Protest Events," also in Rucht et al., *Acts of Dissent.*

19 Sobieraj, *Soundbitten*, 72.

20 Jackie Smith et al., "From Protest to Agenda Building," *Social Forces* 79, no. 4 (2001).

21 James Halloran and Graham Murdock, *Demonstrations and Communication* (Harmondsworth, UK: Penguin, 1970).

22 For more on the protest paradigm, see Joseph Man Chan and Chin-Chuan Lee, "Journalistic 'Paradigms' of Civil Protests," in *The News Media in National and International Conflict*, eds. Andrew Arno and Wimal Dissanayake (Boulder, CO: Westview Press, 1984).

23 Some pillars of scholarship on the protest paradigm include James Hertog and Douglas McLeod, "Anarchists Wreak Havoc in Downtown Minneapolis," *Journalism and Communication Monographs* 151 (1995); McLeod and Hertog, "Social Control, Social Change and the Mass Media's Role in the Regulation of Protest Groups," in *Mass Media, Social Control, and Social Change*, eds. David Demers and K. Viswanath (Ames: Iowa State University Press, 1999); and McLeod, "News Coverage and Social Protest," *Journal of Dispute Resolution* 185 (2007).

24 Jennifer Rauch et al., "From Seattle 1999 to NY 2004," *Social Movement Studies* 6, no. 2 (2007).

25 Danielle Kilgo and Summer Harlow, "Protests, Media Coverage, and a Hierarchy of Social Struggle," *The International Journal of Press/Politics* 24, no. 4 (2019).

26 Des Freedman, "A Return to Prime-Time Activism," in *Media Activism in the Digital Age*, eds. Victor Pickard and Guobin Yang (New York: Routledge, 2017).

27 Freedman, "A Return to Prime-Time Activism."

28 Todd Gitlin, *The Sixties* (New York: Bantam, 1987); Gary Delgado, *Organizing the Movement* (Philadelphia: Temple University Press, 1986).

29 Kevin Howley (ed.), *Understanding Community Media* (London: Sage, 2009); Clemencia Rodriguez, *Citizens' Media Against Armed Conflict* (Minneapolis: University of Minnesota Press, 2011).

30 Nina Eliasoph and Paul Lichterman, "Culture in Interaction," *American Journal of Sociology* 108, no. 4 (2003).

31 For more on empowerment as "a moral vocabulary," see Robert Bellah et al., *Habits of the Heart* (Berkeley: University of California Press, 1985); Eliasoph and Lichterman, "Culture in Interaction," 747–8.

32 Paul Lichterman, *The Search for Political Community* (New York: Cambridge University Press); Nina Eliasoph, *Avoiding Politics* (New York: Cambridge University Press, 1998).

33 *Öffentlichkeit* has no English equivalent that fully conveys the full range of its German meaning. Jürgen Habermas, *The Structural Transformation of the Public Sphere* (Cambridge, MA: MIT Press, 1989).

34 Jürgen Habermas, "Further Reflections on the Public Sphere," in *Habermas and the Public Sphere*, ed. Craig Calhoun (Cambridge, MA: MIT Press, 1993). For criticism of his conceptualization and proposals of alternative "counterpublic spheres," see John Downing, "Alternative Media and the Boston Tea Party," in *Questioning the Media: A Critical Introduction*, eds. Downing, Ali Mohammadi, and Annabelle Sreberny-Mohammadi (Newbury Park, CA: Sage, 1990); and Nancy Fraser, "Rethinking the Public Sphere," *Habermas and the Public Sphere*, ed. Calhoun.

35 Jeffery Alexander and Ronald Jacobs, "Mass Communication, Ritual, and Civil Society," in *Media, Ritual, and Identity*, eds. James Curran and Tamar Liebes (London: Routledge, 2002).

36 Chomsky's writings about media power include titles such as *Necessary Illusions* and *Media Control*.

37 Some scholars argue that alternative media are not always as "alternative" as they seem. See my discussion in Chapter 7 and also Linda Jean Kenix, *Alternative and Mainstream Media* (London: Bloomsbury Academic, 2012). Such assessments sometimes depend on how studies define and operationalize the category of "alternative media."

38 For example, see Chris Atton and Emma Wickenden, "Sourcing Routines and Representation in Alternative Journalism," *Journalism Studies* 6, no. 3 (2005); Tony Harcup, "'The Unspoken—Said'," *Journalism* 4, no. 3 (2003); Summer Harlow

and Dustin Harp, "Alternative Media in a Digital Era," *Communication and Society/ Comunicación y Sociedad* 26, no. 4 (2013); Jennifer Rauch, "Rooted in Nations, Blossoming in Globalization?" *Journal of Communication Inquiry* 27, no. 1 (2003). While many alternative publications, such as urban newsweeklies, do play a watchdog or muckraking role that is more critical of official sources than the mainstream press is, some dispute the notion that they represent alternative voices, because of their emphasis on consumerism: Phyllis Kaniss, *Making Local News* (Chicago, IL: University of Chicago Press, 1991).

39 See Nina Eliasoph, "Routines and the Making of Oppositional News," *Critical Studies in Mass Communication* 5, no. 4 (1988); Chris Atton, "News Cultures and New Social Movements," *Journalism Studies* 3, no. 4 (2002); Sarah Platon and Mark Deuze, "Indymedia Journalism," *Journalism* 4, no. 3 (2003); and Eleanor Lamb, "Power and Resistance," *Discourse and Society* 24, no. 3 (2013); Summer Harlow, "Recognizing the Importance of Alternative Media," *Journalism Studies* 20, no. 1 (2017).

40 Summer Harlow and Thomas Johnson, "Overthrowing the Protest Paradigm?" *International Journal of Communication* 5 (2011).

41 Amoshaun Toft, "Cross-Talk in Political Discourse," in *'Doing Politics': Discursivity, Performativity, and Mediation in Political Discourse*, eds. Michael Kranert and Geraldine Horan (Amsterdam: John Benjamins, 2013).

42 Jacqui Ewart et al., "Through the Ears of the Audience," paper presented to the Journalism Education Conference, Griffith University, November–December 2005, 7–8.

43 Chris Atton, *Alternative Media* (Thousand Oaks, CA: Sage, 2002).

44 Tony Harcup, "Asking the Readers," *Journalism Practice* 10, no. 6 (2016).

45 Robert Entman, "Framing: Toward Clarification of a Fractured Paradigm," *Journal of Communication* 43, no. 4 (2003).

46 Entman, *Democracy without Citizens* (New York and Oxford: Oxford University Press, 1999); and Justin Lewis et al., "Images of Citizenship on Television News," *Journalism Studies* 5, no. 2 (2004).

47 Diane Nicodemus, "Mobilizing Information," *Political Communication* 21, no. 2 (2004): 171; Laura Woliver, *From Outrage to Action* (Urbana: University of Illinois Press, 1993), 70.

48 William Gamson et al., "Media and the Social Construction of Reality," *Annual Review of Sociology* 18 (1992).

49 Eliasoph, "Routines and the Making of Oppositional News."

50 Robert Benford and David Snow, "Framing Processes and Social Movements," *Annual Review of Sociology* 26 (2000); William Gamson, *Talking Politics* (Cambridge, UK: Cambridge University Press, 1992).

51 McCurdy, "Mediation, Practice, and Lay Theories."

52 In this discussion, I have suggested some elements of activist discourse that seem to convey contradictions, oversights, or misconceptions, though I decline to judge their accuracy.

53 Douglas McLeod and James Hertog, "Social Control, Social Change, and the Mass Media's Role in the Regulation of Protest Groups," in *Mass Media, Social Control, and Social Change*, eds. David Demers and K. Viswanath (Ames: Iowa State University Press, 1999).

54 Veronica Barassi, "Ethnographic Cartographies," *Social Movement Studies* 12, no. 1 (January 2013), 58–9.

55 For example, Chris Atton, *An Alternative Internet* (Edinburgh: Edinburgh University Press, 2004); Leah Lievrouw, *Alternative and Activist New Media* (Malden, MA: Polity, 2011); Paolo Gerbaudo, *Tweets in the Streets* (New York: St. Martin's Press, 2012); Graham Meikle, *Future Active* (New York: Routledge, 2002); Jenny Pickerell,

116 Activist Interactions With Journalism

Cyberprotest (Manchester, UK: Manchester University Press, 2003); Clemencia Rodriguez, *Fissures in the Mediascape* (Creskill, NJ: Hampton Press, 2001); Adrienne Russell, *Journalism as Activism* (Cambridge, UK: Polity); Mitzi Waltz, *Alternative and Activist Media* (Edinburgh: Edinburgh University Press, 2005).

56 For example, William Gamson and Andrew Modigliani, "Media Discourse and Public Opinion on Nuclear Power," *American Journal of Sociology* 95, no. 1 (1989); Liesbet Van Zoonen, "The Women's Movement and the Media," *European Journal of Communication* 7, no. 4 (1992); and Charlotte Ryan, "It Takes a Movement to Raise an Issue," *Critical Sociology* 30, no. 2 (2004).

57 For example, Chris Atton, *Alternative Media* (Thousand Oaks, CA: Sage, 2002); Chris Atton and James F. Hamilton, *Alternative Journalism* (Thousand Oaks, CA: Sage, 2008); John Downing et al., *Radical Media* (Thousand Oaks, CA: Sage, 2001); Susan Forde, *Challenging the News* (Houndmills, UK, and New York: Palgrave Mac-Millan, 2001); and Linda Jean Kenix, *Alternative and Mainstream Media* (London: Bloomsbury Academic, 2011).

7

ALTERNATIVE MEDIA RITUALS
AND SUBCULTURAL CAPITAL

"I read it in *Harper's Magazine*," said Nick, a peace activist who attended academic conferences in his spare time.

"There was a good article in *Z Magazine* about it," said Chris, a leader of a radical education collective at Temple University.

"*Philly Weekly* had a cover story about it," said Joni, a volunteer with the local Independent Media Center.

"I looked at it online, at Philly.com," said Janice, who promoted causes such as reproductive choice and separation of church and state.

"There's this really good book called *Amusing Ourselves to Death*," said Jason, an organizer for a national student-led action network.

"I read it in the *Times*," said Sean, who worked as an environmental justice campaigner in West Philadelphia.

"I remember watching [it], I think it was on [regional news channel] CN8," said Liz, a political-science major involved with anti-war, labor rights and human rights groups.

Although the purpose of our conversations was to discuss how these activists interpreted a network newscast, they continually referred to their extratextual experiences reading or watching other media, both mainstream and alternative. The value of context for understanding news was something that they brought up again and again, without prompting from me. "The section about the sniper, there's no context for it," Fred said, explaining how he found outside information essential to making sense of news:

> It's just random acts. How are people supposed to interpret some guy running around on a sniper rampage? I actually read this morning that

this guy used to be in the army, [which is] where he received his marksman's training.

Nick jumped in to say that he, too, understood one news story by reference to others—that is, intertextually. "When I watch this, other thinking goes on. I think back to other reading. I wouldn't rely on this [program] for anything," he said, explaining that he made a game of this interpretive practice:

NICK: My experience was that if I read the news carefully, I could find contradictions within the body of the newspaper. I started reading it as if I were reading a book, looking for lines of argument, connections among the stories. . . . I try to think of things in some context.

Joni, like Fred, thought that events drove mainstream TV news reports, whereas "you have to go outside of the events, looking for contrary or similar information" in order to understand them. Jodi, too, suggested that a media text must be evaluated by reference to external information, saying that "whenever I watch the news, I always think the biggest thing to me is not necessarily what they say but what they don't say." Echoing Todd Gitlin and other critical scholars, Jason remarked that "the biggest problem with mainstream media from what I see is not so much a particular ideological slant, or lack thereof, in what's covered. It's what does not even get brought up."

Where did they look for the contextual knowledge they found so necessary to making sense of the news? How did they learn what's missing from news content, when it's not there? If they didn't rely on this newscast, what other sources did they use? We know that alternative media play an important role in educating and mobilizing activists. In discussions about this mainstream newscast, these activists spontaneously cited a range of alternative sources—including literary magazines such as *Harper's*, books by media critics such as Neil Postman, political publications such as *Z*, and local newspapers such as *Philadelphia Weekly*—in addition to broader-based media like the *New York Times, The Philadelphia Inquirer*, and CN8, a commercial news channel produced by cable giant Comcast, headquartered nearby in Philadelphia. Rather than relying on participants' anecdotal references to alternative-media exposure, I gathered empirical evidence of the range of news sources that they used in daily life. Diary data verified that these activists did rely heavily upon alternative news sources, but it also showed that they consumed a lot of mainstream media, too, in contrast with spoken claims that they didn't really read, watch, or listen to news produced by large corporations. In fact, they used mainstream news sources at a higher rate than the general U.S. public did. My analysis here will demonstrate that this group consisted of news omnivores who formed a hybrid media audience.

By considering the disjuncture between the media consumption that alternative fans recorded in diaries and that which they presented verbally with peers, I uncovered several rituals related to their use of media, including a ritual of abstention from mainstream news and a ritual of interaction through which they performed their rejection of the genre often derided as "MSM." Their verbal communication in focus groups enacted a social performance that drew upon intersubjective meanings specific to this community. In other work, I have described activists as an *interpretive community* with similar understandings of alternative media, mainstream news, and civic engagement.[1] Journalists, television viewers, and media audiences have all been conceptualized as having shared orientations toward social reality and media content.[2] This chapter elaborates on how alternative-media users interact as an interpretive community, a notion that helps explain how audience responses are socially patterned.[3] Media texts are not interpreted in totally idiosyncratic ways; there is relative unity amidst a diversity of interpretations, which provides some stability of meaning and helps make communication possible.[4] As I will show, these resistant communication rituals enact elements of taste and discrimination that contribute to building subcultural capital, pleasure, and identities.

The Diary Phase

In addition to probing interview transcripts for mentions of news sources outside of this program, I asked my informants to record all their media usage for a week. Student and activist groups were instructed to write down for seven consecutive days each source of information that they used: everything they read, listened to, and watched relating to current events, politics, or social issues. Because the diaries were a course requirement for students, 96 percent of them complied with my request, whereas 58 percent of the activists completed this phase of the project. I was pleased that informants showed this level of cooperation, because diaries offered an empirical basis for comparing the extratextual interpretive resources available to students with those of activists, as well as the public at large.[5]

Getting comprehensive data about people's diffused media consumption is difficult. As I could not observe news consumption firsthand, I relied on self-reports. Such data can be inaccurate, because people often forget or misremember their media use, or offer idealized responses rather than accurate ones. Reactivity and response biases often compel people to alter their behavior when they know they're being observed. I cannot know to what extent these diaries disclosed the media that people actually used, the sources they remembered using, and/or those they wanted to present themselves as using. Because the diary phase asked participants to reflect consciously on their media use and record news sources that they found meaningful, it let people define media exposure for themselves.[6] These diaries might say more about the media that people *valued* than the media that people *used*—information that's quite relevant to understanding the resources with which this community made sense of news.

The level of detail in the diaries fluctuated greatly, which could reflect either informants' varying usage or their varying care in recording usage. The activists, perhaps sensing our mutual interest in social change and alternative media, might have kept more conscientious diaries than students did. They may have felt they more invested in the study than the students, who probably identified with me more as a teacher than as a collaborator. Social actors do sometimes mislead themselves and others (including researchers). The diaries may be, to some degree, fabrications or performances, but ones that nonetheless represent their ideas about what media use "should" look like.

Next, we will look at the groups' respective media usage, including patterns of similarity and difference between students and activists. This analysis confirms that the activists took far greater advantage of diverse news sources, including a larger proportion of alternative media, than either the students or the general public did. Then we will contrast the diary data with activists' oral representations of their media intake, in which they de-emphasize and devalue their consumption of mainstream news. Finally, we will consider how activists explained their media usage in both symbolic and instrumental terms.

A Hybrid Audience of News Omnivores

Other chapters of this book explored how activists used different strategies for understanding the news than students did and how they cited alternative media as an important resource in constructing resistant interpretations. In Table 7.1, we establish that the activists actually did experience a distinct range of alternative news texts. The diaries showed some overlap between the information contexts of these students and activists—and suggested that both groups diverged from U.S. audiences as a whole, by comparison to survey data from the Pew Research Center.[7] Survey data are not directly comparable to diary data, but these figures sketch a rough outline of the groups' respective media experiences.[8]

TABLE 7.1 Mainstream news sources used by activists, students, and U.S. population*

	Students %	*U.S. Population* %	*Activists* %
Corporate news magazines	17	13	69
Corporate television news	49	82	64
Corporate online news	39	30+	36
Corporate newspapers	26	42	24
Corporate news radio	9	40	7

*The data sources in Tables 7.1 and 7.2 are student diaries (column 2); 2004 Pew survey of U.S. population (column 3); and activist diaries (column 4). Pew Research Center, "News Audiences Increasingly Politicized." These data reflect media categories used at least once per week (*regularly* or *sometimes*). Note that students *n* = 23, U.S. population *n* = 3,000, activists *n* = 14.

News sources deemed *mainstream* included those produced by the likes of ABC, CBS, Fox, MSNBC, NBC, Clear Channel/IHeartMedia, Sinclair, Advance Publications, Hearst, Time Warner, Cox, Dow Jones, Gannett, Knight Ridder, New York Times Co., Scripps, Tribune, *Washington Post*, Google, and MSN. These mainstream sources represent the news provided by the 30 or so largest U.S. media corporations (ranked by net revenue) and coincide with the monolithic group of corporate, commercial concerns often called "Big Media" by media critics including these activists, who posited an important relationship between the characteristics *big* and *mainstream*.[9]

MSM comprised an important dimension of information for both groups, although levels of usage for all news sources were lower among students than among activists. This difference can partly be explained by the fact that the students were slightly younger overall than the activists; media researchers consistently have found that young people pay less attention to news across all media than older people.[10] Students who participated in the study were 21 or younger, while the activists ranged from 19 to 60 (with about half in their early 20s). In interviews, students said that logs kept during the school year underrepresented their exposure because they had more time to keep up with news during breaks. The important pattern to recognize is that mass advertising media accounted for the top five news sources in this group, with almost no information coming from an alternative context.

As for activists, almost two-thirds reported using commercial TV or newspapers at least once during the sample week. A third said they attended to mainstream news magazines and websites. Rather than eschewing MSM, they used these sources at least as often as students and the general population. The largest mainstream variation between activists and the public at large was the former's infrequent use of commercial radio. (Since these students also listened to mainstream news radio at much lower rates, this could signal a difference in the Philadelphia media market rather than an activist preference per se.)

It is remarkable that 64 percent of activists reported using mainstream TV news and mainstream newspapers/sites in the diary week, while around a third (29–36 percent) of them reported having consumed news from mainstream web platforms and magazines. These levels of usage are comparable to their consumption of alternative TV programs, newspapers/sites, web platforms, and magazines (50–71 percent). Indeed, a majority of the activists used many of the same resources as the rest of the population.[11] This finding supports other research showing that activists use both alternative and mainstream media more than nonmembers do.[12]

This interpretive community of activists and alternative-media fans qualifies as a *hybrid media audience*—which follows from the fact that alternative and mainstream news sources flow through a hybrid media system. Their communal media preference should not be described as "*either* mainstream *or* alternative news sources" but as "*not only* mainstream *but also* alternative news sources" to paraphrase Andrew Chadwick.[13] He concluded that old and new media logics, which have always been deeply intertwined, are now more interdependent than ever as boundaries between technologies, genres, norms, behaviors, and organizational forms have blurred. Nonetheless, some audiences have hybridized more than others. These liberal activists and left-wing media users represent a significantly more blended audience than conservative activists and right-wing media users do.

A Preponderance of Alternatives

While all three groups used MSM at meaningful levels, a striking difference was the absence of alternative media from student news diets (see Table 7.2). Student consumption habits were closer to the U.S. population, especially in regard to the predominance of MSM sources, than to activist ones. "Alternative" media are analytically distinguished here by virtue of their absence from the ranking of largest media corporations. The contours of the mainstream landscape aligned closely with mass advertising media, while the alternative context was largely composed of what can be called *niche, noncommercial* (campus, community, and public broadcasting), and foreign media.

Even allowing for a liberal interpretation of the diaries, a maximum of nine percent of students was exposed to any alternative news source. With a single exposure in the week counting as *sometimes*, the one student out of 24 who read *Ms.* magazine and the two who visited independent news sites *Fark* and *Drudge Report* barely made the charts. None of the students watched or listened to campus, community, or public broadcasting. None attended to any alternative newspapers or activist publications.

By great contrast, the majority of activists used every category of alternative media identified in these diaries at least once during the sample week. Ten out of 14 listened to campus, community, and public radio. Another 10 read niche magazines, including publications that consistently criticize MSM, such as *Adbusters*

TABLE 7.2 Alternative news sources used by activists, students, and U.S. population

	Students %	U.S. Population %	Activists %
Campus, community, public radio	0	35	71
Niche magazines	4	10+	71
Online discussion groups	0	–	71
Campus, community, public TV	0	23	50
Niche newspapers/publications	0	–	50
Niche websites	9	10+	50

and *Extra!* (a newsletter published by media watchdog Fairness and Accuracy In Reporting, or FAIR). At least half watched campus, community, or public television, read niche newspapers and activist publications, and visited niche and foreign news sites (such as Truthout, DemocracyNow!, and the *Guardian*).[14] This usage at least doubled and sometimes tripled the rates at which the rest of the U.S. population consumed news from these same alternative sources.

Sources deemed *alternative* included campus, community, and public organizations such as C-SPAN, NPR, PBS, and PRI; niche and foreign news organizations such as the *Atlantic*, the *Guardian*, *Harper's*, *National Review*, the *New Yorker*, and Slate; local newsweeklies; and online news discussion groups. An interesting pattern emerged: at least half of the activists listened to National Public Radio, read the *Nation*, and looked at Indymedia in this single week.[15] Those three sources, which routinely analyze and criticize MSM, represented the main body of shared interpretive resources among activists. The activists differed further from students by reading current-affairs books (29 percent versus zero) about peace and globalization, watching videos and movies (21 percent versus zero) about politics and the environment, and going to organizational meetings (50 percent versus 13 percent) about issues such as Buddhism, social justice, sustainable energy, death penalty abolition, and labor rights.

Ten out of 14 activists who completed diaries said they participated in online groups—some in as many as five or 24 in this seven-day period—discussing political campaigns, peace, human rights, atheism, the environment, global justice, legal defense, media activism, and other topics. By contrast, the students showed enthusiasm for online entertainment and interpersonal communication; none reported participating in online news discussions during the sample week.

In considering this diary data, I try to not conflate actual exposure and the opportunity for exposure.[16] While self-reports indicated that activists had access to the same core of alternative media, the respondents may not have consumed identical content there. Reading the *Nation* does not guarantee that one has been exposed to articles by media critics Eric Alterman, Naomi Klein, or Robert McChesney, who have regularly contributed to that publication; nor does it guarantee that such messages—even if read—made a meaningful impression. The low proportion of corporate news might not mean that activists were not "exposed" to MSM sources; instead, it suggests they did not attend closely enough to mainstream news to remember and record that experience in diaries—or that they actively chose not to record it.

Active and Passive News Habits

As we talked about mainstream news, students rarely indicated external resources that might have influenced their interpretations the program. In discussing the sniper story, I sought clues as to whether students had learned anything about the shootings or trials reported in this newscast from other sources—and if so, which. Fauve said she hadn't seen anything about it because she doesn't "really watch the news." Ashley had come across something about it at CNN.com. Brandon had read articles about it in his hometown newspaper. Marissa said her mother had sent her letters at camp about the incidents and that she "learned more about it from *The Daily Show*." Adam had heard some coverage on the radio in his dad's car. Matt remembered having seen a made-for-TV movie about the topic on a cable entertainment channel.

Most of the students seemed to think such media exposure "doesn't really count" because they didn't purposely "follow the news." They "just happened to" be in the car with their parents when the radio was on, read "whatever was on the front page," or "caught it on television a couple of times." Marissa suggested she had chanced upon the news because her computer home page was set to MSN.com: "So that's usually where I get it, if I see anything that catches my eye." These students might have underestimated their experiences with news because they often were informed accidentally rather than purposively. Such "incidental news exposure" occurs when people encounter current affairs information when they had not been actively seeking it. Research suggests people can gain political knowledge this way.[17]

The abundance of information flowing online leads many people to believe they no longer have to actively seek the news to be well informed about public affairs. Passive news consumption has become more prevalent as people increasingly choose not to invest time, effort, and money in staying informed and think, instead, that important news will find them through social media or other online channels.[18] Studies have shown that this "news finds me" perception (NFM) is proliferating around the world and that people aged 18–35 have much higher levels of NFM than do their older counterparts.[19] The perception is likely a fallacy, meaning that people are less informed about current affairs than they think they are. High levels of NFM come with low levels of consumption of hard news, of interest in public affairs, of political knowledge, and of voting turnout. Also, NFM is positively correlated with increasing cynicism toward politics. NFM makes people overly reliant on peers and social networks (and hence on algorithms) for important news that might find them—or, indeed, might not.

Jim, a senior who was taking a news analysis class, and Ashley, a sophomore who read *Ms.* as well as *Time*, were the only students to report seeking out (rather than happening upon) information from the media. Both said they preferred to get news online because they valued what Ashley called the "active control" and the links to external sources of information. "If I'm interested in a story, not only can I read about it, I can read about other stories that are related to it," Jim elaborated. The perspective of these two students diverged from their peers, corresponding more closely to activists' practices.

Echoing Jim's preferences, the activists thought they could interpret the news better by actively searching for information that helped them to see "different viewpoints surrounding it," as Janice said. Alternative media helped activists make sense of news in part by triangulating claims among diverse sources. Nick, 60, called this "judging the validity" by "going further and getting into research," which most of them thought the average person was not inclined to do (in line with their critique of mass audiences in an earlier chapter). Yet experiences with alternative media gave these viewers something perhaps more crucial than extratextual information, which served their instrumental communication needs as activists. It offered a sense of communal identity that distinguished them from the mainstream media "dupes" that they imagined other people to be. And it provided a structure of feelings—of belonging, pride, pleasure, irony, and humor—associated with affective and ritual communication.

Communication, Community, Communion

James Carey, one of the most revered journalism scholars of the 20th century, famously contrasted *ritual* communication that values meaning, beauty, and fellowship with the more common *transmission* view that stresses movement, speed, and effectiveness. Carey described ritual communication as "directed not towards the extension of messages in space but towards the maintenance of society in time; not the act of imparting information but the representation of shared beliefs."[20] Media experiences can be something like "attending a mass, a situation in which nothing new is learned but in which a particular view of the world is portrayed and confirmed."[21] Ritual communication provides shared frames through which a community interprets and understands journalism. Carey keenly observed that, with few exceptions, scholars had long focused reductively on the sending and receiving messages while overlooking a larger realm of meanings with which *communication* shares an etymology: *community* and *communion*.

Many studies of activism and alternative media have privileged the transmission mode, perhaps because political action is often understood in instrumental terms. One might argue that sitting on a sofa reading the *Nation* or *Human Events* is a passive activity and that audiences aren't "really" activists unless they're waving placards in the streets or sending online petitions or posting on political blogs. However, choosing to read (and sometimes pay for) alternative media instead of mainstream ones is an intentional act of communication that contributes to the creation and sustenance of activist identities. It certainly matters to alternative-media and activist producers whether you subscribe to their publications or pay attention to their community broadcasts. Such media habits help sustain activist identities, create a sense of belonging, and provoke participation.

I'm not suggesting that transmissive communication is bad while ritual is good—Carey didn't either—merely that a fuller understanding of audiences requires both. Communicative rituals such as reading, watching, and discussing the news coexist with, and can serve as precursors to, instrumental acts. The two modes have a productive, dialectical relationship. "The purpose of news is not to represent and inform but to signal, tell a story, and *activate inquiry*," Carey said (emphasis added).[22] This perspective on news resonates with discourse of my activist-informants. They would likely agree with Carey's view that news stories offer shared frames for understanding, that news embodies community ideals, that news informs and directs action, that news conveys "not pure information but a portrayal of the contending forces in the world."[23]

The ritual perspective showcases how news experiences can bring people together and provide internal solidarity to groups. In advocating for a ritual view, Carey argued that media consumption was less about content and more about the audience's dialogical and emotional responses. Media use is driven partly by a desire to be part of a community—even if the people with whom you sense connection are geographically distant strangers. This is what Benedict Anderson called an *imagined community*, in which we do not know or never meet most of our fellow members. "All communities larger than primordial villages of face-to-face contact (and perhaps even these) are imagined," he said. Anderson credited the existence of nationalism—the sense of "belonging" to a national community whose members are distinct from people in other nations—to shared rituals of reading the same newspapers as one's countrymen. (In the time of which Anderson wrote, they *were* men.)[24]

By considering how activists used news media for symbolic purposes, this chapter examines consumption from the ritual viewpoint wherein communicative acts transmit not only information but also culture.[25] Our conversations about mainstream news demonstrate that contexts of consumption do not just affect the nature of reading and interpretation. As Mark Peterson said of South Asians who shared and discussed news experiences, people engage in narrative and performative constructions of themselves, make claims about their status, reinforce their social relations with other actors, and envision themselves and others as members of broader communities.[26]

Ritual Rejection of the Mainstream

While members of this interpretive community considered themselves alternative-media fans, they actually used quite a lot of mainstream news sources, as we have seen. Another way of characterizing their eclectic media experience is in terms of its omnivorousness. These activists represent *omnivores*, people who consume news and information from multiple media sources, through multiple channels.[27] Such audiences often employ the Internet to check facts and drill deeper into stories. Being a news omnivore requires a great deal of skill, investment, and knowledge. Omnivorous consumers of media and other cultural forms have wide-ranging awareness and a broad taste profile that includes both highbrow and lowbrow genres. Alternative is the former, and mainstream the latter.

People with an omnivorous news repertoire typically sample from both liberal and conservative news, as well as broadcast, TV commentary, print, and online news. According to Stephanie Edgerly, *omnivores* take advantage of the ever-expanding news landscape to seek out an array of media sources, styles, and voices. They have a distinctively "wider lens for what they are willing to consume."[28] This repertoire is common among people who identify as Democrat or Independent. News omnivores engage in online and offline political and civic life at significantly higher rates than those using other repertoires and seem to be more motivated, more confident, and more aware of opportunities to get involved. As Edgerly suggests, omnivores exemplify the "virtuous cycle" between news use and participation.[29]

Alternative-media informants also displayed certain behaviors consistent with what Edgerly calls a *liberal C online* repertoire: use of general online news as well as liberal news via the Internet and radio, with little TV news. This repertoire is associated with Democrats, Independents, and people with higher levels of education. She contrasts omnivores (around 12 percent of the U.S. population) and liberal C onlines (12.2 percent) with other repertoires such as *conservative only* (15.6 percent) and *news avoiders* (18 percent).[30] Conservative only audiences consume content across TV, radio, and the Internet that agrees with their viewpoints. This repertoire is related to being older, male, white, Republican, and perceiving high media bias. News avoiders, who reported the lowest level of political participation, are characterized by low use of news in any medium or any attribute. The study correlated this behavior with having less education, being non-white, and/or identifying as Republican.

While these activists privately behaved like omnivores, they publicly presented themselves as picky eaters and avowed not having eaten junk news. One sign that these viewers saw symbolic value in their news consumption—both actual and perceived—was the way they sought to justify being exposed to mainstream sources. For example, Jodi, cited public broadcasting as a staple of her media diet but seemed apologetic about reading mainstream newspapers, specifying that she neither sought them out nor paid for them. "I wake up to NPR most days," she said. "If I happen to see a *Metro* lying around or an *Inquirer* in the trash, I'll pick it up, sometimes. It just depends on if I'm at a coffeehouse and it's there." And Ryan, 32, claimed that he didn't watch a lot of mainstream U.S. news sources, then made a confession.

RYAN: Well . . . once in a while. Like this afternoon, I was home because I was coming here, and I was upstairs reading and I flipped on MSNBC. Just in the background. I wasn't paying that much attention to it. But for the most part, I don't watch a lot. And we just started watching fairly regularly, in the past few weeks, *The Daily Show.*

As with students, Ryan didn't seem to think that semi-attentive viewing of MSNBC really counted as consuming news. Neither did his interest in *The Daily Show*, although research suggests that people who watched late-night comedy know more about politics than those who do not.[31] A third example of this dismissive tendency arose when Liz mentioned a story about the governor of California that she had seen in the *New York Times.* She not only rationalized reading that mainstream newspaper but also minimized the level of attention she paid it. "I do get the *New York Times*, in my e-mail, because of a class that I had," she explained. "I had to review the *Times*, and I still get it e-mailed to me every day, and sometimes I'll skim through."

Activists talked about mainstream media use in some of the same ways students did: as being incidentally exposed, accidentally informed. They happened upon a news story here, or a news story there caught their eye. This audience of engaged citizens made it clear that they actively sought out alternative media— but that their consumption of mainstream media was mainly passive. While they found alternative news, mainstream news found them. These alternative-media fans denied to their peers, and perhaps to themselves, the true extent to which they followed mainstream news.

Many activists claimed to graze conventional sources merely for ideas about things to research further in alternative media. For them, news fulfilled Carey's function of activating inquiry. Jodi conveyed this kind of activity when she said, "The few times I do watch national news, all it is, is advertising what I should seek out news about from other sources, what I should then go and research." Nathaniel thought that if he still had a TV set, he would find it useful just for topical summaries:

NATHANIEL: It brings up issues, subjects that I might not even think to look at. For example, the prescription-drug benefit is not something that would necessarily interest me at all. But they mentioned it there [in the newscast we watched together] and [I think], "Oh that sounds kind of interesting. I might go and do some research." So it's like the headlines, and I can research it from there.

Ryan, too, considered mainstream programs "a headline service. The evening news should probably be nothing more than a starting point, interesting things to find out more about." Janice, who watched a lot of network programs, used mainstream TV news only to find out "what's making the news today. [Then I] go online and see what's *really* making the news today" (emphasis theirs). Activists saw limited value in mainstream media as a source of information; from a transmission viewpoint, they mainly considered it useful to the extent that it interacted with alternative sources.

Being an *alternative media* user was central to the identity of these audience members. They enjoyed creating distinctions between alternative and mainstream media as well as between themselves and other, presumably more conventional people. The phrase helped them make sense of the world, relate themselves to a larger cultural order, create emotional bonds, and signal membership in an alternative community.[32] These informants presented themselves to me and to each other as alternative-media fans because, for them, denunciation of mainstream media was a marker of collective and individual identity.[33]

Because social movements are voluntary affiliations that cannot compel membership, they "require substantial social cohesion ('we-ness,' 'belonging-ness,' 'solidarity') to exist, persist, and function," sociologists explain.[34] Activist identities depend in part on members' recognition of shared, repeated, and meaningful references that develop collective identity—on what Erving Goffman, one of the 20th century's most influential sociologists, called *interaction rituals*.[35] The concept of ritual illuminates how their communal orientation toward mainstream news helps build unity across a diffused oppositional audience. We form our identities partly by communicating our sense of self to other people, in a sort of performance. Activism frequently involves rhetorical performances through which people publicly display their political identities and knowledge, according to Joshua Atkinson.[36] Both the act of consuming alternative media and the ritual of asserting preferences for alternative media helped create communal bonds.[37]

Among activists, a preference for alternative media signaled not only belonging but also taste. Pierre Bourdieu defined *taste* as a manifested preference of a difference between groups that is, in part, created through words.[38] Taste implies a pattern of cultural knowledge and appreciation that bestows one with cultural capital, the ability to claim higher social status. These discussants communicated their "good" taste by verbally distancing themselves from mainstream media, which represents a low-status genre—yet not so worthless that they refuse to consume it, in reality. This distinction tells us more about the cultural values of these activists and their theories about mainstream media than it does about the empirical reality of their news usage.[39] As Bourdieu noted elsewhere, taste both unites and separates.[40] These activists used the mainstream–alternative distinction, a binary opposition belying an "us-versus-them" worldview, to reinforce symbolic boundaries between themselves and others.

The intersection of liberal activist and alternative-media contexts is sufficiently narrow to qualify this audience as a *subculture*, a group of people who share interests and practices that distinguish them in a significant way from other social groups. Scholars have alternately seen subcultures as "resistant and subordinate, politically hopeful and spectacularly impotent." Members of such groups often jockey for self-esteem and *subcultural capital*, or alternative forms of status.[41] One defining attribute of a subcultural group lies in its self-perception of being more differentiated, active, and creative than the larger culture or mass society, which is "invariably, but not unproblematically, positioned as normal, average, and dominant."[42] People who belong to subcultures like to think of themselves as "not mainstream." The category of *mainstream*, of course, represents something of a myth or a straw man—but a necessary one, because the superiority of an alternative-media community presumes the inferiority of others.

The Pleasure of Distinction

In surveilling mainstream perspectives, some activists said they used corporate news sources to find out what other people think and how media might spread misperceptions about the world.[43] Janice said:

> I want to be aware of ABC—that's what my mother-in-law and [neighbors] watch, though I don't understand why they do—so I can get a general idea of their world view, because I see how it's shaped by their media.

Jodi, who "doesn't really watch TV," said she sometimes flicked on CNN "as a staple of what [other] people may be seeing." This media usage could be considered instrumental as it helps further the goals of social movements—understanding public opinion in order to challenge and change it. Yet the prevalence in these discussions of affective terms such as "love" and "hate" in as well as references to *fun* and *laughter* suggests that media use fulfilled ritual needs for these activists too.

While the majority denied they learned anything from corporate news sources, a few activists admitted to having "a love-hate relationship" with MSM. Janice, for one, explained that she never missed the local ABC news— "It's the only thing I leave my chat-room for"—even though she claimed to "hate" it. Ami, who said she did not watch much TV news, said she had watched CNN that same morning. She thought it was "fucked up" that there were multiple versions of CNN, an American one and an international one, and Chris sarcastically called this "awesome." He minimized his CNN usage by saying he visited the organization's international sites "every once in a while, just to get a laugh." He seemed to read this news content ironically rather than taking it at face value:

CHRIS: If you go to CNN.uk and check the news, it's different news [than CNN.com]. They'll cover the same story, but the information and the words they use are different. There was this one about the death toll in Iraq, and the U.S. version was very sanitized and the British version was still sanitized, but not *as* sanitized. (emphasis theirs)

Chris confessed that he watched a lot of mainstream news, saying, "I actually really enjoy it." The rest of the group laughed, finding humor in this admission of guilt, or guilty pleasure, which rested on their intersubjective understanding that using MSM was a quasi-moral transgression. Some enjoyment of this maligned genre came from "knowing" that mainstream media is "bad," akin to the pleasure that some people find in reading romance novels or watching reality TV. When fans discriminate about which media are worthy or unworthy of their attention, they follow communal criteria of relevance, not merely those of aesthetic quality, as John Fiske underscored.[44] The pleasure that media audiences experience derives—not from "mere" escapism—but from producing meanings that they feel serve their own interests rather dominant ones.

As activists circulating largely among fellow liberals, they found enjoyment in monitoring viewpoints that differed from their own—but not necessarily because they considered those sources informative. In fact, that information is often considered suspect, as demonstrated by what Janice called her "hobby" of looking for erroneous claims made by Fox News commentator Bill O'Reilly. "It was fun to watch and write down what he said and go research it and find out the truth and then e-mail him," Janice said.[45] She used Fox not as a source of information but as a marker of identity to differentiate herself from the kind of viewer who valued the news it provided. Janice said she watched the Fox morning show even though "those people are mean, so I can hate them. I watch their interpretation of the news, and I'm like 'You *cannot* believe that!' I just like the different, fresh perspective" (emphasis theirs).

These alternative-media fans gained pleasure from playing interpretive games and from thinking they knew better.[46] This community's subcultural style of experiencing mainstream news was both ironic and oppositional. While they did engage with low-status media content more than they professed to, they seem to have done so knowingly, with an ample dose of sarcasm and derision.

Rejecting News in Word and Deed

Alternative-media enthusiasts professed paying little attention to mainstream media, while actually using more of it than they realized or admitted. This paradoxical claim expresses symbolic resistance—the *principle* of rejecting mainstream media on account of its structural flaws, as opposed to the *practice* of abstaining from a genre with instrumental and ritual value. Analyzing their habits through the lens of ritual explains how alternative readers experience MSM in ways that support individual and collective identities as well as pleasures such as escape, humor, surveillance, and validation. Ritual communication through and about alternative media helps to produce oppositional consciousness, which first requires identifying with a resistant group.[47] Ritual uses of alternative media help anchor people in activist communities, shape identity narratives, and foster communication across movements.[48] These ritual, affective, and ironic aspects of news interpretations lay beyond the encoding/

decoding model, which oversimplifies what audiences actually do with when they interact with media content.

My analysis supports Mirca Madianou's argument against the assumption of a rational public that only watches the news in order to make informed decisions. Ritual and instrumental uses of the news are "deeply intertwined with the rational and critical dimensions of news consumption, rendering audiences both rational and emotional, both citizens and consumers."[49] She found paradoxes among Turkish news "addicts" similar to those I found among alternative-media fans, including fervent criticism of the style and informational quality of newscasts that was seemingly at odds with their actual viewing habits. "How can one be 'addicted to the news' and then declare that it is no longer 'watchable'?" she wondered, noting that scholars need to investigate both what people say about the media and how they actually use them.[50]

My study confirms that there is more to media use than what informants tell researchers. Scholars tend to rely on surveys, focus groups, and interviews with an assumption that audiences are able to understand, remember, reflect upon, and explain their media use. Indeed, interviews are useful for learning what people think and how they convey their ideas and experiences. But they are less effective at conjuring unconscious thoughts, feelings, and motives. My informants portrayed themselves as rational media consumers, while also acknowledging that their actions were something other than rational. I have tried to triangulate approaches: both taking their statements in diaries and conversations at face value and discussing alternative interpretations that can explain discrepancies between the two data sets. Not *either/or* but *both/and*.

Several other dimensions of these alternative media rituals merit discussion. Rituals of *integration* are social experiences that position individuals within the existing order, following Goffman.[51] Rituals of *suspension* or separation are idiosyncratic experiences that free people from constraints in order to redefine the social structure.[52] The latter are associated with industrialized societies and tend to feature playful experimentation, critique of mainstream institutions and a transforming quality.[53] This interpretive community of liberal activists and alternative-media fans employed both integrative and separative rituals, which coexist in everyday life rather than excluding each other. Their idiosyncratic experiences with alternative media offered separation and transcendence from mainstream reality alongside integration with the order or structure of an alternative-media community.

In addition to the interactions described here, many alternative-media users partake in rituals of news abstention, which can be likened to separation. Abstention is only one way in which social-movement actors respond to their lack of trust in institutional media. Dieter Rucht enumerated four potential responses: "the quadruple As." *Abstention* arises out of negative experiences with media's indifference or outright hostility to social protest. *Attack* refers to explicit written or verbal criticism of media by activists who feel ignored or misrepresented. *Adaption* means the acceptance or exploitation of media agendas and routines in hopes of securing favorable coverage. *Alternatives* signifies the attempt by social movements to create independent media to compensate for bias or lack of interest on the part of mainstream media. The media consumption of these activist-discussants can qualify as a ritual abstention from mainstream news—in words, if not in deeds.

Let's also note similarities and subtle distinctions between "news finds me" behavior, news avoidance, news abstention, and related practices like unplugging, media refusal, and media resistance. NFM implies only passive negligence of news, not active avoidance. Some *news avoiders* and *abstainers* generally lack interest in current events while others take a principled stand against specific kinds of news.[54] Unpluggers practice a range of ritual abstentions from news, media, or technology via fasts, diets and detoxes.[55] Media refusers conspicuously perform their nonconsumption to signal their taste and distinction, their identities and ideologies, perhaps their elitism or nonconformism. Resisters purposefully limit consumption to express their ambivalence toward or dislike of news, mass media, and digital communication technologies.[56]

We can add to this potent mixture such conditions as *chronic information syndrome, information fatigue, information addiction,* and *information overload.*[57] Such practices are often attributed to *news fatigue,* an attitude that apparently proliferated among both older and younger audiences in the wake of Donald Trump's 2016 election and the global COVID-19 pandemic.[58] Regardless of how you label it, a significant portion of news audiences has opted to withdraw from news experiences, due to affective factors and/or critical evaluations.[59] Indifferent or disengaged responses to news are, in their own way, just as interesting as the engaged (and sometimes ironic) ones that are the focus of this book.[60] To paraphrase Anthony Nadler's quip, the invisible hand of the news market seems to be reaching for the remote.[61]

Students' passive approach to news-seeking resembles negligence or avoidance more so than abstention. Their discourse echoes other evidence that young people have abandoned traditional news, due to growing social isolation, alienation from the political process, or mistrust of media and other people. Some blame decreased youth interest in news on apathy, television, air conditioning, or the rise of suburbia. To David Mindich, a decline in communal affinity is the single factor driving young people to avoid or abstain from news: "Perhaps the common means of assassination by all of the above suspects is that each of the accused attacked not only news, but community, too."[62] In addition, there's evidence that people of all ages in many countries avoid news due not to alleged personal moral or intellectual deficiencies but rather due to structural characteristics of their societies, such as press freedom or political stability.[63]

This resistant interpretive community viewed mainstream media as a low-status genre and alternative media as a high-status one. Liberal alternative-media users were omnivores, while conservative ones might be less so. Later we will consider why, while all audiences represent some degree of hybridity in a hybrid media system, some embrace diverse sources more than others do. But first, a substantial question looms: what do people value about alternative news as a genre and devalue about the mainstream? As the next chapter will address, the answer presents new paradoxes.

Notes

1 Jennifer Rauch, "Activists as Interpretive Communities: Rituals of Consumption and Interaction in an Alternative Media Audience," *Media, Culture, and Society* 29, no. 6 (2007): 994–1013.

2 Klaus Jensen, "Television Futures," *Critical Studies in Mass Communication* 7 (1990); Thomas Lindlof, "Media Audiences as Interpretive Communities," *Communication Yearbook* 11 (1987); and Barbie Zelizer, "Journalists as Interpretive Communities," *Critical Studies in Mass Communication* 10, no. 3 (1992).

3 Stanley Fish, *Is There a Text in This Class?* Cambridge, MA: Harvard University Press, 1980.

4 Fish, *Is There a Text?*

5 Those who consented to be diarists specifically (not to mention informants generally) were bound to be atypical because they were not randomly selected. Just as I do not assume participants were necessarily representative of the U.S. population as a whole, I do not assume diarists were strictly representative of the groups to which they belonged.

6 Thomas Lindlof and Debra Grodin, "When Media Use Can't Be Observed," *Journal of Communication* 40, no. 4 (1990); and Don Zimmerman and D. Lawrence Wieder, "The Diary-Interview Method," *Urban Life* 5, no. 4 (1977).

7 The Pew survey was based on phone interviews with a nationwide sample of 3,000 adults, a few months after I collected media-use logs for my study. Pew Research Center, "News Audiences Increasingly Politicized," June 8, 2004.

8 Pew Research Center, "News Audiences Increasingly Politicized." The Pew survey used the terms *regular, sometimes, hardly ever,* and *never* to categorize TV and magazine consumption. It asked about media use "yesterday" (which they defined as *regular,* akin to "at least three times a week") for newspaper, radio, and online sources. I collapsed the Pew categories *regular* and *sometimes* to make them roughly comparable with my diary data. Since Pew nowhere defined *sometimes,* I deemed it "at least once a week" because this frequency exceeds *hardly ever.* To include more data, I reported both *regular* and *sometimes* levels because students used many media categories less than three times per week; using only *regular* consumption would have limited an already narrow range.

9 "Media Companies Ranked 1 to 50," *Advertising Age,* August 22, 2005, 3.

10 For an analysis of young audiences' declining news consumption, which has continued for two generations, see David Mindich, *Tuned Out* (New York: Oxford University Press, 2005). For him, "young audiences" equates with people under 40 years old. Twenty-one of the 24 activists in this study qualified as young people by this standard.

11 One significant variation—and an indicator of the low regard in which activists hold television—was that around a quarter of them had no access to that medium in their homes, in contrast with only 2 percent of the U.S. population. Many of them reported watching TV at work, school, or in other people's homes. This was much more unusual in 2004, when the study was conducted, than it was in 2020, when this book was written.

12 Michael Boyle, "Media and Protest," paper presented to the Association for Education in Journalism and Mass Communication, San Antonio, TX, August 2005. Boyle also found that mainstream media use was negatively related to protest participation for individuals who were not members of activist groups and that alternative-media use shared a positive relationship with protest participation.

13 Andrew Chadwick, *The Hybrid Media System* (New York and London: Oxford University Press, 2013).

14 The *Guardian* qualifies here as foreign media, because the *Guardian U.S.* had not yet launched.

15 Although NPR is often considered a "liberal" news source, more of its listeners identified themselves as *moderate* (38 percent) or *conservative* (36 percent) than *liberal* (20 percent) in 2004. Pew Research Center, "News Audiences Increasingly Polarized."

16 Audience researchers cannot conclude that people actually encountered particular messages of interest to a study simply because those people had opportunity(ies) to encounter those messages. See Michael Slater, "Operationalizing and Analyzing Exposure," *Journalism and Mass Communication Quarterly* 81, no. 1 (2004): 168–9.

17 David Tewksbury et al., "Accidentally Informed," *Journalism and Mass Communication Quarterly* 78, no. 3 (2001): 534.

18 Yonghwan Kim et al., "Stumbling Upon News on the Internet," *Computers in Human Behavior* 29, no. 6 (2013).

19 Homero Gil De Zúñiga et al., "The Proliferation of the 'News Finds Me' Perception Across Societies," *International Journal of Communication* 14 (2020).

20 James Carey, *Communication as Culture* (Boston, MA: Unwin Hyman, 1989), 15.

21 Carey, *Communication as Culture*, 16.

22 Carey, *Communication as Culture*, 82.

23 Carey, *Communication as Culture*, 22.

24 Benedict Anderson, *Imagined Communities* (New York: Verso, 1991).

25 For more on theories of ritual communication, see Carey, *Communication as Culture*, as well as Eric Rothenbuhler, *Ritual Communication* (Thousand Oaks, CA: Sage, 1998).

26 Mark Peterson, "Getting the News in New Delhi," in *The Anthropology of News and Journalism*, ed. S. Elizabeth Bird (Bloomington: Indiana University Press, 2009).

27 Philip Howard and Andrew Chadwick, *The Routledge Handbook of Internet Politics* (Abingdon, UK, and New York: Routledge, 2009), 431.

28 Stephanie Edgerly, "Red Media, Blue Media, and Purple Media: News Repertoires in the Colorful Media Landscape," *Journal of Broadcasting and Electronic Media* 59, no. 1 (2015): 13.

29 Edgerly, "Red Media, Blue Media, and Purple Media," 16.

30 Edgerly's analysis found two other news repertoires: *online only* (17.8 percent of respondents), people using broadcast news, TV news commentary, and print news who tend to be younger and male; and *television C print news* (24.4 percent), the most common repertoire, related to being older, female, White, identifying as Democrat/ Independent, and low levels of perceived media bias. My student informants might seem apt for the *online only* repertoire; however, my diary data were collected in 2004, when getting one's news only online was a less viable option—in contrast with Edgerly's 2008 survey data.

31 Dannagal Young, "*Daily Show* Viewers More Knowledgeable about Presidential Campaign," *National Annenberg Election Survey*, September 21, 2004. This survey does not address whether, or how, viewers might learn about politics from late-night comedy shows. It noted that *Daily Show* viewers were younger, more educated, and more liberal than the average American. Yet those factors did not explain differences in campaign knowledge between people that watched the show and

those that did not. I'm grateful to Carol Polsgrove for calling this study to my attention.

32 Leah Lievrouw, *Alternative and Activist New Media* (Malden, MA: Polity, 2011); Graham Meikle, *Future Active* (New York: Routledge, 2002); Claire Bond Potter, *Political Junkies* (New York: Basic Books, 2020).

33 Erving Goffman, *The Presentation of Self in Everyday Life* (Garden City, NY: Anchor Books, 1959).

34 John Stolte, Gary Alan Fine, and Karen Cook, "Sociological Miniaturism," *Annual Review of Sociology* 27 (2001).

35 Erving Goffman, *Interaction Ritual* (Garden City, NY: Anchor Books, 1967).

36 Joshua Atkinson, *Alternative Media and Politics of Resistance* (New York: Peter Lang, 2010).

37 Anderson, *Imagined Communities*.

38 Pierre Bourdieu, *Distinction* (Cambridge, MA: Harvard University Press, 1984).

39 Pierre Bourdieu, *Distinction*.

40 Pierre Bourdieu, *Distinction*, 56.

41 Thornton, *Club Cultures: Music, Media, and Subcultural Capital* (Hanover, NH: Wesleyan/New England, 1996).

42 Thornton, *Club Cultures*, 5.

43 A University of Maryland poll found that mainstream news can foster public misperceptions. Heavy viewers of Fox News were nearly four times as likely to hold demonstrably untrue positions about the war in Iraq as people who relied on NPR or PBS. Steven Kull et al., "Misperceptions, the Media, and the Iraq War," *Political Science Quarterly* 118, no. 4 (Winter 2003/2004): 569–98.

44 John Fiske, *Television Culture* (New York: Routledge, 1987).

45 Janice e-mailed this correction to O'Reilly, hoping to initiate a dialogue with this mainstream news personality about evidence she found in alternative media that contradicted his statements. When he didn't reply, she was disappointed.

46 Fiske distinguished between games and rituals by defining *games* as cultural forms in which participants start out equal and finish differentiated into winners and losers, whereas *rituals* take differentiated groups and provide them with equalizing communal meanings or identities. Games move from similarity to difference, he said, and rituals from difference to similarity. Fiske, *Television Culture*.

47 Jane Mansbridge, "Complicating Oppositional Consciousness," in *Oppositional Consciousness*, eds. Jane Mansbridge and Aldon Morris (Chicago, IL: University of Chicago Press, 2001).

48 Veronica Barassi, "Ethnographic Cartographies," *Social Movement Studies* 12, no. 1 (January 2013); Amoshaun Toft, "Network Structures in Cross-Movement Talk," *Social Movement Studies* 19, no. 3 (2020).

49 Mirca Madianou, "The Elusive Public of TV News," in *Audiences and Publics*, Vol. 2, ed. Sonia Livingstone (Bristol, UK: Intellect Books Ltd, 2005), 109.

50 Madianou, "The Elusive Public," 102.

51 Goffman, *Interaction Ritual*.

52 Victor Turner, "Liminal to Liminoid, in Play, Flow and Ritual," in *Play, Games, and Sports in Cultural Contexts*, eds. Janet Harris and Roberta Park (Champaign, IL: Human Kinetics Publishers, 2003 [1983]).

53 Bent Steege Larsen and Thomas Tufte, "Rituals in the Modern World," in *Global Media Studies*, eds. Patrick Murphy and Marwan Kraidy (New York: Routledge, 2003).

54 Gil De Zúñiga et al., "The Proliferation of the 'News Finds Me'"; see also Damian Trilling and Klaus Schoenbach, "Skipping Current Affairs," *European Journal of Communication* 28, no. 1 (2013).

55 I discuss diverse practices through which people intentionally avoid media use in Jennifer Rauch, "Constructive Rituals of Demediatization," *Explorations in Media Ecology* 13, no. 3+4 (2014).

56 For more on media resistance and news resistance, see Louise Woodstock, "The News-Democracy Narrative and the Unexpected Benefits of Limited News Consumption," *Journalism* 15, no. 7 (2014); and Trine Syvertsen, *Media Resistance* (Cham, Switzerland: Palgrave Macmillan, 2017). Woodstock's resisters reported benefits such as greater calm and purpose, a constructive attitude toward the present and future, and a willingness to work with others. She concluded these qualities enable resisters to engage in meaningful political participation—challenging the dominant narrative that democracy depends on a citizenry whose knowledge stems from news consumption.

57 Syvertsen, *Media Resistance*.

58 *NY Times*, "Young Adults Suffering from News Fatigue, Study Says," June 2, 2008.

59 Madianou, "The Elusive Public of TV News."

60 For more on the "indifferent audience" and disengaged and ironic responses, see David Morley, "Unanswered Questions in Audience Research," *The Communication Review* 9 (2006), 103.

61 Anthony Nadler, *Making the News Popular* (Chicago, IL: University of Illinois Press, 2016).

62 David Mindich, *Tuned Out* (New York: Oxford University Press, 2005), 9.

63 Benjamin Toff and Antonis Kalogeropoulos, "All the News that's Fit to Ignore," *Public Opinion Quarterly*, July 10, 2020. https://doi.org/10.1093/poq/nfaa016.

8

NEWS OMNIVORES, HYBRID MEDIA, AND ALTERNATIVE IDEALS

When a new network of progressive editors, publishers, and directors gathered in Philadelphia in 2005 to draft a "Declaration of the Independent Media," democracy activist Micah Sifry was among the 25 signatories. An editor of the *Nation*, Sifry believed the playing field had been leveled between "so-called mainstream and so-called alternative media" by the Internet, because "people who used to be called 'the audience' are now co-participants in creating the news":

> I recently heard Amy Goodman brag that her *Democracy Now!* podcast has as many subscribers on iTunes as . . . *Meet the Press*. Surely that tells us that the old notion of creating an "alternative" media in opposition to the "mainstream" has become meaningless. At a time when anyone can find any article or report from almost any news outlet in the world directly and instantaneously, it makes little sense to marginalize ourselves as "alternative."[1]

One wonders what Sifry meant when he used the terms "alternative" and "mainstream," qualified as "so-called" and rendered in quotation marks. The difference between alternative media and mainstream ones has long been blurry, as much an intersubjective perception as an empirical reality. Media scholars, practitioners, and audiences have wrangled for decades to decide what makes some media sources "alternative"—and others not so—with a fixed, universal definition of the category remaining elusive (or, perhaps, being eluded). People have typically bestowed the honorific "alternative" on certain media based on criteria such as the voices, issues, perspectives, and sources that producers include and the ownership, management, financial, or reporting practices that they espouse. The division of alternative, oppositional media from mainstream, dominant ones was difficult already in the early 1970s—"at best superfluous if not irrelevant" per media historian James Hamilton.[2] He later mused, "It would seem that social media have forever rendered conventional conceptions of alternative media . . . quaint if not delusional. All is not as it seems."

By the early 2000s, the task of discerning and describing the differences between these two genres was compounded by drastic changes in the way people produce and consume news, as digital devices and social networks gave audiences unprecedented opportunities to create, distribute, and respond to a vast variety of mediated information. Many once-radical features and practices formerly the province of alternative media were integrated into everyday mainstream media use: horizontal communication, nonhierarchical relationships, a participatory ethic, open access, interactivity. In this context, people working toward democratic communications, as Micah Sifry was, wonder whether the category of alternative media is still distinctive or important—if, indeed it ever was. Many no longer think of alternative-mainstream as a binary opposition, but rather as a spectrum where varying colors of media blend into each other. In a digital media environment of ubiquitous connection to networked information flows, activists and experts alike have questioned the accuracy, necessity, and desirability of labeling any media as "alternative."[3]

This book presents a range of evidence supporting the idea that alternative media continues to be a meaningful, high-status genre to people who read, watch, and listen to such content. This chapter takes a further step toward explaining why. Is the notion indeed meaningless? If not, what does the phrase *alternative media* signify to such audiences? How do users account for differences they see between alternative and mainstream news sources? Previous chapters discussed interview and diary data from earlier phases of my research, with regional activists who valued alternative media. The analysis here introduces a new phase that surveyed a broader, national sample of alternative-media users.[4] I asked respondents a range of quantitative and qualitative questions about the values and practices they associated with alternative media as well as the critiques of mainstream media they supported.

Many conversations about alternative media have centered on how scholars and producers define the category, with little empirical attention to how audiences talk about the genre. Beyond my own research, Chris Atton, Joshua Atkinson, Jacqueline Ewart, Tony Harcup, Dustin Harp, and Summer Harlow have published work that reinforces several themes of this book regarding audiences perceptions that alternative media are more critical of corporations, more supportive of social activism, and less motivated by profit than mainstream journalism. To my knowledge, the present study was the first to ask alternative-media audiences, rather than producers, what alternative media meant to them.[5] This approach provides a richer view of how audiences interact with and view their most trusted and valued news sources, helping to fill the "distinctly disturbing gap" that John Downing located in our knowledge about alternative media.

   This chapter will bring us closer to understanding the connotative and cultural meanings of *alternative* and *mainstream* in this community. Previous discussions emphasized specific contexts of news reception and interpretation, which risks missing the bigger picture. The quantitative data shared in this chapter and the next one will contextualize the insights of my qualitative analysis and help link these micro-differences between actual viewers to macro social processes. Survey data can help map some parameters within which opposition, negotiation, and resistance operate for broader audiences.[6]

   We know that alternative-media fans are omnivorous, that the media system and (some) audiences have been hybridized. Here we dive deeper into the inter-subjective meanings of these two media genres to people who devour both. The survey uncovered audience attitudes toward mainstream news sources that help explain why they distrust and devalue many—but not all—corporate, commercial media outlets. We will address an apparent contradiction that, despite their profligate criticism of corporate, commercial media, these respondents considered news outlets like *The Daily Show*, Facebook, Fox News, and the *Huffington Post* to be "alternative," not mainstream. We also will consider gaps between users' idealized views of alternative media and the realities of alternative-media practices, according to empirical research. In sum, alternative media are not necessarily what these engaged audiences imagine them to be.

Surveying Alternative-Media Users

This phase of research explored what "alternative media" meant to audiences by surveying readers of the *Nation* and *Human Events*.[7] I chose these publications because they were published on similar frequency (weekly in print, continuously online) to readerships of similar size (around 80,000 at the time).[8] I sought a sample that included diverse political orientations (liberal or progressive in the former case, conservative in the latter). Founded in 1865, the leftist *Nation* is the oldest continuously published weekly magazine in the United States and has featured columns by progressive thinkers like Sifry as well as Eric Alterman, Naomi Klein, Robert McChesney, and John Nichols. Launched in 1944 as a vestige of the America First antiwar movement, *Human Events* has been called the "Bible of the Right." With regular contributions from Pat Buchanan, Ann Coulter, Newt Gingrich, and Sean Hannity, it was once some of Ronald Reagan's favorite reading. To my mind, readers of such content were likely to have well-formed opinions about mainstream and alternative media, as well as sufficient motivation to share them in an online survey.

   I recruited participants in 2009 through classified ads in both publications asking "Why Do We Need Alternative Media?" Owing to low response from print ads, additional notices were placed on Facebook. The survey was also mentioned on the *Nation*'s "Altercation" blog by Eric Alterman, author of the book *What Liberal Media? The Truth About Bias and the News*. However, more than 71 percent of respondents did not report being *Nation* readers, which suggests that this outlet's fans did not dominate the sample.[9] The snowball method yielded a convenience or purposive sample of 224 people who identified themselves as using alternative media. The sample was not representative of the U.S. population but was highly appropriate to these research purposes.[10] Although a minority reported using either of the target publications, the demographic profile of participants corresponded closely to the average reader of the *Nation* and *Human Events*, per publishers' data. The majority was white (85 percent), aged 30–59 (64 percent), with a college degree (64 percent), and male (58 percent). Compared with U.S. census data from that year, the sample over-represented males, whites, and people who are older and more educated. Of participants who provided political orientations, 47 percent called themselves *liberal* or *progressive* and 39 percent were *conservative*; the remainder answered *none of the above*. The questionnaire had an 86 percent completion rate.

The survey consisted of around two dozen open- and closed-ended items, plus a few qualifying and demographic questions.[11] I avoided defining "alternative media" in the questionnaire so respondents could self-define this genre. I placed an open-ended question asking participants to name their "favorite alternative media" near the start of the survey to minimize response bias. Closed-ended questions asked, for example, how much they used alternative and mainstream media, which characteristics of alternative media were important to them, and which statements about MSM they agreed with; these latter items were based on conceptions of alternative media in previous scholarship. Participants indicated agreement or disagreement with each item using Likert-style scales, where 1 meant *strongly agree* and 4 meant *strongly disagree*, with 4 points to remove the neutral option. I concluded the survey by asking people to describe alternative media and the problems with mainstream media (MSM) in their own words.

Some critical themes that emerged from my analysis of survey responses include their omnivorous news diets; their desire for diverse content, civic engagement, and social change; and—more surprisingly—their relative ambivalence toward scale, technology, and professionalism.

An Alternative System of Audience Values

While these survey participants identified as alternative-media users, they can be better understood as members of a hybrid audience—as news omnivores. Respondents reported using a lot of both alternative media and mainstream media, as Table 8.1 shows. When asked how often they used alternative media, 81.3 percent of respondents said *regularly*, whereas 52.2 percent reported using MSM *regularly*. Collapsing across frequency categories, those numbers rise to

TABLE 8.1 Frequency of use and time spent with MSM and alternative media*

Type of media	Used regularly %	Used regularly or sometimes %	Spent more than 1 hour daily %
Alternative media	81.3	97.8	65.5
Mainstream media	52.2	78.5	36.1

*For Tables 8.1–8.6, the number of responses ranged from 199 to 224.

97.8 percent of respondents using alternative media *regularly* or *sometimes* and 78.5 percent using MSM *regularly* or *sometimes*. When asked how much time they spent using media on a typical day, 65.5 percent said they used alternative media for more than one hour versus 36.1 percent who said they used MSM for an hour or more. By all three measures, these respondents used alternative media more than they did mainstream media.

The survey started with an open-ended item asking participants to name their "favorite alternative-media source" without prompting. Responses to this question, shown in Table 8.2, indicate how fragmented this audience is. Five media outlets were mentioned by more than 10 percent of respondents: the *Nation* (21.8 percent), *HuffPost* (21.3 percent), Fox News (18.8 percent), *Democracy Now!* (13.4 percent), and *Daily Kos* (10.4 percent). The next most frequently named outlets were *Talking Points Memo* (8.4 percent), Alternet (6.9 percent), *National Public Radio* (6.9 percent), Glenn Beck (5.9 percent), Facebook (5.5 percent), Rush Limbaugh (5.4 percent), *Drudge Report* (4.4 percent), *Human Events* (4.4 percent), and *Mother Jones* (4.4 percent). Rounding out the top 20 were *Altercation*, *The Daily Show*, *Politico*, the *Progressive*, Sean Hannity, and *Truthdig* (all 4 percent). Hundreds of other media outlets—such as *Indymedia, Slate, Common Dreams, Boing Boing, Salon*, the BBC, Bill O'Reilly, *Adbusters, News Busters, Fire Dog Lake*, and *Twitter*—were offered in this question but named by fewer than 4 percent of people surveyed. The *New York Times* and *Village Voice* were each named once.

These results indicate the wide array of outlets that readers, listeners, and viewers thought of when they listed alternative media off the top of their heads: eight current-events blogs; six radio and TV broadcasters focusing on news and opinion; three political magazines; a news-based satirical program; an independent news network, and a corporate-owned social network. Five "favorite alternative media" (Table 8.2) were absent from the responses to subsequent closed-ended items (Table 8.3): Alternet, Facebook, Altercation, *The Daily Show*, and Truthdig. The presence of Altercation here might be partially explained by the fact that its author, Eric Alterman of the *Nation*, posted a link to this survey; some respondents might have clicked through from that blog. Although some people named Alternet, Facebook, and Truthdig as favorite

TABLE 8.2 Favorite alternative news sources

Source	%	Source	%
The Nation	21.8	Rush Limbaugh	5.4
The Huffington Post	21.3	Drudge Report	4.4
Fox News	18.8	*Human Events*	4.4
Democracy Now!	13.4	*Mother Jones*	4.4
Daily Kos	10.4	Altercation	4.0
Talking Points Memo	8.4	*The Daily Show*	4.0
Alternet	6.9	Politico	4.0
National Public Radio	6.9	*The Progressive*	4.0
Glenn Beck	5.9	Sean Hannity	4.0
Facebook	5.5	Truthdig	4.0

TABLE 8.3 News sources used most frequently by hybrid audience

Source	%	Source	%
Daily newspapers	43.4	Talking Points Memo	16.2
National Public Radio	31.4	Daily Kos	16.0
The Huffington Post	30.7	BBC	14.8
The Nation	28.6	*The New Yorker*	14.1
Fox News	22.1	CNN	13.8
Talking Points Memo	21.0	Politico	12.0
Public Broadcasting Service	20.0	Sean Hannity	11.9
MSNBC	18.9	*Time* or *Newsweek*	11.7
Alternative newsweeklies	18.7	C-SPAN	11.3
Democracy Now!	16.8	*The Economist*	11.2

alternative news sources, those media outlets do not show up elsewhere in the data.

The survey collected data about how often people used particular mainstream and alternative outlets. Table 8.3 shows the top 20 media used by this hybrid audience—that is, those used by more than 10 percent of respondents. Legacy print sources included daily newspapers (43.4 percent) and newsweeklies (18.9 percent), as well as news-oriented magazines such as the *Nation* (28.6 percent), *New Yorker* (14.8 percent), *Time* or *Newsweek* (11.7 percent), and *Economist* (11.2 percent), whether in print or online. (Similar publications such as *Harper's*, the *Atlantic, Mother Jones, Human Events, National Review*, the *Progressive*, and the *New Republic* showed levels of support below 10 percent.) Also important were public or nonprofit broadcast media such as National Public Radio (31.4 percent), PBS (21.0 percent), *Democracy Now!* (18.7 percent), the BBC (16.0 percent), and C-SPAN (11.3 percent). The corporate or for-profit broadcast media named most frequently were Fox News (22.1 percent), MSNBC (20.0 percent), Glenn Beck (14.1 percent), CNN (13.8 percent), and Sean Hannity

(11.9 percent). The most-read blog for this sample was *HuffPost* (30.7 percent), followed by *Talking Points Memo* (16.8 percent), *Daily Kos* (16.2 percent), and *Politico* (12.0 percent). This list illustrates the media outlets—commercial and noncommercial alike—that respondents held most in common.

After asking people about their media usage, the survey asked them to rate how important they considered certain characteristics related to alternative media. Respondents believed strongly that alternative media should allow a wide range of people to express their voices and opinions (rating average of 3.51), advocate for a different system of societal values (3.42), and be devoted to issues and events not discussed elsewhere (3.4), as shown in Table 8.4. They thought alternative media should criticize and analyze the work done by MSM (average of 3.36), promote activism and mobilize people to participate (3.11), and be more connected to people in groups and networks that they support (3.04). The ideas that alternative media should use different technology for gathering and sharing information (average of 2.78) and offer favorable coverage to people and groups that respondents supported (2.69) reported the lowest levels of support.

Survey respondents were also asked how much they agreed with certain ideals related to alternative media. The items receiving overall agreement (an average rating of more than 2.5 on a scale of 1 to 4) are shown in Table 8.5. The four most popular ideals were that alternative media should encourage people to get involved in civic life (average of 3.40), use new and interactive technologies (3.33), pursue social justice (3.22), and be produced by small organizations, not big companies (2.92). Somewhat lower support was reported for the ideas that alternative media should be produced by professional journalists (average

TABLE 8.4 Most important characteristics of alternative media, per hybrid audience

How important are the following characteristics of ALTERNATIVE media to you?	Rating average
They allow a wider range of people to express their voices and opinions than MSM do	3.51
They advocate for a different system of values than MSM do	3.42
They devoted to issues and events not discussed elsewhere	3.4
They criticize and analyze the work done by MSM	3.36
They promote activism and mobilize people to participate	3.11
They are more connected to people in groups and networks that I support	3.04
They use different technology for gathering, accessing, and sharing info than MSM do	2.78
They offer more favorable coverage to people and groups that I support	2.69

Source: Scale: 1 = strongly disagree, 2 = somewhat disagree, 3 = somewhat agree, and 4 = strongly agree.

TABLE 8.5 Audience agreement with alternative media ideals★

How much do you support the following ideas about ALTERNATIVE media?	*Rating average*
They encourage people to get involved in civic life	3.40
They use new and interactive technologies	3.33
They pursue social justice	3.22
They are produced by small organizations, not big companies	2.92
They are produced by professional journalists	2.70
They use traditional and familiar technologies	2.62
They aim to be nonprofit	2.60
They are produced by amateur and citizen journalists	2.56

★In Tables 8.5 and 8.6, the number of responses was 205.

Source: Scale: 1 = strongly disagree, 2 = somewhat disagree, 3 = somewhat agree, and 4 = strongly agree.

of 2.70), use traditional and familiar technologies (2.62), aim to be nonprofit (2.6), and be produced by amateur and citizen journalists (2.56).

The items receiving overall disagreement (a rating average of less than 2.5 on a scale of 1 to 4) are shown in Table 8.6. Three of the less popular ideals were that alternative media should help preserve American traditions (average of 2.48), be noncommercial or advertising-free (2.45), and promote family values (2.26). The lowest support was reported for the ideas that alternative media should encourage moral behavior or religious action (average of 2.10), promote a certain political point of view (1.97), and appeal to small or niche audiences (1.84).

Three intriguing themes emerge from the survey data. First, respondents showed similar levels of support for the ideas that alternative media should be produced by both professional and amateur or citizen journalists (rating averages of 2.70 vs. 2.56). This finding makes sense in light of their strong support for a "wide range of people to share their voices and opinions," which could include professional and amateur journalists separately or in collaboration. This attitude also likely relates to respondents' perceptions of media credibility, with research showing that audiences value citizen journalists but view professional ones as more credible.[12] A high proportion of alternative media sources are produced not by amateur, untrained activists but rather by elite, experienced professionals—a significant point to which we will shortly return.

Second, respondents showed more agreement with the idea that alternative media should use new and interactive technologies than that they should traditional and familiar ones (averages of 3.33 vs. 2.62). Question wording might have influenced these results, with being "interactive" carrying more weight than being "different" than the mainstream. Both terms are ambiguous, so that *interactive* and *different* mean diverse things to diverse people. (Most respondents supported both items; 54 percent agreed that "alternative media should use traditional and familiar technologies" while 91 percent supported newer

TABLE 8.6 Audience disagreement with alternative media ideals

How important are the following characteristics of ALTERNATIVE media to you?	Rating average
They help preserve American traditions	2.48
They are noncommercial or advertising-free	2.45
They promote family values	2.26
They encourage moral behavior or religious action	2.10
They promote a certain political point of view	1.97
They appeal to a small or niche audience	1.84

Source: Scale: 1 = strongly disagree, 2 = somewhat disagree, 3 = somewhat agree, and 4 = strongly agree.

technologies.) People valuing activism likely recognize the need to reach diverse communities around the globe through whatever methods necessary, be they older or lower-tech forms of media. These responses represent another instance where binary choices are not forced, where people can choose both/and instead of either/or. Both alternative and mainstream media, both professional and amateur producers, both old and new technologies.

Third, respondents wanted alternative media to be made by small organizations yet appeal to large audiences, not small or niche ones (averages of 2.92 vs. 1.84). Thus, they distinguished between scale of production and scale of circulation. It is reasonable to surmise that, as proponents of social change, they preferred for small media organizations to reach a larger public, rather than remaining in an alternative "ghetto," as Sifry and others have suggested.[13]

Criticizing Capitalist Influences on MSM

In addition to looking at audience conceptions of alternative media, the survey asked people why they used mainstream media and how much they agreed with various ideas about mainstream media. A majority of respondents said they used MSM for surveillance purposes: to monitor what the general public is being exposed to (63.8 percent) or to hear what other people are thinking and saying (52.3 percent). A majority said they used MSM for educational purposes: to get information or knowledge (54.35). A sizable number said they used MSM because they liked to laugh at it or got guilty pleasure from it (19.1 percent). A small portion said they did not use mainstream media at all (9.5 percent).

The eight criticisms of MSM that garnered strong agreement from respondents are shown in Table 8.7. Four economic items received high levels of support: that MSM are compromised by corporations and corporate interests (average of 3.56), by owners' political biases (3.50), by advertising and commercial interests (3.42), and by profit motives (3.36). MSM were amply criticized for supporting the status quo (average of 3.17), for having undemocratic

TABLE 8.7 Audience agreement with mainstream media ideas

How much do you support the following ideas? MAINSTREAM media . . .	Rating average
Are compromised by corporations and corporate interests	3.56
Are biased by politics of their owners	3.50
Are compromised by advertising and commercial interests	3.42
Are motivated too much by profit	3.36
Support the status quo	3.17
Have undemocratic practices	3.06
Disempower the public	3.18
Are compromised by egos or career ambitions of journalists	3.02
Are biased by politics of journalists	2.86

Source: Scale: 1 = strongly disagree, 2 = somewhat disagree, 3 = somewhat agree, and 4 = strongly agree.

practices (3.06), and for disempowering the public (3.18). Mainstream journalists also were blamed for their egos and career ambitions (score of 3.02) and their politic biases (2.86).

The three criticisms of MSM receiving the least support are listed in Table 8.8. Respondents showed ambivalence toward the notion that MSM might have unpatriotic practices (average of 2.5) and disagreed with two criticisms of MSM: that they were compromised by immoral or anti-religious attitudes (2.01) and did not have enough government regulation (1.99).

We now know respondents' prevailing criticisms of mainstream media as well as the alternative media characteristics they most value. What do these responses tell us about the meanings of these media genres to this hybrid audience? They invoked a common set of values associated with the category *alternative media* and distinct from *mainstream media*. Corporate ownership, commercial interests, and profit motives were some of the top problems with MSM that they said necessitated alternative outlets. They perceived corporations, owners, advertising, and profit as major factors compromising MSM—a perspective richly expressed in earlier analysis of group discourse.[14] Yet support for alternative media being nonprofit or shunning advertising was marginal, with averages of 2.60 and 2.45, respectively. However, many of the particular media sources spontaneously named earlier as favorite alternative could qualify as mainstream, by respondents' own standards. These findings complicate assumptions about the primacy of anti-corporate, anti-commercial, and anti-profit concerns often voiced by proponents of alternative media.

Goliaths in the Midst

Let's take a closer look at four popular "alternative" media sources cited by this audience sample: *The Daily Show*, Fox News, *HuffPost*, and Facebook. They frequently

TABLE 8.8 Audience disagreement with mainstream media ideas

How much do you support the following ideas? *MAINSTREAM media . . .*	%
Have unpatriotic practices	2.50
Are compromised by immoral or anti-religious attitudes	2.01
Do not have enough government regulation	1.99

Source: Scale: 1 = strongly disagree, 2 = somewhat disagree, 3 = somewhat agree, and 4 = strongly agree.

cited Facebook as a news source (although it is properly considered a content platform rather than a content producer; people often say they "get their news from" social media, without specifying the original sources of information posted there). The other three sources are large, hierarchical organizations with mass audiences that are corporate-owned, advertising-financed, and profit-oriented—features that ought to disqualify them from being alternative media.

Facebook, of course, has become one of the world's richest companies since its 2004 founding and is one of the few corporations now worth more than $500 billion—higher than the gross domestic product of Belgium, Poland, Sweden, Saudi Arabia, or Taiwan.[15] With 2.5 billion active users, it's one of the most trafficked websites in the world. Its size, wealth, power, and corporate status would seem to preclude it from being an "alternative" news source. Yet Facebook has long been a staple means of communication for activists and social movements. (Its outsized influence over the news ecosystem attracts more public attention now than it did when this survey was conducted.) Recent criticism of Facebook has focused on its role in spreading false and misleading information as well as controversies related to data privacy and psychological effects on users. Survey respondents likely valued the diversity of voices and content offered on Facebook—whose status was decidedly more alternative in 2009, when less than 38 percent of the U.S. population reported getting news through social networks.

Meanwhile, the *Huffington Post* was launched in 2005 by Arianna Huffington, Jonah Peretti, and Andrew Breitbart as a news-aggregation site and semi-professional blog that repurposed a lot of content from news brands like CNN and the *New York Times*.[16] (Later, Brietbart founded his own website to provide news from extremely conservative, alt-right, and right-wing nationalist viewpoints.) Editorially, *HuffPost* offers commentary from public figures and academics, contributions from "an army of several hundred unpaid volunteer writers," and investigative reporting for which it has won Polk and Pulitzer prizes.[17] By the time it was acquired by AOL in 2011 for $315 million, it had "more monthly visitors than the *New York Times* website, a world away from the cliché of the plucky independent blog running on a shoestring budget."[18] (Huffington herself—a celebrity, member of the socioeconomic elite, and vocal advocate for liberal policies—left *HuffPost* in 2016.)[19] This hybrid blog, whose popularity later subsided somewhat, was one of the most widely read online sources of news and left-leaning commentary for more than a decade. Survey respondents might have judged *HuffPost* "alternative" by virtue of its featuring a wide spectrum of voices and interactive technological features.[20]

The Daily Show might also seem an odd choice of "alternative." Its home channel of Comedy Central is owned by Viacom, one of the five largest U.S. media companies, whose other holdings include CBS, Paramount, Showtime, BET, MTV, Nickelodeon, Simon and Schuster, and dozens of TV stations. Viacom counts among the ranks of media monopolies or oligarchies routinely criticized by liberals, activists, and alternative-media fans. In the eyes of viewers, oppositional content in *The Daily Show* might justify its "compromised" form. The show often questions corporate media and challenges journalism routines, punditry, self-interest, and the failures of objectivity (particularly during its Jon Stewart era, 1999–2015). The "culture jamming" potential of such satirical news programs has been widely hailed, especially in the days when the term "fake news" mainly referred to comedic content.[21] Discourse shared in a previous chapter underscored alternative-media users' embrace of news satire. Dannagal Young proposed that political TV satire fills a similar niche for left-wing viewers as opinion talk radio does for right-wing listeners. Both genres are logical extensions of their respective political psychologies, she argued, which express frustration with MSM and offer alternative sources of meaning and information.[22] Irony is a mirror image of outrage.

Outrage, rather than irony, is a hallmark of Fox News, the explicitly conservative cable network owned and run by the Murdoch family since 1996. Despite being a media giant with billions of dollars in annual revenue and one of the largest TV news audiences in the world, Fox News might seem like an "alternative" to traditional journalism in terms of its content and reporting practices, which are often biased in favor of Republican politicians and conservative causes. Many viewers have criticized Fox as "state TV" or a mouthpiece for the Bush and Trump administrations—in a word, as propaganda. Fans of right-wing alternative media find this slant attractive, while some fans of left-wing alternative media watch it nonetheless to surveil the opposition, to see "what other people are watching," or to get ironic pleasure. Survey respondents might have deemed Fox *alternative* due to this sympathy for conservative values, as did an analyst who suggested that the channel be considered alternative rather than mainstream.[23] (Perceived political orientations in news are an intriguing aspect of audience attitudes toward alternative and mainstream media that will receive more discussion in the next chapter, which focuses on partisanship.)

Few alternative-seeming projects live up to all the ideals to which people hold them, while many mainstream-seeming media occasionally meet some of these expectations. Despite ample similarities, alternative media and mainstream ones have meaningful differences in regard to critical content and social motivations.

Alternative Media Ideals Versus Realities

Many respondents named political blogs among their favorite alternative media, including the likes of Daily Kos, Politico, Talking Points Memo, and Truthdig—sources that often feature criticism of elite media. This finding demands closer scrutiny, with research suggesting such online publications do not perforce represent meaningful alternatives to corporate—commercial outlets.

A deep stream of empirical work backs up the argument that alternative media is a porous, flexible, blended, blurred, contentious, and hybrid genre, where some outlets show more (or less) alternative tendencies than others.[24] Linda Jean Kenix's research, for one, offers indispensable insights. Her analysis of political blogs found that they linked more often to mainstream media than to marginal sources, spoke in coded language that only frequent readers could understand, and offered no meaningful two-way communication.[25] Many blogs serve as extensions of corporate news rather than as examples of alternative news, she concluded. Even when blogs critique mainstream content, they often promote dominant values and an "omnipresent commercial ideology."[26] Kenix argued that "traditionally conceptualized mainstream and alternative media now draw so heavily from practices thought to be the purview of the other that it is increasingly difficult to ascertain any clear demarcations of difference."[27] Such findings undermined the idea that alternative and mainstream media are mutually exclusive categories. Instead, she places these media genres on a "converging spectrum" where distinctions like noncommercial/commercial, radical/non-radical, etc. are unsustainable or disappearing, if they ever existed.[28]

Especially in developed nations, alternative and mainstream news sources often share a commercial orientation, similar attitudes toward objectivity and advocacy, a rotating door of personnel, similar organizational structures and management strategies, and activities such as blogging, open-source publishing, native reporting and citizen journalism. A few examples: Chris Atton demonstrated that alternative-media producers have a symbiotic relationship with their mainstream colleagues, often adopting each other's practices.[29] He also illustrated how the global Indymedia network presented hybrid characteristics, with radical content and news values alongside mainstream production values, institutional frameworks, and professionalized reporting.[30] Tony Harcup described alternative personnel and processes as "crossing over"—or, rather, move along the continuum—to mainstream news organizations and vice versa.[31] James Hamilton identified hybrid practices on an alternative news site that addressed neglected issues and used citizen reporters while also limiting nonprofessional contributors and relying on ad revenue.[32] He pointed out the shortcomings of a definitional, essentialist divide between alternative and mainstream media, arguing that we need more nuance than simply assessing the alternative genre "against an ideal set of characteristics." Complex blends of commercial means and social-reform ends have long been evident in media forms and content, from 17th-century religious news to 20th-century Socialist publications, as Hamilton reminds us. Seemingly antithetical media practices— such as selling advertising space while critiquing commercial culture—that we see today as "hybrid" were not only commonplace but also considered "neutral techniques" in other times.[33]

While the two forms have blurred, alternative media remain distinct from MSM in their commitment to contesting power and seeking change.[34] Alternative news producers must face political-economic realities to survive. It's challenging to excoriate certain features of capitalist society when you also need resources from that society.[35] Alternative media do persist in being less commercial, producing more critical content, and being more supportive of social change than their mainstream counterparts.[36] Even some corporate-owned news outlets manage to rebuke media corporations and offer content that articulates a vision of transforming society.[37]

The Blogosphere Goes Mainstream

Some of the "Top 20" favorite alternative news sources named in this survey have ranked among the most popular media—not only legacy institutions like NPR, Fox News, and *Mother Jones* but also born-digital sites like *HuffPost*, Politico, and Daily Kos. In reality, blogs are not what engaged users imagine or hope for them to be, in terms of race, gender, economics, or diversity of opinion.[38] Political communication scholars have provided great insights on the evolving role of so-called "alternative" blogs in the digital mediascape.

One is Matthew Hindman, who proposed that people who praise blogs know little about who writes them or who reads them. Blogs have "amplified the influence of a small group of educational, professional and technological elites in U.S. politics," Hindman said, noting that many elite bloggers were former media critics; they are "not the voice of average citizens."[39] His observation that "vast swaths of the public are systematically unheard in civic debates" online contrasts starkly with the perception that digital alternative media expand the range of ideas and voices participating in public conversations. Audiences mainly search for news organizations they are already familiar with and cluster around a few sources; the top 20 search terms in 2005 (in alphabetical order) included BBC, CNN, *Consumer Reports, Drudge Report*, Fox News, hurricane/weather, MSNBC, the *New York Times, TV Guide*, and *USA Today*. While it takes substantial time, skill, and motivation to read political blogs, it is even harder to build readership for one's own blog. There's a difference between having the ability to speak online and having a realistic expectation of being heard.

A similar view is advanced by Richard Davis, who challenged common wisdom that political blogs are amateur productions that serve niche audiences.[40] An "A-list" of influential blogs, published by upper-class editors with large audiences, dwarfed the readership of "common" bloggers. One telling statistic: the top 10 political blogs of 2008 attracted 48 percent of web traffic. (Some A-list blogs were favorites of my survey respondents: Daily Kos, Huff-Post, Talking Points Memo; meanwhile, Truthdig qualified as "common.") These elite bloggers overwhelmingly relied on establishment sources and produced media criticism, rather than journalism; they aimed to reform traditional media, not destroy or replace it. Davis concluded that the blogosphere had been mainstreamed by 2009, with its agenda significantly overlapping—not quite replicating—that of institutional news outlets.

The U.S. blogosphere has changed in important ways since the mid-2000s, when new digital platforms spurred excitement about "net-roots" media production, an online equivalent of grassroots activism. Blogs and other interactive genres "are no longer the radical departure they once were," according to Andrew Chadwick. These formats have been adopted by public communicators in every sector, with successful bloggers serving as consultants to campaigns, interest groups, government agencies, and traditional media. Many net-roots activists adopted traditional journalism norms while many professionals adopted amateur styles and conversational rhythms. Many bloggers are hybrid semi-professional or semi-amateur journalist-activist-pundits. In the context of this "rapidly pluralizing and fragmenting media system," Chadwick remarked, grassroots media producers have been outflanked by journalists with greater organizational status, prestige, credibility, resources, and the access needed to hold politicians accountable.[41]

Alternative Attitudes in the United States and Latin America

A year after I collected these survey data from alternative-media users, another pair of scholars found similar themes and contradictions in other parts of the world. Summer Harlow and Dustin Harp conducted a 2009 study guided by questions such as: where do activists most often get their news? How much importance do they place on using printed and online alternative media, community radio and television, or social media? What do they think about the role of corporate or mainstream media in democracy and social justice? Their research featured a cross-cultural analysis of how audiences in the United States and Latin America viewed the relationship between activism and mainstream and alternative media.[42]

According to Harlow and Harp, international activists' critique of mainstream media centered on the consequences of a profit-oriented news system for the quality and the accuracy of information. The study confirmed a widespread wariness of corporate media across the Western hemisphere that explains why many activists turn away from mainstream news. More than three-quarters of U.S. respondents and about half of Latin American respondents said they thought corporate media posed a threat to democracy and social justice. These activist-respondents worried about unequal digital access and online censorship but still seemed to see the Internet as the future of alternative media, as creating an online alternative public sphere. Around 80 percent of Latin American respondents said printed alternative media played an important role in activism—compared with around half of U.S. respondents—due perhaps to the "rich tradition of alternative media and a long history of elite-controlled media working in collusion with politicians and business owners" in Latin America.

In addition to other studies cited through this book, Harlow and Harp's research offers complementary empirical evidence of how activist audiences think about and use mainstream and alternative media. Their methods were comparable to mine and their responses parallel in regards to overwhelming distrust of corporate media, a belief that such media restrain social change, and optimism about the Internet's potential for activism. Alternative-media attitudes and behaviors like those reported in my survey appear to hold wider sway beyond the United States.

Impure Alternatives and Necessary Evils

To Micah Sifry, the meaning of alternative media remains rooted in its goal of providing alternative viewpoints to supplement the narrow "ideological spread" visible in corporate media, which corresponds closely to the two major political parties.[43] "There are no open Socialists, Libertarians or Greens on CNN or writing editorial columns for any of the major news outlets," he told me. While the playing field remains off-level and white men still dominate the upper ranks, Sifry sees a much broader variety of high-quality and inclusive content available now than 15 years ago, as well as more possibilities for diligent media creators to "build enough of a paying audience to get by if they super-serve a niche audience."[44]

Despite the ascendance of blogs, social networks, and other forms of communication, the phrase "alternative media" retains a wealth of meaning to audiences. The conceptions of *alternative media* reported here illustrate that the category has substantially consistent meanings to people who read, watch, and listen to such outlets. Intersubjective agreement about what makes alternative media "alternative" was evident among survey respondents. These shared, lay meanings of the category *alternative media* offer new understandings that supplement theories of experts.

In the minds of these alternative-media users, a key distinction between their preferred genre and mainstream media is that the former produces critical content with the primary goal of promoting social change (with financial considerations taking a back seat), while the latter is mainly motivated by the pursuit of profit (with little regard to the social impact of news).[45] We have explored some reasons why they value alternative content more highly than alternative form. User perspectives help us to better understand why alternative media retains its relatively high status in the digital news landscape, while mainstream media are increasingly disparaged. This critique of mainstream media focusing primarily on the undue influence of profit-oriented owners and advertisers sheds light on the roots of their distrust in corporate, commercial news.

These findings underscore the heightened significance of subjective and cultural meanings of alternative media, by comparison to essentialist ones. Exploring how audience conceptions are shaped by their respective contexts helps avoid idealist reduction and underscore possibilities for change.[46] These perspectives echo many themes of identity, community, and resistance among alternative media fans discussed earlier. The label "alternative" might be an expression of lifestyle politics to some extent. Yet it counts as more than self-branding if people are committed to living consistently according to their principles. These audience members profess to put their money where their mouths are, by using and supporting alternative media.

My study bolsters the claim that *alternative media* and *mainstream media* express two ideal types, not empirically distinct phenomena. It also supports the assertion that people who use alternative media are a hybrid audience of news omnivores. This latter merits a few qualifications to account for differences in political orientation, which will be discussed anon. Such audiences represent an area of overlap between alternative and mainstream, where some individuals can be located farther toward one end or another of the media spectrum. Hybridity is a central characteristic of alternative audiences, as it is for media organizations, personnel, and products. The people surveyed here resisted mainstream media to some extent, using alternative media as a complement instead of a replacement. It is easy to imagine that many alternative media enthusiasts attend frequently to news sources on the corporate-commercial end of the spectrum. It is harder to conceive of anyone who wants to avoid—yet alone succeeds in avoiding—the mainstream in favor of a news diet of "pure" alternatives.

While the term "alternative media" represented a distinct system of values and practices for this audience, their responses nonetheless presented many ironies and inconsistencies. One irony is that audiences who criticize mainstream reliance on elite sources themselves rely on blogs produced by elites that do not much expand the socioeconomic range of voices proffered to the public. Respondents professed that corporate-commercial motives and practices were a problem for media outlets—but not for the ones that they liked and considered "alternative." They seemed to view the potential good done by alternative content as mitigating any potential harm done by mainstream form. Put differently, the ends of social transformation might justify the means of corporate-commercial compromise, in their view. These alternative-media users recognized the limitations of capitalism, but they tolerated certain necessary evils in a market society. They idealized the general notion of *alternative media* while holding specific alternative media to pragmatic standards.

A relatively narrow range of news sources was presented here, partly due to the sample population having been drawn from a relatively narrow sliver of the alternative-media audience. These respondents were more concerned with political projects than with cultural ones and leaned toward a particular subset or genre of alternative media: alternative journalism, which reports and comments on factual and topical events. Missing from their responses were many threads in a rich tapestry of radical, community, and grassroots products that lie beyond news: pirate radio, street theater, guerrilla video projects, DIY fanzines, activist fliers, graffiti, quilts, pamphlets, and so on.

While this survey revealed many similarities within this group, it would be instructive to take a closer look at variations among respondents. One of the contexts that shapes audience conceptions of alternative and mainstream news sources is, undoubtedly, political orientation. That's why the next chapter describes a secondary analysis of these survey data that compares and contrasts the perspectives of liberal fans of alternative media with those of conservative fans.

Notes

1 Jessica Clark and Tracy Van Slyke, "Welcome to the Media Revolution," *In These Times* 30, no. 7 (July 2006).
2 James Hamilton, *Democratic Communications* (Washington, DC: Lexington Books, 2008), 4.
3 Chris Atton, *Alternative Media* (Thousand Oaks, CA: Sage, 2002).
4 I would like to thank Kappa Tau Alpha, the national journalism and mass communication honor society, for a research grant that supported the survey phase of this study.
5 Harlow and Harp conducted a similar survey with U.S. and Latin American activists in 2010, which they published in 2013. My survey data were collected in 2009 and published in 2015. Summer Harlow and Dustin Harp, "Alternative Media in a Digital Era: Comparing News and Information Use among Activists in the U.S. and Latin America," *Communication and Society/Comunicación y Sociedad* 26, no. 4 (2013).
6 Andy Ruddock, "Doing It by the Numbers," *Critical Arts* 12 (1998): 115–37.
7 Some material from this chapter appeared in a different version as Jennifer Rauch, "Exploring the Alternative-Mainstream Dialectic'," *Communication, Culture, and Critique* 8, no. 1 (2015).
8 *Human Events* moved to online-only publication in 2013.
9 To wit, 29 percent of participants reported reading the *Nation* and 22 percent named it a favorite alternative source; only 4 percent cited the Altercation blog.
10 Although online audiences might differ qualitatively from print ones, self-identification as an "alternative media user" was the main qualification for this study.
11 See Appendix C for survey questions.
12 Seungahn Nah and Deborah Chung, "When Citizens Meet Both Professional and Citizen Journalists," *Journalism* 13, no. 6 (2012).
13 Chris Atton, "News Cultures and New Social Movements," *Journalism Studies* 3, no. 4 (2002).

14 Left-wing social critics like Chomsky and Herman are virtually invisible in U.S. news media, though they are renowned and respected public figures abroad. See Robert McChesney, *The Problem of the Media* (New York: Monthly Review, 2004).

15 Other members of the "$500 Billion Club" include Alibaba, Alphabet (Google), Amazon, Apple, Microsoft, and Tencent. ExxonMobil, Cisco, General Electric, and Intel have also surpassed that mark.

16 Andrew Chadwick, *The Hybrid Media System* (New York and London: Oxford University Press, 2013).

17 Chadwick, *Hybrid Media System*, 55. HuffPost stopped using unpaid contributors in 2018.

18 Chadwick, *Hybrid Media System*, 55. AOL was in turn acquired in 2015 by Verizon, and the publication later changed name to *HuffPost*. Verizon, which earned around $132 billion in 2019, holds a dominant position in media industries, including cable, digital TV, Internet, and mobile and landline phones services. Verizon has also actively lobbied against net neutrality, even suing the FCC to establish "fast lanes" on the Internet that will give it a competitive advantage over Netflix and YouTube.

19 Huffington was once a California gubernatorial candidate and wife of a U.S. congressman.

20 Elizabeth Ann Roodhouse, "The Voice from the Base(ment)," *First Monday* 14, no. 9 (2009).

21 Geoffrey Baym, "*The Daily Show:* Discursive Integration and the Reinvention of Political Journalism," *Political Communication* 22, no. 3 (2005); and Jamie Warner, "Political Culture Jamming," *Popular Communication* 5, no. 1 (2007).

22 Dannagal Young, *Irony and Outrage* (New York: Oxford University Press, 2019).

23 Sean Aday, "Chasing the Bad News," *Journal of Communication* 60, no. 1 (2010).

24 Atton, *Alternative Media*; Nick Couldry and James Curran, *Contesting Media Power* (Lanham, MD: Rowman and Littlefield, 2003); John Downing et al., *Radical Media* (Thousand Oaks, CA: Sage, 2001); Tony Harcup, "I'm Doing This to Change the World," *Journalism Studies* 6, no. 3 (2005); Olga Guedes Bailey, Bart Cammaerts, and Nico Carpenter, *Understanding Alternative Media* (Maidenhead, UK: Open University Press, 2008); Jennifer Rauch, "Are There Still Alternatives?" *Sociology Compass* 10, no. 9 (2016).

25 Linda Jean Kenix, "Blogs as Alternative," *Journal of Computer-Mediated Communication* 14, no. 4 (2009).

26 See Linda Jean Kenix, "Independent Websites Not So Different from Group-Owned." *Newspaper Research Journal* 35, no. 2 (2014); and Kenix, "Commercialism and the Deconstruction of Alternative and Mainstream Media," in *The Routledge Companion to Alternative and Community Media*, ed. Chris Atton (Oxford and New York: Routledge, 2015), 66.

27 Linda Jean Kenix, *Alternative and Mainstream Media: The Converging Spectrum* (London: Bloomsbury Academic, 2012), 4.

28 Kenix, *Alternative and Mainstream Media*; see also Olga Guedes Bailey, Bart Cammaerts, and Nico Carpenter, *Understanding Alternative Media* (Maidenhead, UK: Open University Press: 2008).

29 Chris Atton, "News Cultures and New Social Movements," *Journalism Studies* 3, no. 4 (2002).

30 Chris Atton, "Reshaping Social Movement Media for a New Millennium?" *Social Movement Studies* 2, no. 1 (2003).

31 Harcup, "I'm Doing This to Change the World."

32 Eun-gyo Kim and James Hamilton, "Capitulation to Capital?" *Media, Culture, and Society* 28, no. 4 (2006).

33 Hamilton, *Democratic Communications*.

34 A small selection of notable recent work not discussed elsewhere in this book documents differences between alternative and mainstream media. This includes Rodney

Benson, "Commercialization and Critique," in *Contesting Media Power*, eds. Nick Couldry and James Curran (Lanham, MD: Rowman and Littlefield, 2003); David Domingo and Ari Heinonen, "Weblogs and Journalism," *Nordicom Review* 29, no. 1 (2008); Susan Forde, *Challenging the News* (Houndmills, UK, and New York: Palgrave MacMillan, 2001); Patricia Gibbs, "Alternative Things Considered," *Media, Culture, and Society* 25, no. 5 (2003); Robert Hackett and Pinar Gurleyen, "Beyond the Binaries?" in *The Routledge Companion to Alternative and Community Media*, ed. Chris Atton (Oxford, UK, and New York: Routledge, 2015); Roman Hájek and Nico Carpentier, "Alternative Mainstream Media in the Czech Republic," *Continuum: Journal of Media & Cultural Studies* (2015); Farooq Kperogi, "Cooperation with the Corporation?" *New Media and Society* 13 (2011); Kperogi, "News with Views," *Review of Communication* 13 (2013); InCheol Min, "Perceptions of the Audience by the Alternative Press Producers," *Media, Culture, and Society* 26, no. 3 (2004).

35 Christian Fuchs, "Alternative Media as Critical Media," *European Journal of Social Theory* 13, no. 2 (2010).

36 Linus Andersson, "There Is No Alternative," *tripleC* 10, no. 2 (2012).

37 David Pritchard et al., "One Owner, One Voice?" *Communication Law and Policy* 13 (2008); Fuchs, "Alternative Media as Critical Media," 180; Marisol Sandoval and Christian Fuchs, "Towards a Critical Theory of Alternative Media," *Telematics and Informatics* 27 (2010).

38 Popular political blogs also overwhelmingly represent the political perspectives of white men. See Dustin Harp and Mark Tremayne, "The Gendered Blogosphere," *Journalism and Mass Communication Quarterly* 83, no. 2 (2006).

39 News and political content is a tiny niche market online, representing about 3 percent of audience traffic, per Hindman. This figure is likely inflated by the fact that the "news and media" category also includes weather, a huge magnet for Internet traffic. Even a popular outlet like the *Huffington Post* ranked only 796th among nonpornographic websites in 2007. Matthew Hindman, *The Myth of Digital Democracy* (Princeton, NJ: Princeton University Press, 2009).

40 Richard Davis, *Typing Politics* (Cary, NC: Oxford University Press, 2009).

41 Chadwick, *Hybrid Media System*.

42 Harlow and Harp also used the snowball sampling method, which yielded 128 U.S. participants and 133 Latin American participants for their study; see "Alternative Media in a Digital Era."

43 Personal communication with the author, July 1, 2020.

44 Ibid.

45 This audience viewpoint supports Kristoffer Holt et al.'s proposal that alternative news media are primarily self-perceived correctives to the shortcomings of traditional, legacy, dominant, or mainstream news media in any given system or sociocultural and historical context. Kristoffer Holt et al., "Key Dimensions of Alternative News Media," *Digital Journalism* 7, no. 7 (2019).

46 James F. Hamilton, "Theory Through History," *The Communication Review* 4 (2001).

9

PARTISAN INTERPRETATIONS OF MEDIA PROBLEMS AND SOLUTIONS

In the minds of many people, alternative media were long linked to sociopolitical movements for peace, environmental protection, racial equity, global justice, labor, LGBT rights, gender equality, and other left-wing causes.[1] Until recently, a preponderance of academic and public conversations about alternative media, activism, and social change focused on organizations, messages, and audiences with liberal and progressive leanings. The broad, deep influence of U.S. right-wing media on popular discourse received much less attention from scholars in this field—until a surge of "alt-right" media accompanied the 2016 presidential election that "shook the foundations of the American political system."[2] During that campaign season, the alt-right website Breitbart News received more audience traffic than CNN.com.[3] This moment signaled a decisive confluence of alternative media and mainstream news systems, with a political valence quite opposite to what many left-leaning observers had anticipated.

So far, this book has examined how alternative-media ideals and practices resonate with left-leaning audiences. To what extent can these attitudes and behaviors be explained by the fact that people are liberals and progressives, rather than their being activists or alternative-media users? Left-wing interpretive communities might have intersubjective understandings of alternative media that are distinct from those of right-wing media users. The present chapter explores how the perspectives of alternative-media audiences with a conservative political orientation are similar to and different from those of liberals and progressives. Here, I describe a reanalysis of the previously introduced survey that explicitly addresses partisanship. In addition to quantitative data, I share open-ended responses to questions about what alternative media meant to respondents and how they view the problems of mainstream media, with the aim of giving more voice to these audiences. This phase of the study yielded thought-provoking convergences and divergences of opinion between the two groups regarding their lay theories of news media and their attitudes toward journalism.

Alternative-media scholarship once focused largely on progressive and left-wing sources, to the relative exclusion of regressive and right-wing ones.[4] Scholars have now produced a fascinating body of work on conservative alternative media. The history of right-wing alternative media was long obscured due to their being subsumed under the label "conservative media." Radical-right news institutions founded by conservative media activists in the United States in the mid-20th century started popularizing "the myth of the liberal media" and promoting fear of "big government."[5] The rhetorical claim that mainstream news producers are biased against conservatives is an enduring legacy of post-World War II alternative publishers such as *Human Events* and the John Birch Society, whose disparagements of "liberal media," "big government," democracy, and socialism are now mainstream features of right-wing politics.[6] According to one study, popular right-wing alternative websites in the United States routinely displayed a conspiratorial worldview akin to the Birchers', in which "anyone (liberal, foreigner, Muslim) may be a potential enemy, or working to aid enemies."[7]

While U.S. liberal activist media have focused on themes like democracy, unity, "be the media," and human rights, conservative ones have fixated on the ideological "impurity" of mainstream politicians regarded as bogus conservatives.[8] Analysis of an Italian fascist website found use of "doublespeak" and "dog whistles"—polysemous messages that seem to mimic liberal democratic ideas but that target audiences read in racist, anti-immigrant, anti-Semitic, and Islamophobic ways.[9] Far-right alternative publications in the United States use rhetorical techniques such as sarcasm, parentheses, mock quotations, and ambiguity that audiences pride themselves on knowing how to decode.[10] Just like left-wing ones, right-wing readers are an interpretive community whose collective identity, sense of superiority, and lay theories are fostered by alternative-media use.

While attention to right-wing news sources and audiences has been noticeably sparse in scholarship related to alternative media, the same is not true of research in political communication.[11] Since the turn of the millennium, key works such as Kathleen Hall Jamieson and Joseph Capella's 2010 *Echo Chamber*, Jeffrey Berry and Sarah Sobieraj's 2014 *The Outrage Industry*, and Yochai Benkler and colleagues' 2018 *Network Propaganda* have explained how partisanship interacts with public perceptions of media. Jamieson and Capella likened the conservative media establishment to an interpretive community, an insular feedback loop, an alternative or "balkanized" knowledge base that fosters an in-group identity.[12] According to Berry and Sobieraj, conservative audiences chose purveyors of outrage like Sean Hannity over traditional right-wing sources like *The Weekly Standard* for ritual and affective reasons: to combat social isolation and enjoy para-social relationships with relatable, charismatic hosts. Conservative alternative media tend to flatter, ennoble, and validate their audiences and their values, they wrote, offering "empowerment zones that bolster self-assuredness rather than challenging their beliefs" in a cultural climate where conservatives feel "more precarious and vulnerable" than liberals do.[13] In analyzing the media sources most trusted by audiences on the left and right, Benkler et al. found an asymmetrical pattern. Liberals engaged with an ecosystem mixing partisan and objective news while conservatives inordinately attended to hyper-partisan sources not anchored in journalistic truth-seeking norms.[14]

Scholars and reporters have taken great strides toward filling gaps in our knowledge of the interactions among right-wing activists, conservative media, and mainstream culture. My survey adds to this stream of research by revealing distinctive partisan perspectives on alternative media that challenges existing conceptions of "alternative media."

The Emergence of Alt-Right Media Activism

After the 2016 presidential election, researchers and commentators avidly scrutinized far-right media activism by a loose coalition of Internet trolls, techno-libertarians, "men's rights" activists, anti-immigration advocates, pick-up artists, Gamergate supporters, and "bored young people" who spread their beliefs through online subcultures.[15] Thanks in large part to novel uses of media, an amalgamation of right-wing actors achieved wide recognition for ideas that might have remained subcultural and politically marginal. Participants in this realm of media were variously motivated by ideology, financial gain (including ad revenue, book deals, speaking fees), fame, influence, status in their communities, and a *schadenfreude* sense of pleasure. The alt-right leveraged many techniques of participatory culture and affordances of social media, assembling agile teams to gather information, organize meet-ups, swap strategies, and share memes.

Though the term remains ambiguous, "alt-right" was coined in 2008 by a white supremacist leader to describe right-wing actors with views diverging from and critical of the conservative establishment. By contrast, the term "alt-light" refers to conservative media that parrot some far-right talking points while shying away from more extreme beliefs. In recent years, a growing number of news websites, blogs, and forums have labeled themselves as "alt-right" or simply "alternative media."[16] While this ideology was not necessarily new, the alt-right label served in part to rebrand white nationalism by appealing to millennials and taking advantage of the media's fascination with novelty, which helped give broader exposure to racist and misogynist ideas.[17] Whereas left-wing critics tend to frame right-wing movements as marginal or threatening by using terms such as *ultra, far, radical, extreme, repressive*, and *regressive*, the alt-right presents itself more neutrally, simply as an "alternative."

Alternative media offer an effective means of ritual and transmissive communication to people with right-wing viewpoints, as well as those with left-wing views. Online platforms help such audiences find each other and collaborate on media production and dissemination, while mainstream news outlets amplify their messages. Alt-right networks endeavor to boost the visibility of radical ideas by manipulating news frames and agendas—by targeting journalists, bloggers, and social influencers through memes, bots, and other tactics. Right-wing activists cooperate online to move their messages "up the chain" of news media from smaller, alternative outlets to larger, mainstream ones.[18] One common practice is planting a story (sometimes a hoax, a conspiracy theory, or a false claim) with a local news outlet ill-equipped to adequately fact-check it; if the story performs well, national news outlets might pick it up. Radical activists can thus succeed in influencing the public agenda, regardless of whether journalists eventually debunk their stories.

Marwick and Lewis characterize many common alt-right media practices as manipulation. Many of these actions are motivated by antipathy toward mainstream media (widely known and belittled as MSM), which they perceive as driven by sensationalism, spectacle, novelty, and sentiment. (I use the acronym MSM through this chapter to save considerable time and space.) In their view, the multitudinous flaws of MSM justify activist campaigns to "expose" its hypocrisy, ignorance, and stupidity. A common practice is to send deliberately ambiguous messages, so audiences have difficulty interpreting whether the media producers are being serious or ironic. This playful ambiguity is a key strategy in alt-right subcultural spaces, allowing participants to hide their intent and "dissociate themselves with particularly unappetizing elements while still promoting the overall movement."[19] Whether their messages are sincere or sarcastic, the outcome is the same: public attention.[20]

Beyond the academy, researchers have produced detailed studies of hard-right groups that use or advocate violence, including through online activities.[21] David Neiwert, a researcher and writer for the Southern Poverty Law Center, traced the rise of the right that presaged Trump's win in the 2017 book *Alt-America*.[22] His work explains how once-fringe media figures like Steve Bannon and Alex Jones nurtured an audience of white supremacists, xenophobes, patriot militias, and conspiracy theorists for decades until their radical ideas began to permeate mainstream journalism and national politics. Alt-right co-optation of language and tactics from the left is a central theme of such research.[23] For instance, a white supremacist think-tank called the National Policy Institute, which lobbies for the alt-right, publishes what it calls "critical theory" in the journal *Radix*, which resembles a left-wing academic journal.[24]

The alt-right also strategically applied leftist notions of rebellion in building its own Internet culture from the ground up, as Angela Nagle observed.[25]

A contributor to *The Baffler* and other alternative publications, Nagle detailed how the radical right bypassed MSM by communicating in online forums such as 4chan and Reddit. In the book *Alt-Right*, Mike Wendling described right-wing media activism as a leaderless constellation that has thrived since the 1990s due to horizontal and participatory communication in online forums. Wendling, a BBC reporter, said this relatively youthful movement conceives of itself as a counterculture akin to punks and hippies—though he concludes the alt-right has failed to generate music, films, or books as significant as leftist countercultural products were.[26]

Alt-right media have "cribbed" aesthetic elements such as memes, 80s sci-fi, anime, Italo disco, and synthpop music from 4chan-related subcultures. One alt-right leader, who described his media style as "Non-ironic Nazism masquerading as ironic Nazism," cited Saul Alinsky's *Rules for Radicals* as a major influence.[27] One of Alinsky's memorable tips regarded the importance of humor and satire in activist campaigns: "The most potent weapons known to mankind," he wrote, "are satire and ridicule."[28]

Conservative media activities have eluded the scholarly agenda partly due to presumptions that alternative media are inherently progressive and partly because right-wing projects have often sought to evade attention. Chip Berlet, a researcher who followed the rise of U.S. right-wing alternative media through the 1990s, noted the surreptitious nature of these projects, which "seldom step from behind the curtain into the spotlight of mass culture; instead, they circulate backstage among specific subcultures."[29] For decades, alternative media played a central role in the long-term strategies of secular conservative, theocratic, and far-right activists, according to Berlet. He regards the "first major U.S. social movement organized extensively via horizontal telecommunications networks" to be the Patriot and militia movement—whose ideology is distinctly *not* progressive-left.[30]

Partisanship Among Alternative Media Users

The original purpose of the survey reported in the previous chapter was to compare what "alternative media" meant to audiences of varying political orientations. To that end, I recruited participants through ads in the liberal-progressive news source the *Nation* and in the conservative *Human Events,* as well as on Facebook. This self-selected convenience sample yielded 224 respondents, of whom 95 reported their political orientation as *liberal or progressive*, 44 called themselves *conservative*, and the remainder either declined to report their political leaning or answered "none of the above." (The responses of survey participants who did not report a political orientation are not analyzed in this chapter. They are provided in full in Appendix C.) Of the conservatives, 25 provided open-ended responses to a penultimate question about alternative media, and 26 answered a final question about MSM problems. Of the liberals-progressives, 23 provided responses to the alternative media question and 25 answered the final MSM question. The following discussion presents a census of all 99 qualitative responses.[31]

As the survey attracted comparatively few conservative participants, I originally opted not to divide responses based on political orientation and instead analyzed the data as one group. If the responses of alternative media users of different political orientations were considered separately, how much would the conservative perspectives differ, or perhaps resemble, liberal-progressive ones? That's what the current reanalysis aims to find out. Dividing these survey data into two groups by political orientation gives us a richer view of how alternative-media fans understand the meanings of alternative and mainstream media genres.

Why *was* the number of responses to this survey so low from right-wing readers? Perhaps right-leaning audiences think of their media as not *alternative* but rather *conservative* or some other qualifier. Perhaps the phrase "alternative media," which I used in ads to recruit participants, does not resonate widely among conservatives. (Similarly, I wonder if right-wing actors commonly identify themselves as "activists," or if this term has a left-wing valence.) Perhaps the term is more meaningful to this group now than it was at the time the survey was conducted, in 2009. Explicit conceptions of "alternative media" seem to have developed later among right-wing audiences than among left-wing ones. The term "alt-right" began its ascendance into popular usage shortly thereafter.

At the time, conservative activists rarely linked the phrase "alternative media" with right-wing politics, two exceptions being Richard Viguerie and David Franke. Viguerie was a pioneer of computerized direct-mail fundraising who used alternative media to activate a "New Right" populist base through newsletters that pumped out news, opinions, and analyses to an audience of politicians and political junkies.[32] Franke was a conservative writer and editor for *Human Events* and *National Review*. In their 2003 book, *America's Right Turn: How Conservatives Used New and Alternative Media to Take Power*, they detailed how right-wing activists had used various alternative media since the 1950s "below the radar of the liberal establishment" to achieve a "conservative political revolution" through the elections of Ronald Reagan and George W. Bush. By "alternative media," they primarily meant direct mail, talk radio, cable TV news, and the Internet—which they declared "the four horseman of the conservative apocalypse."[33]

Earlier, I summarized participant responses to an initial question asking them to name their favorite alternative media. When people self-identifying as liberal/progressive were isolated for analysis, their most frequently cited alternative sources were: *Adbusters, Alternet, Center for American Progress, Common Dreams, Counterpunch, Crooks and Liars, Democracy Now!, Free Speech TV, Indymedia, The Indypendent, In These Times, Jim Hightower, Media Matters, Mother Jones, MoveOn*, the *Nation*, the *Progressive, Rachel Maddow, Think Progress, Truthdig,*

Truthout, the *Washington Spectator*, and *Z Magazine*. (In the following discussion, I will refer to people self-identifying as liberal or progressive as "liberals," for brevity's sake.)

By contrast, the 44 respondents self-identifying as conservative named alternative sources, including secular, theocratic and far-right outlets such as *American Family Association, Americans for Prosperity, Ann Coulter, Breitbart News, Conservative Christian News, Drudge Report, Family Research Council, Glenn Beck, Heritage Foundation, InfoWars/Alex Jones, Laura Ingraham, Michael Medved, Michael Savage, Michele Malkin, The New American, NewsBusters, Patriot Post, Rush Limbaugh, Sean Hannity, Townhall*, and *WorldNetDaily*.

This open-ended question generated intriguing indications of the specific alternative media sources that spring to mind when fans of this genre are invited to spontaneously name their favorites. Other interesting results emerged in response to subsequent quantitative questions about media bias, objectivity, and political orientation.

Quantitative Audience Evaluations of Media

The survey asked people how strongly they approved or disapproved of two dozen statements about alternative media and MSM, using Likert-style scales where 1 meant strongly agree and 4 meant strongly disagree. (These questions are provided in Appendix C.) I have discussed some of these quantitative results in other work, so I will give a brief overview of them here before presenting and probing my qualitative findings in greater detail.[34]

Let's look first at the biggest similarities regarding alternative media, in Table 9.1. Left- and right-wing users reported comparably high agreement with statements that alternative media should encourage people to get involved in civic life (rating averages of 3.51 among liberals vs. 3.41 among conservatives) and use new and interactive technologies (3.31 vs. 3.43). They reported comparably lower agreement that alternative media should: be produced by amateur and citizen journalists (2.69 vs. 2.41), promote a certain political point of view (averages of 2.12 for liberals vs. 1.86 for conservatives), use traditional and familiar technologies (2.53 vs. 2.80), be produced by professional journalists (2.85 vs. 2.52), and appeal to small or niche audiences (2.00 vs. 1.61).

Next, the greatest differences regarding alternative media are presented in Table 9.2. Conservatives were more likely to say that alternative media should promote family values (average rating of 3.61 vs. 1.91 among liberals), preserve American traditions (3.57 vs. 2.16), and encourage moral or religious behavior (3.23 vs. 1.81). Liberals were more likely to think that alternative media should pursue social justice (3.59 vs. 2.82 for conservatives), be produced by small organizations, not big companies (3.25 vs. 2.30), be nonprofit (2.93 vs. 1.95), and be noncommercial or advertising-free (2.75 vs. 1.86). The items with the largest differences in average ratings between the two groups were that

TABLE 9.1 Similarities in alternative media views of conservative and liberal audiences

ALTERNATIVE media should . . .	Average conservative rating	Average liberal rating	Difference
. . . encourage people to get involved in civic life	3.41	3.51	−0.10
. . . use new and interactive technologies	3.43	3.31	0.12
. . . be produced by professional journalists	2.52	2.85	−0.23
. . . promote a certain political point of view	1.86	2.12	−0.26
. . . use traditional and familiar technologies	2.80	2.53	0.27
. . . be produced by amateur and citizen journalists	2.41	2.69	−0.28
. . . appeal to small or niche audiences	1.61	2.00	−0.39

Source: Scale: 1 = strongly disagree, 2 = somewhat disagree, 3 = somewhat agree, and 4 = strongly agree.

TABLE 9.2 Differences in alternative media views of conservative and liberal audiences

ALTERNATIVE media should . . .	Average conservative rating	Average liberal rating	Difference
. . . promote family values	3.61	1.91	1.70
. . . encourage moral behavior or religious action	3.23	1.81	1.42
. . . help preserve American traditions	3.57	2.16	1.41
. . . be nonprofit	1.95	2.93	−0.98
. . . be produced by small organizations, not big companies	2.30	3.25	−0.95
. . . be noncommercial or advertising-free	1.86	2.75	−0.89
. . . pursue social justice	2.82	3.59	−0.77

Source: Scale: 1 = strongly disagree, 2 = somewhat disagree, 3 = somewhat agree, and 4 = strongly agree.

alternative media should help preserve American traditions (3.57 among conservatives vs. 2.16 for liberals), encourage moral behavior or religious action (3.23 vs. 1.81), and promote family values (3.61 vs. 1.91).

The biggest similarities regarding MSM are presented in Table 9.3. Users of left- and right-wing alternative media reported comparably high agreement with statements that MSM are biased because of the politics of their owners (average ratings of 3.64 vs. 3.8), compromised by corporations/corporate

TABLE 9.3 Similarities in mainstream media views of conservative and liberal audiences

MAINSTREAM media are/have . . .	Average conservative rating	Average liberal rating	Difference
. . . biased due to politics of owners	3.80	3.64	0.16
. . . compromised by corporations/ corporate interests	3.45	3.68	−0.23
. . . compromised by advertising/ commercial interests	3.23	3.54	−0.31
. . . motivated too much by profit	3.25	3.59	−0.34
. . . un–democratic practices	3.43	3.05	0.38
. . . disempowering the public	3.61	3.18	0.43

Source: Scale: 1 = strongly disagree, 2 = somewhat disagree, 3 = somewhat agree, and 4 = strongly agree.

interests (3.68 vs. 3.45), compromised by advertising/commercial interests (3.54 vs. 3.23), motivated too much by profit (3.59 vs. 3.25), have un–democratic practices (3.05 vs. 3.43), and disempower the public (3.18 vs. 3.61).

Finally, the greatest differences regarding MSM are presented in Table 9.4. Conservatives agreed more than liberals did with statements that MSM are compromised by anti-religious or immoral attitudes of journalists (average rating of 3.57 vs. 1.51 for liberals), by the political biases of journalists (3.84 vs. 2.66), and by journalists' egos or career ambitions (3.48 vs. 2.86). Conservatives also showed higher agreement than liberals with the idea that MSM were unpatriotic (averages of 3.41 vs. 2.31). On the other hand, liberals agreed more with statements that MSM support the status quo (3.36 vs. 2.77 for conservatives) and need more government regulation (2.25 vs. 1.43), though agreement with the latter was the lowest level of any item in the survey.

Among these responses, some showed a much larger gap between the two groups than others did. The idea that MSM are compromised by the anti-religious or immoral attitudes of journalists showed the widest difference: two full points higher on the four-point Likert scale among conservatives than among liberals. The ideas that alternative media should promote family values, encourage moral behavior or religious action, and help preserve American traditions rated around 1.5 points higher among conservatives than liberals. The ideas that MSM are unpatriotic and biased due to journalists' own politics rated one full point higher among conservatives than liberals. Meanwhile, the ideas that alternative media should be nonprofit, noncommercial, and produced by small organizations rated almost one point higher among liberals than conservatives. All other responses ranged more closely, within approximately +/− one point on the four-point Likert scale, between the two groups.

Responding to questions about bias and objectivity, both liberal and conservative respondents perceived MSM as biased against their own political orientation (Table 9.5). Ninety-three percent of conservatives who used right-wing

TABLE 9.4 Differences in mainstream media views of conservative and liberal audiences

MAINSTREAM media are . . .	Average conservative rating	Average liberal rating	Difference
. . . compromised by anti-religious or immoral attitudes of journalists	3.57	1.51	2.06
. . . biased due to politics of journalists	3.84	2.66	1.18
. . . un-patriotic	3.41	2.31	1.10
. . . in need of more government regulation	2.25	1.43	0.82
. . . compromised by journalists' egos or career ambitions	3.48	2.86	0.62
. . . support the status quo	2.77	3.36	−0.59

Source: Scale: 1 = strongly disagree, 2 = somewhat disagree, 3 = somewhat agree, and 4 = strongly agree.

TABLE 9.5 Audience perceptions of political perspective in mainstream media

	Conservatives %	Liberals %	Difference
They're very liberal	93.0	0	93.0
They're slightly liberal	3.5	5.7	−2.2
They're neutral	0	5.7	−5.7
They're slightly conservative	0	37.0	−37.0
They're very conservative	3.5	37.0	−33.5
There's a wide range of political perspectives	0	14.3	−14.3

alternative media viewed MSM as *very liberal*, while 37 percent of left-wing users viewed MSM as *very conservative*. The other 7 percent of conservatives split between saying MSM were slightly liberal or very conservative, with none reporting that MSM were neutral, slightly conservative, or diverse in political perspective. Meanwhile, the remaining liberals were more likely than conservatives to say MSM were slightly liberal (5.7 percent), neutral (5.7 percent), slightly conservative (37 percent), or represented diverse political voices (14.2 percent).

By contrast, respondents perceived less bias in "their" alternative media (Table 9.6). The plurality of both groups agreed that alternative media featured *a wide range of political perspectives*: 44.8 percent of conservatives and 51.4 percent of liberals. Conservatives reported viewing alternative media as *slightly conservative* (20.7 percent) or *very conservative* (20.7 percent), while liberals viewed alternative media as *slightly liberal* (22.9 percent) or *very liberal* (17.1). Both groups agreed that alternative media held more diverse political views than MSM did.

TABLE 9.6 Audience perceptions of political perspective in alternative media

	Conservatives %	Liberals %	Difference
They're very liberal	0	17.1	−17.1
They're slightly liberal	0	22.9	−22.9
They're neutral	13.8	5.7	8.1
They're slightly conservative	20.7	2.9	17.8
They're very conservative	20.7	0	20.7
There's a wide range of political perspectives	44.8	51.4	−6.6

TABLE 9.7 Audience perspectives on objectivity in alternative media

	Average conservative rating	Average liberal rating	Difference
I like alternative media when their journalists seem to hold a point of view similar to mine	2.93	2.94	−0.01
I like alternative media when their journalists seem objective or detached	3.38	3.22	0.14
I like alternative media when they're run by international or foreign organizations, who give a non-U.S. viewpoint	1.76	3.17	−1.41

Source: Scale: 1 = strongly disagree, 2 = somewhat disagree, 3 = somewhat agree, and 4 = strongly agree.

Table 9.7 shows audience preferences regarding diverse viewpoints offered by alternative media. When asked if they liked for alternative media to hold a similar perspective to theirs, conservatives and liberals responded with similar levels of agreement (average ratings of 2.93 vs. 2.94), suggesting that they somewhat agreed. When asked if they liked alternative media to be objective or detached, both groups agreed at similarly strong levels, 3.38 for conservatives and 3.22 for liberals. However, the two groups diverged on the matter of alternative media from international or foreign organizations. Liberals supported non-U.S. viewpoints on the news at a much higher level (average rating of 3.17) than conservatives did (1.76).

Yet there are striking contradictions in some of their responses. Large majorities in both groups wanted alternative media to simultaneously "have a point of view similar to mine" and "be objective or detached." Perhaps they valued a range of alternative sources—some sharing their views, some striving for neutrality. Perhaps they believed their viewpoint *was* objectively and verifiably correct. The preference for alternative media with a similar viewpoint in this question also would seem to conflict with an earlier question, where they gave low support to "Promoting a certain political view" as an alternative media ideal. These results will help us understand the discussion to follow, in which conservative and liberal respondents share their views on media bias, objectivity, politics, and economics in their own words.

Views of Alternative Media From the Right

A primary concern that emerged in both groups' open-ended comments involved the role of *bias* and *objectivity* in journalism. (Other themes we shall address momentarily are *politics* and *economics*.) Of the 25 open-ended answers from right-wing users, a majority said alternative media were necessary because MSM excluded information, especially from conservative perspectives. Alternative media "report on many issues that the other media will not," they said, giving you a "broader offering of all views" and "both sides of the news." They said alternative media were "a place where I can get the whole story," "a great way to hear the other side of the story that MSM doesn't give," and worked hard "to give us 'the rest of the story' that we do not read in the mainstream press, major networks, most newspapers."

Conservative comments frequently contrasted alternative media with a perceived bias and lack of fairness, balance, and integrity in mainstream news. "Alternative media has allowed people to express their opinion, no matter what it is," one respondent wrote, continuing, "It is important to be non-biased when delivering news." According to right-wing users, alternative media were "fair and balanced in their reporting" and "fair and balanced and the only place you can hear conservative viewpoints." Several referred to a need for truth and honesty. They called alternative media "honest, with no strings attached," "very important to those of us who are continually searching for the truth," "the only place you can hear the truth," and "honest and truthful. They are not hiding anything; they expose corruption and show politicians and their politics for what it really is." One wrote, "If you care about our nation and want to hear the truth you should watch or listen to alternative-media sources." One of the most extensive responses from a conservative user said alternative media have

> more journalistic integrity and ability than the so-called "MSM." With "alternative media," you will get information that cuts through the rhetoric and asks tough questions. "MSM" has forgotten how to do that. I want the truth, I want answers, and I want people who are making the news to have to answer to the public, answer to the people who put them in the position of power.

While these conservative users valued fairness, balance, and truth, they also appreciated right-leaning alternative-media sources partly due to partisanship. Alternative media both "provide no slant" and "promote conservative viewpoints," according to one respondent. Others describe alternative media as "any outlet that does not continually promote the Obama administration and the Democratic Party talking points," not "controlled by the state/Obama," and "not in the direct control of hard-core left-wing progressives such as ABC, CBS, NY Times, etc." This genre was important to them because "about 90 percent of the MSM is very liberal (due to) their anti-Bush coverage and falling all over themselves for Obama, who has a radical leftist background." They preferred a conservative perspective on news to a *Democratic, left-wing,* or *progressive* one.

Few respondents in this group mentioned features of this genre beyond the partisanship, bias, objectivity, or truth of its content. Only two conservative comments out of 25 referred to economic factors such as a diminished influence of corporate owners, advertisers, or profit motives on alternative media structures. One said alternative media "exist because MSM has sold out their viewers, especially the ones owned by GE" and another said they were "independently owned, not owned in concert with several other media by large corporations, generally not ABC, CBS, NBC, CNN, NYT." By contrast, liberal comments were fixated on the MSM business model, as you shall see.

Views of Alternative Media From the Left

Like the conservative responses, a majority of the 95 open-ended statements from left-wing users described alternative media explicitly by reference to the shortcomings of MSM content. Alternative media "tell you what MSM doesn't say," "attempt to bring information and stories to light that would not be covered by MSM," "cover what is relevant and what may be left behind by MSM," and deliver "that which we need to know and cannot learn from MSM." Liberal respondents said alternative media presented "a range of issues relevant to the world," "other points of views than mainstream," and "perspectives that are silenced or severely under-represented in the MSM, such as the voices of people of color, poor people, gays and lesbians, the disabled, and other marginalized groups."

Several liberal respondents said alternative media adopted a viewpoint, rather than being objective. They said alternative media were "coming from a specific point of view," holding "a point of view held by the makers, writers, publishers, etc., and makes it clear in the writing or ad space," and expressing "a varied viewpoint on social, political, and economic issues. It may not be my viewpoint, but it allows me to see more than one side of an issue." These commenters did not specify which political viewpoint they thought alternative media represented.

Most liberal respondents suggested certain information, stories, issues, and perspectives were absent from MSM. A few thought alternative media were needed because MSM actively hid the truth or lied. Alternative media put MSM "to shame with the lies they tell and they constant lean one way or the other politically," one stated. Two said alternative media gave "the real facts" and "a real-time view of what is happening," implying that MSM did not. The words *truth* and *true* appeared nowhere in the liberal responses, as they often had in conservative ones. The majority of liberals seemed to believe that MSM were not untrue, merely incomplete.

How did these liberal fans of alternative media explain MSM's failure to provide comprehensive coverage from varied viewpoints? Whereas conservative comments frequently blamed partisan actors such as the Democratic Party and Democratic president for corrupting MSM, no liberal comments did so. Instead they concentrated on economic factors. Alternative media were "not controlled by corporate interests and not funded by advertising," "with a non-corporate perspective, not funded by a large company," and "somebody other than the big three news networks and isn't doing their job for profit, but 'cause they feel the story needs to get out."

A few liberal respondents said alternative media had a more oppositional relationship to the political elite than MSM did. One thought alternative media exposed "propaganda and motivation for that propaganda"—the only liberal who used the word *propaganda*, which no conservatives did. More often than not, they mentioned financial and partisan interests in the same breath. Alternative media were "independent, well researched, and not beholden to any corporate interest or political parties" and sought "to inform without the restrictions of corporate or government interest." They were not "sponsored by corporations that have a hand in the government or foreign policy," another wrote, continuing "MSM is state-run media. All for-profit media supports the ruling party's side of the story." One respondent cited MSM healthcare debates that he/she thought neglected a single-payer option out of allegiance to "Big Pharma" and commented, "Health insurance companies are filling the pockets of politicians (Dems and Repubs); therefore MSM will not often talk about [single-payer options]." This comment expresses a progressive view that MSM support the interests of a business and political elite that includes Democrats and Republicans.

To these left-wing respondents, a crucial function of alternative media was to "translate what we hear from MSM to reveal their true motivations." The real motives of MSM, to them, were revenue, ratings, and profit. Liberal commentators viewed alternative media as "not entirely sponsored by advertisement revenue," "not bound by commercial interests and therefore better able to give an accurate depiction of the state of the world," "structured in alternative formats (i.e. not vertically integrated)," and "less concerned about ratings and more concerned about getting a story out there. They aren't worried about pissing off their advertisers and losing revenue." Some appreciated alternative media for being "viewer or listener supported" and "supported by means other than corporations or big company advertisers," with one comment placing NPR "on the fringe" of alternative media because of its "government and profit motives." Thus liberal respondents recognized compromises related to ad-revenue reliance and valued an alternative funding model, neither of which conservative respondents had mentioned.

Now that we have heard voices from conservatives and liberals regarding alternative media, let's turn to their ideas about mainstream news. In reading conservative comments, you might note, as I did, that the tone of responses became more hostile and aggressive when discussing MSM than it had been when describing alternative media. As before, the dominant theme that emerged in analysis of the conservative responses was *political* whereas in liberal responses it was *economic*.

Conservatives and the Politics of MSM

Concerns about bias and lack of objectivity continued in this set of conservative comments. MSM were "totally devoid of any objectivity" and were "biased opinion presented as news and/or fact." Unlike liberal respondents, conservative ones connected media failures to political as well as moral ones—a point that we shall revisit anon. MSM were "politically biased and void of morals" and had "no journalistic integrity, driven by a political agenda and a hatred for traditional American moral values." Yet partisanship lay at the crux of the bias problem, in conservative comments. To illustrate this point, I'll share four of the lengthier, more detailed responses here:

- The first said, "What I really would like is a news source that reported all the news about our government without an opinion from a Democrat or Republican. I really would rather hear the full story and the truth than someone else's opinion. I have my own opinion, I do not need theirs."
- The second said MSM were "neutered. There's no more in-your-face investigative reporting, no edge, no principles that are worth upholding, only the 'party line' and political correctness. No one reporting really seems to care anymore."
- A third said MSM were "predictably partisan. Infested with the news anchor's personal opinion—smirks, eye rolls, mockery, outright disdain of opposing views, and too often false interest in the topics of a 24-hour news cycle. Commentators are partially to blame as they cloak themselves in Ivy League respectability yet Joe Citizen like myself recognizes that the days of accurate impartial reporting have long since disappeared, opening the door to alternative-media outlets."
- A fourth said there was "nothing wrong" with MSM in the past, when news broadcasts "didn't even display the American flag for fear of showing a bias" [presumably meaning they were more objective]. But "as of late, there are too many broadcasters that enter their own opinion, their viewpoints, and have swayed to one side of the pendulum. It is so obvious that they

refuse to speak about certain topics and cover certain stories because it is contrary to their beliefs."

Some of these evaluations were based on perceptions that individual TV news anchors and broadcasters specifically—rather than media owners, advertisers, or print journalists—injected their own political perspectives into the news.

They were concerned not only about the general presence of political bias in the news but also about the specific direction of this bias: *liberal*. Conservative respondents professed that MSM were too liberal or not conservative enough—rather than neutral or multi-perspectival. Representative comments in this vein stated that MSM were "not neutral in their reporting, liberal in whatever they report" and "liberal, one-sided, too far left, not honest, trying to steer the public to benefit their goals, not what is good and beneficial for America." One person said MSM "coddles idiots, liberal idiots, animal-rights idiots, ACLU idiots, environmental idiots, etc. etc." Another believed there were "no conservatives in MSM. Not one on ABC, NBC, CBS—all of their anchors are very liberal. Most newspapers are also liberal" so there was "no balance in the media"—or rather, "just one: Fox News leans to the right." A third said MSM

> do not give both sides of the story if it does not fit the liberal agenda. . . . They do not lead with all the NEWS, but only cover it to prevent from looking completely inept (which I don't think they are). They need to DROP THEIR AGENDA and get back to reporting the latest news if they want to survive much longer. Or maybe when they lose ALL their readers (viewers) and the government will bail them out, too [all caps in the original].

In contrast with liberal respondents, conservative ones said they believed MSM personnel not only had liberal personal beliefs but also were controlled by Democrats and the Obama administration (which held power at the time). The majority of conservative responses were devoted to this perception. Here are five sample comments that convey the scope and prevalence of such views:

- The first said MSM were "extremely biased to the left and did not hold Democrats to the fire as they did Bush. I have not seen in my lifetime such bias and outright, unabashed hatred for a president [Bush]. Their performance was hideous as is their current role of being nothing more than a cheerleader for the Obama administration."
- A second said MSM were "in the pocket of the current administration. They make up news stories, they lie, they are VERY BIASED, they only tell one side. They don't report the news, they only tell what they are told to report. Press conferences are pre-approved questions that the administration wants them to ask. They are not reporting the news" [all caps in the original].

- According to a third, MSM "make me so sick with their undying love and adoration for their messiah Obama. Chris Matthews with his man-crush. Compromising their journalistic values and then becoming downright corrupt and unbelievable."
- A fourth said, "They do not report the 'news' at all. They are only interested in their slobbering love affair with B. Hussein Obama and are not even ashamed of it one bit. They are financed by extremely wealthy liberals such as George Soros and Al Gore, and they follow their orders, come hell or high water. If there were suddenly NO other media available (by means of the 'Fairness' Doctrine or something similar), then I would choose to not follow any news at all, over listening to that trash" [all caps in the original].
- Finally, a fifth example: MSM are "no longer capable of asking tough questions. . . . Obama has the 'MSM' as his lap dog. It gets very old to those of us who care about his policies and the damage it has done and is doing to our great country."

The use of ALL CAPS, hyperbole, affective language, and sensational imagery (as well as, perhaps, sarcasm or irony, which is hard to detect in text) such as *messiah, hideous* performance, *no edge/no principles, outright, unabashed hatred, nothing more than a cheerleader, come hell or high water, that trash, I have not seen in my lifetime, undying love and adoration, slobbering love affair,* and *downright corrupt and unbelievable* suggests the depth of partisan animosity that conservative news users feel toward MSM. While some conservative respondents said individual journalists had the power to express their own partisan views and entertain political "crushes" in the news, some said even those reporters who might have investigative initiative are impotent: merely *following orders, in the pocket of, neutered,* and *told what to cover* and how by the White House and its presumed allies.

Beyond liberalism, right-wing audience disapproval of MSM extended to "problems" such as progressivism, socialism, and fascism—often connected to a lack of morals, religious principles, patriotism, and respect for individuals. One conservative said, MSM "promote secular humanism, progressive socialism from left, progressive fascism from the 'right'; work against God, the Bible, individual liberties, and freedoms; promote nation over states and government over individual rights." A second said, MSM "think that they will be in the inner circle when the statists take over this country but at that point they will no longer be of value (see the media in Venezuela, for example)." A third said, MSM are "too fascist and controlled by special interest groups. Reporters are too biased and anti-American. They remind me of National Socialists of Nazi Germany." A fourth said, MSM were "overwhelmed by secular humanist progressive socialism, a hate of God, a love of amoral 'anything goes, nothing is wrong with anything' perverse mentalities, anti-constitutional, anti-individual person."

A single outlying conservative respondent looked beyond ideology to practical factors that compromise MSM. He/she said MSM were "the reason we have talk radio. They (MSM) are mostly biased and run by major corporations like GE," more akin to liberal respondents.

Liberals and the Economics of MSM

Similar to conservative respondents, liberal ones were concerned about truth, bias, objectivity, and partisanship in journalism—though not uniformly. Some said MSM were "biased," "not telling the truth," putting "journalism to shame with the lies that they tell," and misrepresenting "the truth. Their coverage is limited in issues. I want the facts, all sides of who, what, where, when, and why—and make up my own mind. Why oh why did Bill Clinton kill the Fairness Doctrine???" Liberal commenters said MSM were variously "objective," "slightly conservative," and "constantly [leaning] one way or the other politically." One stated:

> All for-profit media supports the ruling party's side of the story. All MSM provides an authoritarian and right-wing view point of the issues. That leaves me, a left libertarian, out of the picture and yelling at the TV screen or newspaper. Mainstream maintains the status quo and doesn't question authority (unless it's Fox questioning Obama or MSNBC questioning Bush).

To some extent, these liberal responses described MSM as "state-run media," but in a different way than conservatives did. They referred to a "ruling class" that included both parties, with sparse references to Republican politics. In the words of one liberal, MSM "only gives you a spectrum that supports the ideas of the ruling class and the two capitalist parties in Washington." One person described MSM as "groupthink, an inability to speak truth to power, and way too much emphasis on access 'journalism.' They are whores, bought and paid for." But who bought and paid for them, from this liberal perspective? In their view, the capitalist ruling class included not only national politicians but also corporate owners and advertisers, which brings the discussion back once again to the question of media economics.

Liberal respondents described MSM as "corporate owned and commercially maintained," "driven by politics and profit, not interested in the integrity of the field or in educating the public," and "bound to economic needs for its success; (it's) not in its own interest to report fairly and accurately." Other factors they cited were "conglomeration, a lack of independence, too much control from outside sources," "having to pander to companies or advertisers, or worrying about what people will think," and "money, advertising dollars, owning too many other outlets (TV, radio, print), trying to satisfy all their stock holders, only worrying about ratings, or if they do a particular report it will offend a current or potential advertiser." Some noted that "sponsors have their own agendas" and that "focusing on the need to sell ad time leads to a dumbing down of important issues facing our nation and world." Another associated MSM with "mass corporate ownership, fear of changing the status quo, desire to capitulate to the ignorance of middle America in the name of ratings." Someone contrasted this profit orientation with alternative funding models: "In America there is no MSM that was not created for the sole purpose of generating profits (i.e. we have nothing similar to BBC or the CBC)."

Here, I will highlight three especially thoughtful comments that conveyed this economics theme.

- One liberal respondent named five problems with MSM, of which four were economic: "1. Too much advertising distracts from the news. 2. Influence of advertisers and corporate interests skews the political perspective. 3. Conservatism due to needing to support the status quo in order to continue making a profit. 4. Focus on increasing market share causes journalists to focus on sensationalist and horrifying news items instead of emphasizing positive, peaceful initiatives." The fifth problem was cultural: "5. Unaware and unacknowledged racial profiling, sexism, classism, and stereotyping of people with disabilities and immigrants."
- A second articulated a critique of MSM being "too concerned about ratings. Most are owned by giant corporations who don't know a thing about true journalism, and see media as a money-making machine. Therefore, agendas can be slid into stories and topics can be ignored if it's in the best interest of the company. But the biggest problem is that too few own too much. This is scary and very dangerous to democracy."
- A third described MSM in terms of its representation of social movements, saying they "tend to be corporate-biased, sound bite focused, pundit-driven, and shallow. I participated in the million-plus March for Women's Lives and when I came home, was dismayed that our million participants *barely* made any news." (This echoes observations made by liberal activists and alternative-media users in earlier chapters.)

By paying attention to MSM's business motives, these respondents brought sensationalism and audience expectations to the fore. They said MSM were "aimed at a general audience rather than a specific audience" and appealed "to a mass population of the people, but does not offer various viewpoints on social, political and economic issues." These liberal views implied both that MSM gives audiences sensationalism because that's what people want and that the masses are ignorant, gullible, easily manipulated. One respondent said MSM capitulated "to the ignorance of middle America." A second said, "The danger is the masses are gullible and have no idea no clue they are being so manipulated." A third pointed to "sound bites and sensationalization. They want to add sports and gossip to fill air-time. If I wanted sports or celeb glamor, Hollywood crap, I would go to those outlets!" In line with liberal interpretations of mainstream news shared earlier, these respondents believed that mainstream news aims to appeal to a large, general, or mass audience—rather than the targeted, specific, affluent one that scholars cite as a dominant influence on the nature of MSM.

Liberal respondents were concerned that MSM treated audiences as passive and that this mode of address had negative effects on the public. One said MSM featured "topics and approaches to coverage (that are) uniform and predictable, mind-numbing and fear-inducing, that don't invite or promote participation." A second said MSM were "taking away the possibility for true democracy by keeping the masses ignorant and hysterical with misdirected rage." A third contrasted MSM with alternative media that "enables and encourages active participation on the part of readers/listeners/viewers." Such liberal comments find few echoes in conservative ones. Let's recall that one conservative outlier accused MSM of condescending to its audience, saying "They only publish, broadcast what they want you to know. It is as if they think their audience is mindless and ignorant and cannot think for themselves. MSM spoon-feeds its audience and does not allow them to think!" Perhaps alternative-media fans of both political orientations value journalism that addresses its audiences as active interpreters, not passive consumers of news.

Asymmetrical Perceptions of the News

Before continuing, I want to share some additional results regarding conservative and liberal preferences of news *medium* that help interpret their comments. When asked which medium they normally got their news from, the predominance of TV was the biggest difference between the two groups of alternative-media fans. Television was the second most popular medium for these conservatives; around 38 percent said it was their main source of news. By contrast, around 6 percent of these liberals reported getting news from television. When asked to rate how useful various mediums were for getting news and information, 79 percent of conservatives deemed TV *useful* or *very useful*, compared to 57 percent of liberals who did so. Another large divergence arose in views of magazines and newspapers, which 60–70 percent of liberals declared *useful or very useful* vs. 20–28 percent of conservatives. This conservative audience signaled a strong preference for broadcast news sources and a strong aversion to traditional print ones, while the liberal one valued print more and television less.[35]

These figures suggest that when conservative respondents criticized mainstream news, they primarily envisioned TV journalism—while liberals did not. Several data points suggest that conservatives had mainstream TV news in mind, whose nature is very distinct from print, radio, and online forms.

Their comments referred repeatedly to "anchors," who represent a tiny portion of mainstream journalists and are often not, in a strict sense, reporters. Conservatives mainly referred to networks such as ABC, CBS, NBC, Fox, and CNN as well as TV personalities such as the commentator Chris Matthews. In questions about what news sources they used, 83 percent of these conservatives said they watched Fox News regularly. No other source received such high attention from either group; Rush Limbaugh, Glenn Beck, Sean Hannity, and *Drudge Report* were runners-up, with usage in the 35–60 percent range among conservatives. These preferences resound with Viguerie and Frank's vision of conservative alternative media: cable TV news, talk radio, and the Internet.

For comparison, the news sources that liberals said they used most regularly included more legacy and non-televisual media: newspapers, *The New Yorker*, MSNBC, NPR, PBS, BBC, *HuffPost*, and *Democracy Now!* These liberal respondents mixed partisan and objective news while conservatives used hyper-partisan sources that eschew journalistic norms, in line with the broader asymmetrical patterns that Benkler et al. have described. Most audiences live in a "mixed-media ecosystem" that distributes attention around a core of traditional professional news outlets—except for the roughly 30 percent of the populace that pays attention primarily to right-wing media.[36] "People on the left certainly read left-oriented materials, but they also read and engage with publications and media outlets anchored in professional journalistic norms," they wrote. The same appears less true of people on the right, whose experience is dominated by sources like Breitbart, Fox, Gateway Pundit, *InfoWars*, and *The Washington Times*—which counted among favorites in my conservative sample.

As these survey data show, liberal and conservative fans of alternative media have both convergent and divergent perceptions of news. Among the commonalities was a perception of mainstream media bias. Both groups displayed the well-known "hostile media perception" in which partisans view mainstream sources as opposing their own political perspective.[37] It might be due to perceptions of hostile biases in MSM that partisans now use more alternative sources of news. People with strong political views tend to seek out information consistent with those views—and thus to self-select into distinct audiences. In a competitive and diverse information environment, audiences can choose between different messages and different sets of "facts." The greater availability of alternative news outlets with increasingly divergent views has accelerated ideological polarization of Americans, some say.[38] Republicans and conservatives are more prone to watch Fox News, whereas Democrats and liberals avoid Fox in favor of NPR or CNN.[39] Cynical assessments of media have surged more dramatically among conservatives, who are twice as likely as Democrats to rate major news outlets as biased.[40] Yet perceptions of bias are not evenly distributed across the U.S. public: 57 percent of Republicans view media as hostile toward their viewpoint, while only 3 percent of Democrats do.[41]

The attitudes and behaviors of alternative-media enthusiasts underscore the "marked asymmetry" that reigns among partisan media.[42] Elements of this imbalance include the right-wing audience's higher reliance on television, greater loyalty to ideological media, greater perception of media hostility, stronger conviction that news media are liberal, and stronger belief in the autonomy of individual journalists. Asymmetries extend beyond the perspectives of this audience to the actions of conservative elites, who have conducted decade-long campaigns to delegitimize mainstream media as "liberal." Powerful, wealthy conservatives devoted to pushing journalism toward the right helped create commercially-successful outlets such as Fox News, talk radio programs hosted by the likes of Rush Limbaugh and Glenn Beck, and online platforms such as Brietbart.com—a corporate behemoth that marketed itself as part of a populist movement.[43] There is no liberal or progressive equivalent of this well-financed conservative organizing. Left-wing media criticism such as Noam Chomsky's is largely absent from the mainstream press, whose personnel likely prefer to conceive of themselves as autonomous professionals than as pawns of powerful elites.[44] References to the liberal bias of news outnumbered references to a conservative bias by a factor of more than 17 to 1 in press coverage per study.[45] Lopsided news discussion of media bias has yielded lopsided public opinion about media bias; a Gallup poll found that 45 percent of Americans thought news media were too liberal while only 15 percent found them too conservative.[46]

Of particular interest is my finding that conservative respondents had a distinct tendency to cite *individual* failures of journalists and owners (their political views, egos, career ambitions), while liberal ones focused primarily on *structural* deficiencies of MSM, grounded in a capitalist critique. This resonates with Figenschou and Ihlebæk's finding that right-wing European populists widely regard mainstream journalists as "vain."[47] It also aligns squarely with conservative arguments that journalists (not owners or advertisers) have decisive power over news content, that these journalists are liberals, that they use their power to advance personal politics, and that "objective" journalists would present the world exactly as conservatives see it.[48] (These claims have little credibility among journalism scholars.) My research goes further in discerning similarities and differences between left- and right-wing perspectives. This analysis suggests that while liberal audiences might reject assumptions about journalists' empowerment and partisan proclivities, they similarly believe that "objective" journalists would present the world exactly as liberals see it. This raises intriguing questions about what people understand (or misunderstand) by terms like *objectivity, impartiality, detachment,* and *neutrality* in journalism—as principles as well as practices.

Mainstream Problems, Alternative Solutions

This exploratory study helps fill gaps in our knowledge of interactions between right-wing audiences and alternative media. In particular, it clarifies and differentiates conservative and liberal perceptions regarding individual and structural biases of mainstream news media. In some ways, the conservative responses seem to confirm that the battle against alleged "liberal media bias" begun via right-wing alternative media in the 1940s had been won by the early aughts.[49] Right-wing commentators have characterized this press criticism as a successful strategy, likening it to an attempt to "work the refs," "a genuine triumph," a steady "drumbeat" that the mainstream press eventually internalized.[50] By 2002, the "traditional liberal media monopoly" did not even exist anymore, according to Rush Limbaugh—assuming it ever had.[51] (Some conservative pundits have admitted that the claim was a myth and a "great little racket.")[52]

My research offers reasons to believe the supposed right-wing victory is incomplete. In the closed-ended portion of the survey, conservatives expressed strong disapproval of the corporate, commercial nature of MSM systems—indeed, at levels comparable to the liberals. Right-leaning respondents were almost as likely as left-leaning ones to say MSM were compromised by corporate owners and commercial interests. In open-ended comments, however, conservatives talked almost exclusively about political (viz. liberal) corrupters of MSM, neglecting economic ones. By contrast, liberals did not view partisanship as the driving influence on MSM failures, despite perceiving strong conservative tendencies. In both quantitative and qualitative portions of the survey, liberals fixated on economic corrupters of MSM. I attribute this to liberal audiences having access to more cultural venues and interpretive resources that support a political-economic critique of MSM, including an alternative public sphere where they are accustomed to reading, watching, listening to, and participating in such conversations. Many conservatives who dislike the MSM business model are unlikely to have experienced or rehearsed those arguments to the extent that liberals have. The multiple-choice options on this survey might have spurred them to voice nascent or latent individual attitudes about the financial dilemmas of MSM, whereas in open-ended responses they reverted to collective scripts about liberal media/liberal journalists prevalent throughout right-wing media and the conservative public sphere. This explanation jibes with other conclusions that the conservative interpretive community inhabits a mediated echo chamber with limited exposure to dissenting cultural views.[53]

Although alternative-media fans of both political orientations identified many of the same problems, they reached different conclusions about why MSM is broken and how to fix it. The liberal respondents, who stressed economic influences, were alone in seeing potential solutions. One indicator was their comparatively high support for alternative-media ideals such as being nonprofit and being noncommercial/advertising-free. When this survey dataset was analyzed as a whole, alternative-media users on average seemed ambivalent toward both prospects, with rating averages of 2.4 on the nonprofit item and 2.55 on the noncommercial item. However, dividing the conservative responses from the liberal ones tells a different story. In reality, conservatives disagreed somewhat (2.75) with the idea that alternative media should be non-commercial or advertising free, while liberals agreed much more strongly with that statement (1.86). Conservative respondents also were ambivalent toward the ideal of being nonprofit (2.93), while liberal ones supported it (1.95). And, conservatives accepted the role of big companies over small organizations at a much higher rate than liberals did (3.25 vs. 2.30).

In addition, let's note that liberals strongly favored member-supported and publicly funded alternatives such as PBS, NPR, and the BBC—whose funding models at least partially address economic threats to the quality of mainstream news. Among liberals, 73 percent watched PBS *regularly* or *sometimes*, 71 percent listened to NPR, 57 percent listened to the BBC, and 47 percent visited the BBC website. Among conservatives, these percentages dropped dramatically: 23 percent watched PBS often, 16 percent listened to NPR, 18 percent listened to the BBC, and 12 percent visited the BBC website. These right-wing audiences largely ignored noncorporate, noncommercial, nonprofit news media with alternative economic structures and dismissed alternative ways of financing journalism beyond the supposedly free market.

The binary split of liberals vs. conservatives enabled us to draw some broad distinctions between these two groups. However, it likely masked some differences between moderate and radical partisans—for example, between so-called alt-light users (mainstream conservatives) and the more radical alt-right (the hard, ultra, or far right). The discussion here did not analytically distinguish between "alternative media" and "alternative journalism" because respondents used solely the former phrase and tended to elide the meanings of *media, journalism*, and *news*. Other limitations of the study were its small sample size, the age of data, and a preponderance of white males. These survey respondents were more racially homogeneous (85 percent white), educated (64 percent had college degrees), older (77 percent were over 30) and male (58 percent) than the general U.S. population. Future research could recruit a larger, more diverse population of alternative-media users with a higher ratio of conservative respondents, which would enable statistically meaningful analysis. There's certainly more to the conservative view of alternative media than what was expressed in this single study.

This chapter has identified some conservative *lay* theories of news that greatly resemble conservative *elite* theories of news. They explain the deficiencies in mainstream media in political terms that ignore the reality that traditional journalism organizations are first and foremost businesses. The real competition is for advertising dollars, not between left- and right-wing views.[54] News organizations have strong economic incentives to cater to audience's political preferences—a fact that conflicts with the perception that coverage is driven by journalists' own opinions.[55] To paraphrase Eric Alterman: you're only as liberal as the person who pays you will let you be. The discourse of talk radio, political blogs, and news commentators results from a "perfect storm" of business trends, commercial needs, technological advances, and regulatory shifts—not from public political attitudes or antagonisms.[56] While the sociocultural biases of news are often liberal, it's economic biases are consistently conservative and pro-business—indicating that liberal and conservative critics of mainstream media are talking about different kinds of bias.[57]

Notes

1 See Robert Glessing, *The Underground Press in America* (Bloomington: Indiana University Press, 1970); Michael Johnson, *The New Journalism* (Lawrence: University Press of Kansas, 1971); Roger Lewis, *Outlaws of America* (Middlesex, UK: Penguin, 1972); David Armstrong, *A Trumpet to Arms* (Boston, MA: South End Press, 1981); Abe Peck, *Uncovering the Sixties* (New York: Pantheon, 1985); Chris Atton, *Alternative Media* (Thousand Oaks, CA: Sage, 2002); John McMillian, *Smoking Typewriters* (New York: Oxford University Press, 2011); and Mitzi Waltz, *Alternative and Activist Media* (Edinburgh: Edinburgh University Press, 2005).

2 Yochai Benkler, Hal Roberts, and Ethan Zuckerman, "Study: Breitbart-Led Right-Wing Media Ecosystem Altered Broader Media Agenda," *Columbia Journalism Review*, March 3, 2017.

3 Robert Entman and Nikki Usher, "Framing in a Fractured Democracy," *Journal of Communication* 68 (2018).

4 Joshua Atkinson and Suzanne Valerie Leon Berg, "Right-Wing Activism," in *Activist Media and Biopolitics*, eds. Wolfgang Sutzl and Theo Hug (Innsbruck: Innsbruck University Press, 2012); Chris Atton, "Far-Right Media on the Internet," *New Media and Society* 8, no. 4 (2006); John Downing et al., *Radical Media* (Thousand Oaks, CA: Sage, 2001); and Patricia Mazepa, "Regressive Social Relations, Activism, and Media," in *Alternative Media in Canada*, eds. Kirsten Kozolanka, Patricia Mazepa, and David Skinner (Vancouver: University of British Columbia Press, 2012).

5 Nicole Hemmer, *Messengers of the Right* (Philadelphia: University of Pennsylvania Press, 2016); Claire Bond Potter, *Political Junkies* (New York: Basic Books, 2020); Charles Stewart, "The Master Conspiracy of the John Birch Society," *Western Journal of Communication* 66, no. 4 (2002).

6 See Hemmer, *Messengers of the Right*; and Yochai Benkler, Robert Faris, and Hal Roberts, *Network Propaganda* (Oxford and New York: Oxford University Press, 2016), 316.

7 Atkinson and Berg, "Right-Wing Activism."

8 Joshua Atkinson and Suzanne Valerie Leon Berg, "Narrow Mobilization and Tea Party Activism," *Communication Studies* 63, no. 5 (2012).

9 Cinzia Padovani, "The Media of the Ultra-Right," *Journal of Language and Politics* 15, no. 4 (2016); see also Chip Berlet, "Who's Mediating the Storm?" in *Media, Culture and the Religious Right*, eds. Linda Kintz and Julie Lesage (Minneapolis: University of Minnesota Press, 1998).

10 Alice Krieg, "Vacance Argumentative," *Mots/Les Langages du Politique* 58 (1999).

11 For a summary of research on right-wing alternative media, see Rauch, "Comparing Progressive and Conservative Audiences."

12 Kathleen Hall Jamieson and Joseph Cappella, *Echo Chamber* (New York: Oxford University Press, 2010).

13 Jeffrey Berry and Sarah Sobieraj, *The Outrage Industry* (New York and Oxford: Oxford University Press, 2014), 140.

14 Benkler et al., *Network Propaganda*.

15 The Gamergate controversy stemmed from online harassment of women and centered on sexism in video game culture. The men's rights movement focuses on

social policies and government services that adherents believe structurally discriminate against men and boys; some describe it as a "backlash" against feminism and women's rights. Alice Marwick and Rebecca Lewis, *Media Manipulation and Disinformation Online* (New York: Data and Society Research Institute, 2016), 5.

16 Kristoffer Holt, "Alternative Media and the Notion of Anti-Systemness," *Media and Communication* 6, no. 4 (2018).

17 Marwick and Lewis, *Media Manipulation and Disinformation Online.*

18 See also Ryan Holiday, *Trust Me, I'm Lying* (New York: Portfolio, 2013).

19 Marwick and Lewis, *Media Manipulation and Disinformation Online*, 11.

20 For more on how trolling and hoaxing subcultures interact with mainstream media, including Fox News, see Gabriella Coleman, *Hacker, Hoaxer, Whistleblower, Spy* (New York: Verso Books, 2014), and Whitney Phillips, *This is Why We Can't Have Nice Things* (Cambridge, MA: MIT Press, 2015).

21 A series of investigative reports by *BuzzFeed* is helpful in understanding the emergence of alt-right media, including Joseph Bernstein, "Alt-White," *BuzzFeed*, October 5, 2017; and Charlie Warzel, "The Right Is Building a New Media 'Upside-Down' to Tell Trump's Story," *BuzzFeed*, January 23, 2017.

22 David Neiwert, *Alt-America* (New York: Verso, 2017).

23 Some scholars note that alt-right media use leftist discursive strategies to position themselves as outsiders and critics marginalized by the mainstream. André Haller and Kristoffer Holt, "Paradoxical Populism," *Information, Communication, and Society* 22, no. 12 (2019).

24 According to Marwick and Lewis, *Media Manipulation and Disinformation Online.* The National Policy Institute describes itself online as "dedicated to the heritage, identity, and future of European people in the U.S. and around the world" and "an indispensable part of nationalist and identitarian culture"; https://altright.com/the-national-policy-institute.

25 Angela Nagle, *Kill All Normies* (London: Pluto Press, 2017).

26 Mike Wendling, *Alt-Right* (London: Pluto Press, 2018).

27 Andrew Anglin, "A Normie's Guide to the Alt-Right," *Daily Stormer*, December 1, 2018.

28 Saul Alinsky, *Rules for Radicals* (New York: Vintage, 1989), 85.

29 Berlet, "Who's Mediating the Storm?" Conservative activist-publishers Richard Viguerie and David Franke also described their own movement as secretive in *America's Right Turn* (Chicago, IL: Bonus Books, 2004).

30 Berlet, "Who's Mediating the Storm?" 255.

31 The ten ambiguous responses I was not able to interpret, categorize, and analyze included the following. Conservatives describing alternative media: "Alternative media are the future"; and "Anything other than the alphabets and most daily newspapers." Liberals describing alternative media: "Badly needed for democracy"; "Free"; and "I think it is part of modern life." Conservatives describing MSM problems: "Dishonest with ties to the 'mob' and I'm not referring to the 'Tea Party protesters'"; "They are not doing their jobs!!" and "Waste of time." Liberals describing MSM problems: "It remains to be portable to the extent of the improvement."

32 Claire Bond Potter, *Political Junkies* (New York: Basic Books, 2020).

33 Viguerie and Frank, *America's Right Turn*, 2.

34 This chapter corrects some scale discrepancies presented in earlier discussion of this data in Jennifer Rauch, "Comparing Progressive and Conservative Audiences for Alternative Media and Their Attitudes toward Journalism," in *Alternative Media Meets Mainstream Politics*, eds. Joshua Atkinson and Linda Jean Kenix (Lanham, MD: Lexington Books, 2019).

35 Both groups valued the Internet and radio similarly, describing these mediums as *useful* or *very useful*. Internet was the top news medium for both groups, with around 41 percent of conservatives and around 54 percent of liberals/progressives naming it

their main source of news. Radio was the main source of news for around 21 percent of conservatives and around 29 percent of liberals/progressives. Neither group showed a strong preference for newspapers or magazines. It's not clear whether they interpreted *newspaper* and *magazine* as printed forms only or subsumed such content under *Internet*.

36 Benkler et al., *Network Propaganda*, 291.

37 Robert Vallone et al., "The Hostile Media Phenomenon," *Journal of Personality and Social Psychology* 49, no. 3 (1985).

38 Jamieson and Cappella, *Echo Chamber.*

39 Jonathan Ladd, *Why Americans Hate the Media and How It Matters* (Princeton, NJ: Princeton University Press, 2012).

40 Ladd, *Why Americans Hate the Media.*

41 Pew Research Center, "Campaign Leads the Pack as Campaign News Source," February 7, 2012.

42 Entman and Usher, "Framing in a Fractured Democracy."

43 Robert McChesney, *The Problem of the Media* (New York: Monthly Review, 2004); Entman and Usher, "Framing in a Fractured Democracy."

44 McChesney, *Problem of the Media.*

45 Geoffrey Nunberg, "Label Whores," *American Prospect* (May 6, 2002).

46 McChesney, *Problem of the Media.*

47 Tine Ustad Figenschou and Karoline Andrea Ihlebæk. "Challenging Journalistic Authority: Media Criticism in Far-Right Alternative Media," *Journalism Studies* 19 (2018): 9.

48 Research suggests that journalists lean liberal on social issues and lean conservative on economic issues. Yet, their political views are immaterial if they have neither the power nor the desire to insert personal opinion in their news-work. See McChesney, *Problem of the Media.*

49 A left-wing mass media ecosystem never emerged to parallel the right-wing one that began forming in the 1990s, as Benkler et al. explain in *Network Propaganda*, 318. The corollary "conservative media bias" argument remains largely in the academic and activist domain and never became a popular narrative like "liberal media bias."

50 Republican Party chair Rich Bond quoted on TomPaine.com and E.J. Dionne in the *Washington Post*, cited in McChesney, *Problem of the Media*, 110, 116.

51 Joe Conason, *Big Lies* (New York: St. Martin's Press, 2003), 34.

52 A writer for the right-wing *Weekly Standard* said, "We've created this cottage industry in which it pays to be un-objective. It's a great way to have your cake and eat it too. Criticize other people for not being objective. Be as subjective as you want" (quoted in McChesney, *Problem of the Media*, 109). For more on liberal media bias as a decades-long core rhetorical strategy of conservative elites, see Eric Alterman, *What Liberal Media?* (New York: Basic Books, 2003); he cites op-ed columnist E.J. Dionne saying "It took conservatives a lot of hard and steady work to push the media rightward . . . It adds up to a media heavily biased toward conservative politics and conservative politicians" (145). See also Edward Herman, *The Myth of the Liberal Media* (New York: Peter Lang, 1999); and David Edwards and David Cromwell, *Guardians of Power* (London: Pluto Press, 2005).

53 Jamieson and Cappella proposed that the conservative "insular feedback loop" could be erased by omnivorousness, a claim that other scholars challenge. See Ladd, *Why Americans Hate the Media*, and Benkler et al., *Networked Propaganda.*

54 Berry and Sobieraj, *Outrage Industry.*

55 W. Lance Bennett and Shanto Iyengar, "A New Era of Minimal Effects?" *Journal of Communication* 58, no. 4 (2008).

56 Berry and Sobieraj, *Outrage Industry.*

57 See Alterman, *What Liberal Media?*; and James T. Hamilton, *All the News That's Fit to Sell* (Princeton, NJ: Princeton University Press, 2004).

10

JOURNALISM IN AN AGE OF ALTERNATIVES

There are three ways to look at how society is informed, someone once enumerated: that people are gullible and will read, listen to, or watch just about anything; that people are intellectually redeemable but need capable intermediaries to tell them what is important and meaningful; and that people are pretty smart and can, given the means, "sort things out for the themselves, find their own version of the truth."[1]

One might put people like Walter Lippmann, Theodor Adorno, Max Horkheimer, and Stuart Hall in the first category—critics associated with Mass Culture theory, the Frankfurt School, and the Incorporation/Resistance Paradigm. Progressive reformers and pragmatic thinkers might rank among the second group—people like John Dewey, James Carey, maybe Jürgen Habermas. More sanguine, populist scholars focused on playful, autonomous, participatory aspects of audience activity, like John Fiske and Henry Jenkins, might be placed in the third.

What about the alternative-media fans whose voices you have heard in this book? What kind of intermediaries, if any, do they think society needs? What role do they believe the press plays, or should play, in helping people decide what's important and what's meaningful? Do they view the public as gullible, redeemable, autonomous, or some combination thereof?

In many regards, the lay theories of this alternative audience resonated with those of the Frankfurt School, a mid-20th-century critical perspective that has broadly influenced leftist social movements. Stuart Hall drew on Frankfurt School thinkers (as well as on Karl Marx, Friedrich Engels, and Antonio Gramsci) in formulating his incorporation/resistance model. Influenced by the rise of authoritarianism in Hitler's Germany and of wartime propaganda in the United States, Adorno and Horkheimer viewed "the mass culture industry" as a powerful ideological system that promoted escapism, sowed false consciousness, produced illusory material needs, and reduced citizens to consumers.[2] From this viewpoint, journalism serves mainly to amplify the voices of powerful elites—uncritically reflecting and legitimizing the status quo instead of being a force for social change and progress. Proponents of this critique tend to see "the media" as powerful manipulators and the public as "cultural dupes" who are powerless to resist the persuasion in news. Much as Frankfurt-inflected scholars do, these research participants tended to portray most audiences as passive victims—distracted, exploited, and sedated by news media.

In other ways, the activists' vision of journalism resembled that of progressive intellectuals who believed a socially responsible press could advance participatory democracy. The idealistic John Dewey observed that the Industrial Revolution generated a society based on extended, impersonal relationships rather than more intimate, geographically bound ones. He hoped to convert this "Great Society" into a "Great Community" by reforming news media, "so that genuinely shared interest in the consequences of interdependent activities may inform desire and effort and thereby direct action," as he wrote in *The Public and Its Problems*. Carey shared this philosophy and drew upon Dewey's ideas in formulating the ritual view of communication. Journalism should not just give audiences information, he said. An effective press should also provide discursive, interpretive, and mobilizing resources to aid audiences in forming opinions, following arguments, understanding other people's viewpoints, and debating communal goals. According to Carey, "The press, by seeing its role as that of informing the public, abandons its role as an agency for carrying on the conversation of our culture."[3] In a similar vein, Habermas—one of the most influential critics of commercial mass media of the 20th century—advanced a radical version of the "public sphere" as a domain of popular power, deliberation, and decision-making. Like these activists, he viewed media as distorted by financial and corporate power, necessitating independent news sources with "unpolluted" information that citizens need to exercise sovereignty over the state.[4]

What's more: these alternative-media fans approximated Fiske, Jenkins, and kindred popular-culture proponents in seeing the news as a semiotic democracy, where people are capable of detecting and rejecting ideological coercion, of using media rather than being used by it. The activists saw themselves and select "other people" as smart, creative members of an interpretive democracy. This view jibes with opponents of the Incorporation/Resistance Paradigm who believe audiences find pleasure and power in making their own meanings. My informants expressed tensions among the three conceptions of audience competence mentioned earlier and ultimately leaned toward the perspective that trusted (preferably noncorporate) intermediaries were necessary because people (including themselves) did not always have the time or expertise to master an enormous range of complicated social issues.

These three categorizations are not mutually exclusive or incompatible. Aternative-media enthusiasts blended multiple conceptions of news that slid along a scale from pessimism to optimism and back again. One advantage of the pluralistic methods of my audience research was capturing a fuller range of lay theories, which oscillate from moment to moment and sometimes coexist. Scholarly attitudes toward audiences are likewise variable and ambivalent. Because he doubted that most people were up to the task of being informed citizens, Lippmann is often labeled an elitist or pessimist. He likened the public to a deaf spectator in the back row who can't manage to stay awake. (As for the populist Dewey, he thought news of his era was too dull to attract a mass readership and should be *more* sensational.) Yet Lippmann claimed not to doubt the public's abilities to participate in public life. He thought the expectations of democratic citizenship were unrealistic, noting that ordinary people do not have an "unlimited quantity of public spirit, interest, curiosity, and effort" (and, I would add, time—as work has expanded and leisure contracted, for many of us).

Likewise, Fiske is often caricatured as a populist and optimist. Yet many nuances of his arguments have been lost in translation and repetition.[5] While Fiske said audiences were "already equipped" with discursive competences to make their own meanings from media, he also described semiotic productivity as not "an innate gift" but "an acquired ability" that resulted from "social experience or training, whether formal or informal."[6] Autonomous interpretive agents are made, not born.

Myths About the News

This book described manifold lay theories shared by liberal activists and alternative-media users. Together, these theories comprise a well-rounded and well-informed popular critique of journalism. If you piece together these beliefs about mainstream news, alternative media, and mass audiences, it creates à story that goes like this: mainstream media (which are big and bad) are largely dependent upon advertising revenue to earn profits. That's why corporate owners need to produce large audiences and ideological messages that satisfy commercial sponsors; their interests align more closely with elite colleagues in business and politics than with the public, whose well-being is irrelevant to them. Top-level managers call the shots, and rank-and-file journalists don't have much control over the news they gather, produce, and disseminate. Mainstream media give advertisers and the public what they want: sensational, dumbed-down, biased stories. This fosters a passive consumer culture that disempowers citizens, who are too brainwashed to realize what's happening. On the other hand, alternative media (which are smaller, and good) place the public interest ahead of—or, at least, on equal footing with—their own economic gain. The purpose of alternative media is to produce serious, factual (though not necessarily objective) news that addresses audiences as citizens rather than consumers and that motivates people to get involved with civic life and political action.

In order for this cultural narrative to work, one must assume, among other things, that sensational news is popular with a mass audience, rather than with marginal consumers; that sensational news is detrimental to citizenship, rather than potentially beneficial; that most viewers are ignorant rather than critically aware of media biases in various forms; that professional journalists have little autonomy vis-à-vis owners; that alternative-media content is more informative and less tabloid-esque than its mainstream counterpart; and that alternative-media producers are motivated by public spiritedness more so than by profit. This subcultural understanding of "the way mainstream journalism works"—which shares many elements with public intellectuals and alternative-media producers—helps fuel this audience's critique of the news landscape. This framework of lay knowledge both shapes and constrains this audience's media engagements, as well as their social-change efforts. Some of these theories, though widespread in the U.S. public, are based on flawed assumptions.

First, this critique of journalism is undermined by the common perception that news media operate on a democratic basis whereby audiences "vote" for content. Victor Pickard calls this a "market ontology," an assumption that the journalism crisis results from supply and demand, or of consumer preferences.[7] The idea that mainstream news "gives the people what they want" is one of the most prevalent myths about U.S. media. Robert McChesney calls this belief "a half truth at best" that "serves as an ideological fig leaf to protect naked commercial interests."[8] For-profit news is driven *über alles* by economic considerations—regardless of what audiences might (or might not) want. News producers aim to satisfy consumer demand with only the limited range of content that can generate the greatest profits.[9] Programmers prioritize what's cheapest, which yields "economical fare such as recycled exploits of reality TV celebrities; fluffy features on fashion, health, and food; and dramatic scandals and political clashes that resemble food fights," as W. Lance Bennett said.[10] Soft, sensational news content is typically less expensive to produce than hard-hitting investigations, with the added benefit of being less likely to offend sponsors. Audiences "are not asked whether they would prefer alternatives to news formulas; they are simply asked which formulas they like best," per Bennett. Mainstream news does not respond to popular demand; it merely reflects what people prefer among those choices that are profitable and convenient. "The market compels firms to give us plenty of what we don't want, whether we like it or not, and gives us no recourse to address these flaws within the market," McChesney noted.[11] We merely choose items from the menu offered, not from an ideal menu we created ourselves.

The news industry characterizes its audience as these informants did: as busy and distracted people craving scannable, graphic, bite-size morsels of information.

Producers often imagine their audiences as spectators captivated by personalities, sensation, drama, and opinion-driven talk more so than news, as Anthony Nadler noted.[12] They don't conceive of viewers as practical, self-interested consumers, yet alone as citizens. Much of the industry's own audience research relies on preconceived master narratives and questionable data interpretations, Nadler showed. The purpose of market research is to test whether certain cost-effective news strategies are viable in certain environments—not to give audiences a venue for expressing their true desires. These industry perceptions deviate from academic research on what audiences want.[13] Research suggests that practices such as doing more enterprise reporting, covering more of the community, airing longer stories, sourcing stories better, hiring more reporters, and giving journalists more time were effective in attracting and holding viewers.[14] High-quality news can be good for ratings—a fact that does not explain its mainstream rarity.

Many people assume, as my discussants did, that media organizations seek the biggest possible audience. This is not the case. Programmers aim to attract a specific niche audience, not merely a *large* one. One example is urban reporters who are under commercial pressure to appeal to wealthy suburbanites. As local journalists told Phyllis Kaniss, their selection and presentation of news reflected the psychographics and demographics of that target audience, regardless of what reporters or less affluent audiences might have wanted.[15] Other evidence is offered by economist James T. Hamilton, who examined factors such as high first-copy costs and low additional costs per copy that distinguish news from other products. In his analysis, the news emphasizes issues and perspectives that appeal to *marginal consumers*, rather than to base audiences (those likely to tune in anyway). Female readers, listeners, and viewers aged 18 to 34 are frequently targeted because they spend more and are prized by advertisers. (They also tend to vote Democratic, which incentivizes journalists to address liberal political issues; Hamilton concludes that perceptions of media bias arise in part from the economic realities of news markets.) Journalists produce soft news to attract this minority of swing audiences—not the majority that values hard news. The current media system is not democratic; it gives considerably more "votes" to affluent and spendthrift audiences than to poor, middle-class, and frugal ones.

I could point to other elements of this master story that might not bear scrutiny. Specific iterations of alternative media do not live up to the idealized expectations that audiences set for them, as earlier discussion has addressed. Mainstream audiences do not crave sensationalism at the levels this narrative presumes; to the extent that they do, the appetite might be a learned response rather than an innate one. Furthermore, the assumption that sensationalism is the enemy of citizenship has been credibly challenged by those who propose sensational approaches can productively inform people and motivate them to care about issues they might otherwise disregard.[16] Theories of mainstream audiences being naive about or oblivious toward the news do not hold a great volume of water—although, as we have seen, they do hold some.

Hashtag #Resist

Resisting the News offers significant insights into how alternative-media audiences interpret journalism in ways that diverge from the mainstream public. This spectrum of alternative strategies can be characterized as more resistant and more competent than those of a control group of college students with negligible use of independent news sources. My research demonstrates that experience with alternative media and liberal activism makes exceptional contributions to shaping this audience's interpretations. These contextual factors recursively inform popular criticism of mainstream news and appreciation of alternative media. These new insights came from peering through the lens of ritual communication, from employing mixed methods with comparative group analyses, and from embracing multiple theoretical perspectives.

Media experiences are sufficiently complex that any single narrative about power and pleasure, about ritual and transmission, can only capture certain aspects of how people negotiate the images, narratives, forms, and forces that permeate our lives. The most effective strategy is to accept the mutual incompleteness of Frankfurt School, cultural studies, and political-economic narratives and to synthesize diverse perspectives in one's analysis, so that each can correct for the others' limitations.[17] The differences among these viewpoints pale in comparison to their "compatible attempts to improve the human condition by creating a more harmonious, egalitarian, just, and democratic world," as Joshua Meyrowitz observed.[18] We can minimize blind spots and tell a fuller story about human interactions with news by combining our "toolkit of narratives."

Indeed, a bigger, more diverse toolkit of narratives can be credited for the high competency in news evaluation and resistance displayed by these engaged audiences. In proposing this, I follow Ann Swidler's view of culture as a toolkit of symbols, stories, rituals, and worldviews that people use in varying configurations to solve different kinds of problems.[19] Omnivorous audiences for liberal alternative media brought a broader range of tools to bear on their news interpretations than did audiences who experienced only mainstream news sources or only conservative alternative media. The cultural repertoire of activists was further enlarged by firsthand observation of journalism processes and closeness to scholarly discourses. Wider cultural resources and deeper news literacy can help audiences develop thicker imaginations.

This book depicts myriad discursive practices through which people engaged with alternative media presented themselves as hostile toward mainstream news, as resisting its persuasion, as impervious to its effects. This audience criticized the political-economic system in which mainstream news is produced, refused to interpret that news in "obedient" ways, opposed—or, at least, performed opposition to—consuming such content, and claimed to reject the ideology they perceive therein. (By contrast, they gave little indication of resisting the content, structures, interpretations, or ideologies of alternative media—an oversight of their otherwise sensitive critical radar.) Such interpretive activities and actions are not only resistant but also potentially emancipatory. Potentially.

I use the term *resistance* in its interpretive, semiotic, or symbolic sense, as "a refusal to accept the social identity, meanings, and control proposed by the dominant ideological system," as Nina Eliasoph and Paul Lichterman put it.[20] The power to construct one's own meanings, pleasures, and identities is quite distinct from the power to influence our collective social, economic, and political system. These two forms of resistance are simultaneously related and autonomous. Eliasoph, Lichterman, and countless others have observed that symbolic resistance itself does not challenge the system or involve any sociopolitical action. Indeed, this variety of resistance can have exactly the opposite political valence from the one that resistance theorists like Michel De Certeau imagined.[21] Symbolic resistance is a prerequisite to practical rebellion, because it helps people maintain a sense of social difference in which to ground direct action.

Eliasoph and Lichterman studied how conservative patrons of a Midwestern social club/bar talked with each other about politics and other topics in culturally patterned, socially situated ways. Akin to my liberal informants, these club members considered themselves to be *active, critical, autonomous, realistic,* and *rational*—rather than passive, deferential, dependent, distorted, or irrational. But in this context, many of those words were inverted so that *active* meant actively avoiding politics; being *realistic* and *rational* meant appearing passionate and wild. Their research showed that people can rebel against something without being "for" anything in a meaningful way. These quasi-resistant bar habitués resembled the right-wing fans of alternative media in my survey, who criticized corporate influence on the news but did not conceive of an alternative, yet alone pursue one. They demonstrated the tendency toward "anti-systemness" that Kristoffer Holt identified in the right-wing alternative-media ecosystem of Sweden.[22] The conservative audience's resistant response to mainstream news recognizes problems with the for-profit system that are both political *and* economic yet envisions no viable alternatives beyond burrowing deeper into ideological bunkers. The liberal audience's resistance sees and supports alternative news organizations that provide not only content from diverse political perspectives but also nonprofit and publicly funded models that offer correctives to deficiencies of a corporate, commercial structure. Being *against the current system* represents a less constructive response than being *for* a better system.

Let's dig deeper into what *resistance* means in light of the profusion of meanings and forms it can take—or, perhaps, not take. Perhaps resistance is futile, as proposed by both Star Trek's Borg and media theorist Douglas Rushkoff, who called the word "a relic of an electronic age, when a resistor on a circuit board could attenuate the current passing through it."[23] In a digital environment, there is only *on* or *off*, he argues; anything in-between is relegated to one or the other. There is no attenuation, only opposition. The workings of human society, however, need not be analogized to those of binary code. Dichotomies like on/off, and/or, alternative/mainstream, elite/mass, and conservative/liberal are useful tools for thinking, to a point, but can gloss over the beguiling nuances and contradictions of human life. Social-change actors more likely associate *resistance* not with electrical currents but with hashtag #resist, with an upraised fist, or with the French resistance that fought Nazi occupation. In lay terms—which are this books' raison d'être—resistance and opposition mean roughly the same thing.

Resistance has much to learn from opposition. The subtle semantic difference signals a shift in strategies from defense to offense, from reaction to action. Rushkoff compares resistance to jamming a paddle into whitewater turbulence to steady one's raft—an act that still leaves one at the river's mercy. A more constructive resistance would take the form of steering one's own course—of engaging with the torrent, not just withstanding its effects. This hews closer to Gramsci's notion of resistance as overcoming domination by a ruling class with a coherent, convincing alternative.[24] Resisting the power of mainstream news can take a range of potential forms with varying levels of passivity/activity and negativity/positivity: abstaining from them, trying to be impervious to their effects, being hostile toward them, taking an informed critical stance against them, striving to alter their course, struggling to create alternatives.

The So-Called News

This book has highlighted some limitations of resistance as a principle and as a practice. Resisting forces of social domination is a good thing, to be sure. While mainstream journalism as now practiced does contribute to legitimizing the status quo, it also does more than that. Journalism informs citizens about collective problems and guides them toward finding solutions. In order to thrive—indeed, to survive—democratic societies need people to trust and attend to the shared corpus of knowledge and interpretive resources that institutional journalism can provide. Alternative-media outlets supplement but do not replace the information available from mainstream news sources.

In this light, popular resistance to not only the perceived influence of mainstream news but the very existence of mainstream news is deeply problematic. Large swathes of the public do more than challenge the ideological content of news; they avoid partaking of journalism altogether. Young people and conservatives, in particular, resist mainstream news not by consuming its messages and interpreting them in oppositional ways but rather by declining to consume journalism much at all. Recent years have brought a continued increase in news fatigue and avoidance. In 2019, 32 percent of people worldwide, 35 percent in the United Kingdom, and 41 percent in the United States said they often or sometimes avoid the news.[25] The leading reasons for news avoidance among Americans were "It can have a negative effect on my mood" (57 percent) and "I can't rely on news to be true" (35 percent). Some people seem "debilitated by information overload and unsatisfying news experiences," one survey concluded, likening news fatigue to a learned helplessness response. The more overwhelmed or unsatisfied people were, the more they tuned out.[26] News fatigue was common among young consumers who craved more in-depth news but were unable or unwilling to get it.

There's reason to believe that growing reliance on alternative media diminishes public support for established journalism. Such news outlets often fervently attack the institutional press, as Jonathan Ladd details in *Why Americans Hate the Media*. Criticism of "lamestream" media is a staple of talk radio, political blogs, and alternative news sites—which have become major routes through which politicians, activists, and pundits give flak to journalists. Ladd's research identified elite media criticism and tabloid-style coverage as two main factors nurturing mistrust of journalism—more so than partisanship, ideological bias, and public cynicism.[27] (It is no small irony that increasing competitive pressure from alternative media in the 2000s likely pushed mainstream outlets toward more sensational approaches to news.) Audience distrust of mainstream journalism is related to their use of partisan alternative media, but which comes first?[28]

Alternative-media pioneers have strived since the 1950s to make the public more interested in politics and more supportive of diverse perspectives, according to Claire Potter.[29] Many enthusiasts think alternative media can promote better democracy by being more transparent and more explicitly ideological. In many ways, alternative media have succeeded in transforming the news ecosystem, while also fracturing and polarizing it. Mainstream journalism is viewed by many in alternative-media communities as "insufficiently ideological, part of a political, media and corporate establishment that cannot be trusted to tell the truth," she said. Ironically, partisan news sources, many of which are as profitable and entrenched as establishment media, "have made us more contemptuous of our democracy."

Media criticism and sensationalism probably pose more significant obstacles to the goal of repairing journalism's credibility than does partisan bias. The latter provides red meat for cable news, which thrives on conflict, but it's a red herring in terms of understanding how the mainstream news system operates. News outlets devote much time and space to accusations of political bias in media, which reinforces public perceptions of partisanship. Unfortunately, the more people talk about partisan bias, the more people think it exists.[30] Many people do not view the world through red- or blue-colored glasses. Activists, academics, journalists, and politicians steeped in ideological thinking might find it hard to imagine: most people do not follow politics or have strong political opinions. All evidence says that 85–90 percent of Americans lack a "full-blown political ideology."[31] While most people's values lean toward conservative or liberal (labels that don't meaningfully align with a left-right continuum because they are not opposites), only a minority of Americans can identify what *liberal* or *conservative* means.[32] According to Morgan Marietta and David Barker, our values and identities both shape what we see and structure what we look for in the first place—irrespective of whether we have ever watched Fox News or MSNBC.[33] Partisanship is a minor influence on our worldviews by comparison to "the constellation of values and premises" through which we envision a good society. Marietta describes values as "how the world *should* work" and premises as assumptions about "how the world *does* work," as value-laden or idealized facts. That's why understanding the lay theories of media that underlie popular evaluations of news is important, not just knowing whether audience members identify themselves as liberal or conservative.

It's the People, Stupid

Some of the most serious media critics of the 21st century have been comedians. Jon Stewart, Stephen Colbert, John Oliver, Samantha Bee, and their kin have shone spotlights on news displaying false balance, doublespeak, misrepresentation, over-dramatization, superficiality, and hypocrisy. Stewart famously accused the hosts of CNN's Crossfire of being partisan extremists who neglected their democratic duty by amplifying political misinformation and "doing theater when you should be doing debate." Colbert tapped the spirit of the aughts when he coined the term "truthiness" to describe "the quality by which one purports to know something emotionally or instinctively, without regard to evidence or intellectual examination." Oliver once brought 97 climate-change-confirming researchers on stage with three deniers to visually represent the weight of scientific agreement behind an issue often depicted in news as a "debate" between equally credible positions. (Liberal comedians aren't alone in deriving entertainment value from the foibles of mainstream news, of course. Multiple content analyses of conservative media programming like the *Rush Limbaugh Show* find that MSM is one of the two most frequent "issues" discussed, sometimes trailing only "election/politics" coverage.)[34]

Despite being a keen observer of journalism's shortcomings, Stewart did little to illuminate the financial structures that impede news from fulfilling its public responsibilities. In *Irony and Outrage*, Dannagal Young wondered why Jon Stewart "never tackled media deregulation or the consolidation of media ownership. He never discussed the conundrum posed by journalism being charged with serving the public good and simultaneously being squeezed for corporate profit."[35] (She credits Oliver and Bee for segments examining the dangers of media conglomeration and the economics of investigative journalism.) Maybe Stewart declined to dwell on corporate media's threat to democracy because his network was part of the problem, Young suggests. Or maybe the subject just did not seem funny. My own delight in such satirical antics is tempered by this oversight. I suspect that media criticism plus irony equals people who feel cynical toward journalism, instead of appreciating what it can, could, should do.

Media criticism has the potential to start conversations about how journalism can improve.[36] However, criticism often moves in less constructive directions, such as skepticism and cynicism.[37] News coverage that disparages politics and political talk that disparages media together create a "spiral of cynicism" that erodes popular trust, interest, and participation in journalism and government alike.[38] My findings support other scholarship related to media criticism, skepticism, and cynicism, showing that alternative-media audiences in the United States, Latin America, and Europe distrust mainstream and corporate media.[39] The public cynicism propelled by media criticism is further boosted by commercial culture itself, which sends a persistent message that "all our most treasured values—democracy, freedom, individuality, equality, education, community, love, and health—are reduced in one way or another to commodities provided by the market," McChesney said.[40] Skepticism spawns greater alienation from and mistrust toward journalism.[41] When people are cynical about media, they are likely to perceive all news sources as equally bad, biased, and unfair.[42] Whereas cynicism is an emotional judgment that seeks to create mistrust, criticism should (ideally) be a constructive and rational act that seeks to improve the status quo.[43]

When people disparage MSM, they usually mean mainstream *news* media, by which they mean mainstream *journalism*. The elision of genres is troublesome, because journalism is a tiny subset of phenomena deemed "the media." People unwittingly throw diverse genres of truth-y, news-y content into the same bucket, where facts co-mingle with opinions and demonstrably untrue tidbits of misinformation, disinformation, and malinformation. When people do not like or trust journalism, it's often because they do not distinguish journalism from news or opinion or information or, especially, televised infotainment. Many of the loudest and most influential voices in MSM are not and have never been or claimed to be journalists. Besides the aforementioned comedians, many news commentators come from the ranks of entertainers as well as former political advisers, speechwriters, consultants, strategists, and politicians.[44] Think Tucker Carlson, Paul Begala, Sean Hannity, Chris Matthews, George Stephanopolous, James Carville, Laura Ingraham, and Joe Scarborough. No wonder the trouble with news is often diagnosed through a political lens. Maybe we need some entertaining accountants to guide public discourse. They might pursue that classic journalism instinct: follow the money.

News Literacy and Objectivity

Resisting the News has illustrated how and why particular people mistrusted mainstream news by reference to an alternative system of journalistic values and principles in the early decades of the 21st century—a time of upheaval in journalism and in public orientations toward media. This audience's skepticism toward corporate news evinced ample cynicism as well as a style of criticism with the potential for serving constructive ends. Three productive responses to the crisis of confidence in journalism present themselves at this juncture: we can fix the public, we can fix journalism, or we can do both.

While this book has focused on discrete pockets of interpretive resistance, my aim as a critical-cultural scholar is to better understand the cultural repertoire of alternative news users so this toolkit can be promulgated. Doing so would empower more audiences to interrogate mainstream news genres and structures. My central point is that resistant interpretations of news are *skilled accomplishments*. Reception of media products depends on automatic deployment of extremely diverse skills and competences so engrained in individuals that they are rarely recognized as "complex, and often very sophisticated, social acquisitions," in the words of John Thompson.[45] If some liberal activists and alternative-media enthusiasts have acquired this range of skills and competences, other people can, too.

People are not naturally literate about news media. I am not the first, and will not be the last, to propose that the public would benefit from gaining additional critical tools for discerning, understanding, and choosing to resist (or not) the messages, values, and ideologies that infuse media culture.[46] Many of the interpretive strategies displayed in active audience research like mine are integral to the project of news literacy, which aims to make citizen engagements with media more democratic.[47] Some media literacy educators have stressed the need for young people to understand propaganda and inserted a new verb in an earlier triad of audience activities: analyze, *resist*, critique, and create.[48]

Critical pedagogy helps people better understand how journalism is different from other news content, which is no easy task. It educates people in recognizing news stereotypes and formulas, in seeking varied sources of information (including alternative ones), in finding new perspectives (such as political satire), and in becoming not cynical but productively skeptical, critical, even self-critical.[49] There's little use in doubting and rejecting everything that mainstream news has to offer. This is not to say that journalism is not deserving of critique; it indubitably is. The majority of news outlets do not live up to the high standards to which a critical public holds them and to which some still hold themselves. The sliver of content that ranks high on the journalism scale—think Polk- and Pulitzer-winning coverage—does. Audiences who "hate the news" might be reading, watching, or listening to the wrong so-called news. Educators can guide people toward being better informed about news options, more productively critical of journalism, and more effective advocates for improving the media system.

News literacy can help people to better grasp the practice of *objectivity*—what it means and doesn't mean to "be objective" in the context of journalism (which is different from what it means in science and philosophy.) My research confirms that, for better or worse, many of the categories and concepts through which the public evaluates and critiques journalism are related to objectivity. Although both its meaning and value are very much contested, objectivity can be understood as "an ensemble of ideals, assumptions, practices, and institutions that have become a fixture of public philosophy."[50] It offers a supposed form of "self-regulation" for news professionals, who are suppressed indirectly or internally through objective production routines rather than through direct, external, or anticipated censorship and coercion by owners, advertisers, and governments.[51] As my informants intuited, objectivity is intimately tied to larger questions of journalism's credibility and autonomy as well as its responsibilities to democracy and the public.

The people whom I interviewed and surveyed raised provocative questions about objectivity both as a professional standard and as an ontological stance. They criticized mainstream news' predilection for presenting "objective" facts, which they thought portrayed current events as faits accomplis in which audiences could play no part, instead of as sociopolitical processes in which the public could participate. Yet in other regards, my informants showed uncertainty about objectivity as a professional journalism norm. They wondered whether journalistic objectivity was possible, yet alone desirable. They expressed conflicting views on the subject of whether alternative media did or should reject objectivity in favor of assuming an overt stance of political advocacy and social responsibility. Although the "regime of objectivity" has been "fraying at the edges" since the 1990s, it is still central to audience expectations, still integral to journalists' professional identities, and still a benchmark against which alternative approaches to journalism are measured.[52]

It's enlightening to examine how objectivity and related terms like bias, impartiality, neutrality, and independence are understood and used by journalism audiences. Many public evaluations of news involve assumptions about individual political biases: that journalists wittingly or unwittingly express their own partisan interests. Media scholars per contra tend to analyze objectivity from an economic perspective. "Reporters are small cogs in large business organizations that have a vested interested in producing a marketable, neutral product," as Bennett said. "For the most part, constructing an attention-grabbing story is more important than introducing political slant in the news."[53] The development of objectivity norms during the 20th century was driven by commercial factors like rising ownership consolidation and reliance on ad revenue. Objectivity helps justify owners, publishers, and managers having more control over journalists, restricting writing styles, and limiting opportunities for public commentary.[54] Bennett stressed the "peculiar nature" of objectivity, which employs a circular logic to equate the official views that dominate the mainstream press with "being somehow objective."[55] When a certain viewpoint predominates, it starts to seem like the objective one. Audiences might comprehend the complex notion of objective journalism insufficiently to assess its causes, merits, and implications.[56]

Saving the News

From the viewpoint of alternative-media activists, professional objectivity often seems like a ruse, a way of "smuggling a particular view of society into the social order as if it were neutral 'reality'," according to Anthony Nadler.[57] For populist audiences, the objective tone of journalism often appears "stuffy and condescending." News professionals themselves are divided on the issue. The ideal is so problematic that the Society of Professional Journalists declines to use the word "objectivity" in its Code of Ethics; instead, journalists prefer to talk about *fairness, balance,* or *credibility.*[58] Like activists, alternative journalists often question the pursuit of objectivity, the desirability of being detached, and the possibility of achieving this state. Asymmetrical tendencies arise again. Many centrist and liberal alternative news practitioners do operate under norms of objectivity and adopt a neutral standpoint. Many right-wing ones like Fox News, *Daily Caller,* and Breitbart either claim to follow such norms and do not in fact do so, or do not even make that claim.[59] Meanwhile, many mainstream journalists increasingly deviate from this norm by adopting practices of subjectivity, including opinion-based narratives and emotive subject matter.[60]

One notable challenge to the regime of objectivity was the reform movement called *public journalism* (née civic journalism), a collective project to transform the profession's relationship to the people it serves. A subset of news practitioners began promoting this approach in the 1990s, aiming to develop a "journalism of conversation" akin to what alternative-media activists seek. Public journalism advocated for more civic participation and community dialogue, for providing "some oppositional force to the next wave in the global concentration of power and the tyranny of the market."[61] Controversial at its onset, the movement was resisted by news professionals who feared that advocating for the public interest meant abandoning objectivity. Proponents of this journalistic revitalization underestimated how inhospitable the corporate news sphere was (and is) toward such reforms, which were oriented toward the public in ways fundamentally at odds with commercialism.[62] Public journalism later morphed into *participatory journalism,* which welcomed ordinary citizens and amateurs as players in an alternative public sphere.[63] While many tenets of public journalism have been incorporated into mainstream practices, this approach is largely absent from commercial news organizations such as CNN and Fox.

The profession's willingness and ability to evolve has stemmed partly from its recognition that both journalism and democracy are in crisis, and partly from the affordances of digital media and social networks. Journalists are not oblivious to the low regard in which their industry is widely held and often share some popular complaints about mainstream media. Newer iterations of the public journalism impulse include *slow journalism* and *solutions journalism.* The former arose as a corrective to the increasing quantity and decreasing quality of mainstream news. Borrowing a metaphor from the Slow movement, its adherents see corporate news production as an industrial process that makes standardized, unhealthful news akin to the junk food exuded by fast-food restaurants. Slow journalists devote more time and reflection to producing their work, embrace values like community participation, and provide audiences with an alternative to "churnalism" and news overload.[64] Solutions journalism goes beyond reporting on social problems to investigate examples of public responses and offer insights on how communities can effectively tackle serious issues. Solutions-oriented news stories aims to change the tone of public discourse, to make it less divisive and more constructive.[65]

This profusion of participatory, slow, solutions, and other new approaches shows that journalism has entered an era of high theorization and experimentation.[66] Many innovative public-oriented projects like these struggle to find sustainable sources of financial support, often favoring crowd-funding and membership models that make news professionals accountable to audiences instead of advertisers. Re-envisioning the norms of news production is one piece of the puzzle. Reinforcing the public's news literacy through systemic education is another. And there's a third: reimagining the system that finances journalism.

Time for a Fifth "A"

Alternative-media users and liberal activists are at the vanguard of a new attitude recognizing journalism as a public good like clean air and clean water, "something that market forces, left to their own devices, won't produce enough of."[67] These engaged audiences consume news from independent sources that they view as serving the public interest. They support public media, including NPR and PBS and the BBC, in practice and principle. They reject the market model for news in favor of a public-service one. Let's recall my discussants' observations about news having some "inherent goodness" beyond its ability to make a profit, about the "fantasy of what news used to be" when it "didn't have to cover its expenses," that "major media would probably have to divorce themselves of all their sponsors" in order to serve the public. In light of these values and practices, it's somewhat surprising that media reform activism is relatively low on the agenda of people engaged in efforts for social and political change.

Protest groups who feel their viewpoints are ignored or distorted by mainstream news respond to that lack of media resonance with a variety of strategies that Gerhard Rucht called the "quadruple A": *Abstention, Attack, Adaptation,* and *Alternatives.*[68] Different strategies have been adopted at different times, according to a group's goals and resources. Rucht observed that in a first period, informed by New Left experiences of the 1960s, the alternative strategy predominated. In a second, less confrontational period, activists shifted toward the adaptation strategy and conformed more or less to mainstream media expectations. Now is the time for a new strategic period, when social-change proponents must address in earnest what Downing called the "tiresome and daunting problems of trying to democratize the actually existing mainstream media."[69]

There's another A that Rucht did not include in his typology, what Des Freedman calls *Amelioration*: campaigns to reform the failing institutions that make up the news media.[70] He notes, as I do, that media policy activism has a relatively low profile in social-movement literature, as well as in movement activities. Many progressive activists are wary of liberal reforms and would prefer to replace a media system founded upon injustice, rather than try to fix it. Freedman argues that people have not merely overlooked campaigns for an ethical press or more democratic media ownership but deliberately rejected them as a waste of time and energy. "Why prioritize an environment that is fundamentally hostile to our interests when we have the ability to produce our own materials that we can disseminate through our own networks?" he asked. Additionally, policymaking is not a space in which grassroots activists typically feel comfortable. Policy venues are often depoliticized and top-down, as well as white, male, and middle class—exactly the features that many activists oppose. To boot, media policy activism lacks excitement and passion, Freedman says; it is "kind of boring."

James Carey thought journalism could only be revived by disconnecting news organizations from the global information and entertainment industries that constrain them. For more than a century, the news industry was financially founded upon ad revenue. In the 21st century, that model is broken. Advertisers need not reach news audiences to market their wares, and journalism can no longer sustain its problematic business model. We are witnessing the "slow-but-sure structural collapse of professional journalism," Pickard writes in *Democracy Without Journalism?*, which argues that the commercial news system's days have always been numbered.[71] In the past two decades, the newspaper industry shed more than half of its employees—and that was before the coronavirus struck.[72] (An example: Cleveland's daily paper, the *Plain Dealer*, had 340 journalists at the turn of the millennium; it now has four.) Post COVID-19, journalism both alternative and mainstream is facing an existential crisis. Alternative newsweeklies and small dailies were hit hard by the pandemic, due to reliance on advertising from local businesses requiring spatial proximity: concerts, restaurants, bars, theaters, movies.

Alternative news audiences want and need the original, local, and investigative reporting that mainstream journalists do. Institutional news sources remain distinct and retain an important role in the U.S. political system. Although a guiding objective of alternative media is to serve as a corrective to mainstream ones, at some point there are simply too many errors and omissions to compensate for. Posing the dilemma as a choice between building an alternative news system or fixing the current one is fundamentally wrong. We must do both. Alternative and mainstream news sources are integrated into a hybrid eco-system where the former supplement but do not replace the latter—especially when it comes to provision of fact-based local reporting.[73] The fates of alternative media, mainstream news, local communities, and democratic processes are irrevocably joined. Audiences for alternative and mainstream publications suffer or flourish together.

Both liberal and conservative audiences for alternative media recognize that journalism is compromised by its commercial framework. Because that now-failing structure has been around for so long, some regard it as inevitable or natural while others recognize it as a political choice—and a contingent one, open to human intervention. The mainstream news system did not result from a free market but from explicit government laws, regulations, and subsidies, as McChesney explains.[74] When mail was the public's primary means of exchanging information, the U.S. government's largest expenditure after national defense was its federal subsidy for the postal service. "Every major communication system from the postal system to broadcasting to the Internet flourished thanks to government resources," Pickard said. "Media subsidies are as American as apple pie."[75] Today, news corporations still get substantial tax deductions for their advertising expenses, which is effectively a public subsidy. While the federal government increasingly underfunds and undermines the post office, it spends an enormous amount of public money on corporate subsidies and tax breaks for private businesses and billionaires. Instead, we could shift a tiny portion of public funds toward supporting an independent, noncommercial news eco-system that would encourage diverse views, voices, and formats.

Democracy requires not just alternative approaches to journalism but an alternative model for financing those approaches. The United States spends only $3 per citizen on public media—far less than other advanced democracies. By comparison, many Western and Northern European countries spend around $68 to $180 per person on public media.[76] A modest outlay of around $100 per citizen devoted to alternative and local media infrastructures would yield more than $30 billion annually, proportionate to what U.S. postal subsidies for newspapers were in the 1800s.[77] One idea is to establish a citizen news voucher giving all taxpayers an annual credit to allocate to the nonprofit or publicly owned news organization of their choice. This would allow for democratic input regarding which news projects, formats, and approaches receive public subsidies. Besides offering new financial support for journalism, such policy reforms would remove economic incentives for flooding the public with so many advertisements. Many Americans of various ideologies are united in their contempt for advertising and rampant commercialism.[78] The aphorism bears repeating: when you don't pay for media content, it's because *you* are the product.

The idea of a small subsidy through which citizens participate in creating reliable journalism should be uncontroversial. These nonprofit newsrooms could be overseen in a decentralized, bottom-up way that responds to community needs. Many people have renewed appreciation for journalism as "the last bulwark of civil society, protecting them from everything from fake news to fascism" in the wake of Trump's election, per Pickard.[79] Until now, the myth of the United States having a free press was propped up by public support for corporate ownership of news media, resistance to government support of public broadcasting, and the belief that news should be objective or politically neutral.[80] (McChesney notes that such attitudes deviate from public opinion prior to the 20th century.) The popular critique of journalism shared in *Resisting the News* indicates that some of these conventional wisdoms are less sturdy than they once were.

Another Journalism Is Possible

A century ago, John Dewey and Walter Lippmann deliberated not only whether the public was intellectually redeemable but also whether the press was too. The so-called "Lippmann-Dewey debate"—a conversation, really, between two social-change proponents who held much common ground—looks as relevant as ever today. In the early 1920s, optimism about democracy was "under a cloud," according to Dewey, with mistrustful citizens questioning the legitimacy of a divisive political system.[81] The two men agreed broadly in their diagnosis of society's and journalism's ills but disagreed on remedies; both conflated democracy with capitalism, and neither proposed transforming the economic structure of news.[82]

Lippmann pled for improving ethics in journalism but saw no real possibility of reform that would enable the press to "carry the whole burden of popular sovereignty."[83] The nation made unrealistic and asymmetrical demands from its press and its public, he said. The obligation of the press to the people far outweighed the commitment that citizens were willing to make journalism, he said. "We expect the newspaper to serve us with truth however unprofitable the truth might be," Lippmann wrote. "For this difficult and dangerous service, which we realize as fundamental, we expected to pay until recently the smallest coin turned out by the mint."[84] Lippmann worried that elite players who opposed the public interest would overwhelm reform efforts.

Dewey similarly saw journalism being constrained by the market model and by the manipulations of powerful interests. Yet he argued that the failure of news to inform the citizenry coincided with a failure of the educational system to enlighten them. Dewey said his counterpart "seemed to surrender the case for the press too readily—to assume too easily that what the press is it must continue to be." He believed that another journalism was possible.

The journalism critique proffered by alternative-media activists suggests that another audience is possible, too.

Notes

1 Dale Peskin, co-director of The Media Center at the American Press Institute, in the introduction to Shayne Bowman and Chris Willis, *We Media* (Reston, VA: The Media Center at the American Press Institute, 2003), v.

2 See Theodor Adorno and Max Horkheimer, *The Dialectic of Enlightenment* (New York: Herder and Herder, 1972); and Herbert Marcuse, *Counterrevolution and Revolt* (Boston, MA: Beacon, 1972).

3 James Carey, *Communication as Culture* (Boston, MA: Unwin Hyman, 1989), 82.

4 Jeffery Alexander and Ronald Jacobs, "Mass Communication, Ritual, and Civil Society," in *Media, Ritual and Identity*, eds. James Curran and Tamar Liebes (London: Routledge, 2002).

5 David Morley, "Unanswered Questions in Audience Research," *The Communication Review* 9 (2006).

6 John Fiske, *Television Culture* (New York: Routledge, 1987), 17.

7 Victor Pickard, *Democracy Without Journalism?* (New York: Oxford University Press, 2020), 58.

8 Robert McChesney, *The Problem of the Media* (New York: Monthly Review Press, 2004), 199.

9 McChesney, *Problem of the Media*, 199.

10 W. Lance Bennett, *News: The Politics of Illusion* (Chicago, IL: University of Chicago Press, 2016).

11 McChesney, *Problem of the Media*, 176.

12 Anthony Nadler, *Making the News Popular* (Chicago, IL: University of Illinois Press, 2016).

13 See James Ettema and David Charles Whitney, *Audiencemaking* (Newbury Park, CA: Sage, 1994); Charles Layton, "What Readers Want," *American Journalism Review* 21 (1999); and Dustin Harp, *Desperately Seeking Women Readers* (Lanham, MD: Lexington Books, 2017).

14 See Tom Rosenstiel and Marion Just, "Five Ways to Build Viewership," *Columbia Journalism Review/Project for Excellence in Journalism* (November/December 2002), 92–3.

15 Phyllis Kaniss, *Making Local News* (Chicago: University of Chicago Press, 1991).

16 For example, see Matthew Baum, "Sex, Lies, and War," *American Political Science Review* 96, no. 1 (March 2002); S. Elizabeth Bird, "Seeking the Audience for News," in *The Handbook of Media Audiences*, ed. Virginia Nightingale (New York: Wiley-Blackwell, 2014); Henrik Örnebring and Anna Maria Jönsson, "Tabloid Journalism and the Public Sphere," *Journalism Studies* 5, no. 3 (2004); and John Zaller, "A New Standard of News Quality: Burglar Alarms for the Monitorial Citizen," *Political Communication* 20 (2003).

17 Douglas Kellner, *Media Culture* (New York: Routledge, 1995); and Joshua Meyrowitz, "Power, Pleasure, Patterns," *Journal of Communication* 58, no. 4 (December 2008).

18 Meyrowitz, "Power, Pleasure, Patterns," 661.

19 Ann Swidler, "Culture in Action," *American Sociological Review* 51 (1986).

20 Eliasoph and Lichterman, "Culture in Interaction."

21 Eliasoph and Lichterman, "Culture in Interaction."

22 Kristoffer Holt, "Alternative Media and the Notion of Anti-Systemness," *Media and Communication* 6, no. 4 (2018).

23 Douglas Rushkoff, *Team Human* (New York: W.W. Norton, 2019), n.p.

24 John Downing et al., *Radical Media* (Thousand Oaks, CA: Sage, 2001), 4.

25 Nic Newman, Richard Fletcher, Antonis Kalogeropoulos, and Rasmus Kleis Nielsen, *Digital News Report 2019*, Reuters Institute.

26 Bree Nordenson, "Overload! Journalism's Battle for Relevance," *Columbia Journalism Review* (November/December 2008).

27 Jonathan Ladd found little evidence that the political bias of a news item directly alters how it is evaluated by either Democrats or Republican audiences. (This is not to claim that news media are free of bias). He suggests that the beliefs and preferences of alternative-media audiences and activists, who might be more astute and

sophisticated than the broader public, are important harbingers of the health and future of the political system. Ladd, *Why Americans Hate the Media and How It Matters* (Princeton, NJ: Princeton University Press, 2012); see also Ladd, "Affective and Perceptive Polarization among Party Activists," working paper, January 5, 2018.

28 While Ladd thought distrust of mainstream media might result from alternative media persuading people to trust MSM less, he acknowledged that it could be another factor or that the causation could be reversed.

29 Claire Bond Potter, *Political Junkies* (New York: Basic Books, 2020).

30 Kathleen Hall Jamieson and Joseph Cappella, *Echo Chamber* (New York: Oxford University Press, 2010).

31 Morgan Marietta, *A Citizen's Guide to American Ideology* (New York: Routledge, 2011).

32 Philip Converse, "The Nature of Belief Systems in Mass Publics," in *Ideology and Discontent*, ed. David Apter (New York: Free Press, 1964).

33 Morgan Marietta and David C. Baker, *One Nation, Two Realities* (New York: Oxford University Press, 2019).

34 Jamieson and Cappella, *Echo Chamber*, 169; also Project for Excellence in Journalism, "Winning the Media Campaign: How the Press Reported the 2008 General Election," October 22, 2008.

35 Satirical news shows have proven effective at educating viewers on complex matters of public policy, Dannagal Young notes in *Irony and Outrage* (New York: Oxford University Press, 2019), 65.

36 Wendy Wyatt, *Critical Conversations* (Cresskill, NJ: Hampton Press, 2007).

37 Kristoffer Holt et al., "Key Dimensions of Alternative News Media," *Digital Journalism* 7, no. 7 (2019).

38 James Cappella and Kathleen Hall Jamieson, *Spiral of Cynicism* (New York: Oxford University Press, 1997).

39 Tine Ustad Figenschou and Karoline Andrea Ihlebæk, "Challenging Journalistic Authority," *Journalism Studies* 20, no. 9 (2019); and Summer Harlow and Dustin Harp, "Alternative Media in a Digital Era," *Communication and Society/Comunicacion y Sociedad* 26, no. 4 (2013).

40 McChesney, *Problem of the Media*, 166.

41 Yariv Tsfati, "Media Skepticism and Climate of Opinion Perception," *International Journal of Public Opinion Research* 15, no. 1 (2003).

42 Wyatt, *Critical Conversations*.

43 Holt et al., "Key Dimensions of Alternative News Media."

44 Ronald Jacobs and Eleanor Townsley, *The Space of Opinion* (New York: Oxford University Press, 2011).

45 John Thompson, *Media and Modernity* (Stanford, CA: Stanford University Press, 1995), 40.

46 Kellner, *Media Culture*, 60.

47 Sonia Livingstone, "Engaging with Media," *Communication, Culture, and Critique* 1, no. 1 (2008). For an introduction to media literacy, see Renee Hobbs, "Literacy: Understanding Media and How they Work," in *What Society Needs From Media in the Age of Digital Communication: Media XXI*, ed. Robert Picard (New York and Barcelona, Social Trends Institute, 2016).

48 See Renee Hobbs, *Mind Over Media: Propaganda Education for a Digital Age* (New York: Norton, forthcoming).

49 McChesney, *Problem of the Media*, 222.

50 See Robert A. Hackett and Yuezhi Zhao, *Sustaining Democracy?* (Toronto: Garamond Press, 1998), 1.

51 Hackett and Zhao, *Sustaining Democracy?*

52 Hackett and Zhao, *Sustaining Democracy?* 9.

53 Bennett, *News: The Politics of Illusion*, 31.

54 Nadler, *Making the News Popular*, 37–8.

55 Bennett, *News: The Politics of Illusion*, 175.

56 See Robert McChesney, *Rich Media, Poor Democracy: Communication Politics in Dubious Times* (New York: The New Press, 2015 [1999]).

57 Nadler, *Making the News Popular*, 27. See also Mayer Zald and John McCarthy (eds.), *The Dynamics of Social Movements* (Cambridge, MA: Winthrop, 1979).

58 See Hackett and Zhao, *Sustaining Democracy?* 8.

59 Yochai Benkler, Robert Faris, and Hal Roberts, *Network Propaganda* (Oxford and New York: Oxford University Press, 2016), 14.

60 For more on objectivity and subjectivity in alternative journalism, see Chris Atton, "What Is 'Alternative' Journalism?" *Journalism* 4, no. 3 (2003); David Domingo and Ari Heinonen, "Weblogs and Journalism," *Nordicom Review* 29, no. 1 (2008); Robert A. Hackett and Pinar Gurleyen, "Beyond the Binaries?" in *The Routledge Companion to Alternative and Community Media*, ed. Chris Atton (Oxford and New York: Routledge, 2015); Farooq Kperogi, "News With Views," *Review of Communication* 13 (2013); Susan Robinson, "The Mission of the J-blog," *Journalism* 7, no. 1 (2006).

61 James Carey, "In Defense of Public Journalism," in *The Idea of Public Journalism*, ed. Theodore Glasser (New York: Guilford, 1999), 64. For more on public journalism principles and practices, see Tanni Haas, *The Pursuit of Public Journalism* (New York and Abingdon, UK: Routledge, 2012); and Richard C. Harwood and Jeff McCrehan, *Tapping Civic Life* (College Park, MD: Pew Center for Civic Journalism/Harwood Institute for Public Innovation, 1998).

62 James Compton, "Communicative Politics and Public Journalism," *Journalism Studies* 1, no. 3 (2000), 462.

63 For more on participatory journalism and participatory news, see Bowman and Willis, *We Media*; and Herbert Gans, *Democracy and the News* (New York: Oxford University Press, 2003).

64 For more on Slow Journalism, see Jennifer Rauch, *Slow Media* (New York: Oxford University Press, 2018); Megan Le Masurier, "Slow Journalism," *Journalism Practice* (2016); and Peter Laufer, *Slow News* (Corvallis: Oregon State University Press, 2011).

65 Solutions Journalism Network, "What Is Solutions Journalism?"

66 Megan Le Masurier, "Slow Journalism," *Journalism Practice* (2016): 7.

67 Bennett, *News: The Politics of Illusion*, 209.

68 Dieter Rucht, "The Quadruple 'A's," in *Cyberprotest*, eds. Wim van der Donk et al. (London and New York: Routledge, 2004).

69 Downing et al., *Radical Media*, 42.

70 Des Freedman, "A Return to Prime-Time Activism," in *Media Activism in the Digital Age*, eds. Victor Pickard and Guobin Yang (New York: Routledge, 2017).

71 For Pickard, two other major failures of media are the tremendous amount of misinformation circulating on social media platforms, especially Facebook, and the domination of profit over public service. He quotes the head of a major news network unabashedly declare that the Trump candidacy "may not be good for America but it's damn great for CBS. . . . The money's rolling in and this is fun . . . bring it on, Donald. Keep going." Pickard, *Democracy without Journalism?*

72 Victor Pickard, "Coronavirus Is Hammering the News Industry," *Jacobin*, April 20, 2020.

73 A fascinating, thoroughgoing study of interactions between alternative and mainstream media in an urban news ecology combined survey data and focus groups to explore how individual citizens of Leeds made sense of their collective media experiences. Stephen Coleman et al., *The Mediated City* (London: Zed Books, 2016).

74 Robert McChesney, *Digital Disconnect* (Boston, MA: New Press, 2014).

75 Pickard, "Coronavirus Is Hammering."

76 Bennett, *News: The Politics of Illusion*, 239.

77 Pickard, "Coronavirus Is Hammering."
78 McChesney, *Rich Media, Poor Democracy.*
79 Pickard, *Democracy Without Journalism?* 5.
80 Bennett, *News: The Politics of Illusion*, 213.
81 Stuart Allan, "Journalism and Its Publics," in *The Routledge Companion to News and Journalism*, ed. Stuart Allan. (London and New York: Routledge, 2010).
82 Allan, "Journalism and Its Publics."
83 "Burden" is a pet word of Lippmann's. In addition to popular sovereignty, he describes thought, meaning, citizenship, decision-making, the enforcement of peace, the interpretation of expert opinions, and the delivery of news as burdensome, as well as "debts, confusions, and disreputabilities," *Public Opinion* (New Brunswick, NJ, and London: Transaction Publishers, 1922).
84 Lippmann, *Public Opinion*, 362.

APPENDIX A

Interview Guide

I'm conducting research about how people interpret the news.

I'm trying to understand what messages you think the program is trying to convey, and what gives you that impression.

We're going to watch a TV news segment together It's *ABC World News Tonight*, recorded on November 17. It's about 20 minutes long.

Afterwards, we'll talk about your reactions.

1   What did you find interesting in the program? What stands out in your mind?
2   What do you feel you learned from the news segment?
3   Was there anything you didn't like about the segment? Did anything you saw or heard rub you the wrong way?
4   How did this program make you feel about the news, your life, the world?
5   When you were watching, what did you find yourselves thinking about?
6   Does everything in this program jibe with things you've learned elsewhere, that you've seen and heard from other sources? (What's different? Where did you see or read that?).

Probes

- (Repeat term.) What do you mean by _____?
- That's interesting. . . . Why?/Why not?/In what way?
- What's the difference between X and Y?
- Do you have a particular _____ in mind? Can you give me an example?
- You mentioned _____. How did you get that impression? What brought out that idea?

- You seemed to like/dislike the part where _____. What did you think about it? What did you find interesting in that?
- How did it make you feel when you saw/heard _____? What made you feel like that?
- How about the rest of you on that? I don't expect all of you to agree.
- Are there any other reactions to that?

7   Did anything else about this program catch your attention, that we haven't talked about?

8   If you were producing the show, what would you have shown or said that they didn't?

9   If you had one minute to give advice to the producers, what would you tell them?

APPENDIX B

Diary Instructions and Sample Page

Each day, take some time to jot down all the sources of news and information that you've used in the previous 24 hours.

Include everything you've read, listened to, and watched in the types of media listed here.

Also note any informational exchanges related to news, political events or social activism (you don't need to share anything private) that you've had with people face-to-face, over the phone or Internet, etc.

If anything doesn't fit in the boxes provided, just make a note of it at the bottom of the page.

You can start on any day of the week that's convenient, as long as you fill in the diary for seven consecutive days.

Example Diary Entries: (Researcher filled in some examples by hand)

	Morning (6 a.m.-noon)	Afternoon (noon-6 p.m.)	Evening (6 p.m.-midnight)	Wee hours (midnight-6 a.m.)
Radio				
Program/station				
Total time spent				
Program/station				
Total time spent				
Website visits				
Website name/URL				
Total time spent				
Website name/URL				
Total time spent				
E-mails (non-listserv)				
Total # of e-mails				
Total # w/articles or action alerts included				
Total time spent				
In-person conversation				
Friend/family/colleague				
Place where talked				
Total time spent				
Friend/family/colleague				
Place where talked				
Total time spent				
Newspapers				
Publication title				
Total time spent				
Publication title				
Total time spent				
Magazines				
Publication title				
Total time spent				
Publication title				
Total time spent				
Newsletters/flyers				
Organization name				
Total time spent				
Organization name				
Total time spent				
Television				
Program/station				
Total time spent				
Program/station				
Total time spent				

	Morning (6 a.m.-noon)	Afternoon (noon-6 p.m.)	Evening (6 p.m.-midnight)	Wee hours (midnight-6 a.m.)
Discussion groups				
Group/listserv name				
Total time spent				
Group/listserv name				
Total time spent				
Telephone conversation				
Friend/family/colleague				
Total time spent				
Friend/family/colleague				
Total time spent				
Meetings/lectures/etc.				
Name of organization				
Total time spent				
Name of organization				
Total time spent				
Films/videos				
Title of film/video				
Total time spent				
Title of film/video				
Total time spent				

Source: Notes . . . Clarifications . . . Anything else that didn't fit the grid?

APPENDIX C

Survey Questions

How often do you use ALTERNATIVE news media?

Regularly—Sometimes—Hardly Ever—Never

How often do you use MAINSTREAM news media?

Regularly—Sometimes—Hardly Ever—Never

About how much time do you spend using ALTERNATIVE media sources on a typical day?

-30 mins—30 min-1 hr—1–2 hrs—2–3 hrs—3–4 hrs—4 hrs+

About how much time do you spend using MAINSTREAM media sources on a typical day?

-30 mins—30 min-1 hr—1–2 hrs—2–3 hrs—3–4 hrs—4 hrs+

What are your favorite ALTERNATIVE media sources—in print, broadcast, online or whatever? Please type their names in the box below.

How important are the following characteristics of ALTERNATIVE media, to you? Please check the appropriate boxes.

Very important—Important—Somewhat important—Not important at all

They . . .

. . . use different technology for gathering, accessing, and sharing information than mainstream media do

. . . are devoted to issues and events not discussed elsewhere.

. . . allow a wider range of people to express their voices and opinions.

. . . advocate for a different system of values than mainstream media.

. . . criticize and analyze the work done by mainstream media.

. . . *promote activism and mobilize people to participate more than main-stream media do.*

. . . *offer more favorable coverage to people and groups that I support.*

. . . *are more connected to people in groups and networks that I identify with.*

How much do you support the following perspectives in ALTERNATIVE media? Please indicate whether you agree or disagree with each statement.

Strongly agree—Somewhat agree—Somewhat disagree—Strongly disagree

I like alternative media when . . .

. . . *their journalists seem to hold a point of view similar to mine.*

. . . *their journalists seem objective or detached.*

. . . *they're run by international or foreign organizations, who give a non-U.S. viewpoint.*

In terms of political perspective, how do you view ALTERNATIVE media?

Strongly agree—Somewhat agree—Somewhat disagree—Strongly disagree

They are . . .

. . . *very liberal.*

. . . *slightly liberal.*

. . . *slightly conservative.*

. . . *very conservative.*

. . . *there is a wide range.*

In terms of political perspective, how do you view MAINSTREAM media?

Strongly agree—Somewhat agree—Somewhat disagree—Strongly disagree

They are . . .

. . . *very liberal.*

. . . *slightly liberal.*

. . . *slightly conservative.*

. . . *very conservative.*

. . . *there is a wide range.*

How much do you support the following ideas about MAINSTREAM media? Please indicate how much you agree or disagree with each statement.

Strongly agree—Somewhat agree—Somewhat disagree—Strongly disagree

Mainstream media . . .

> . . . *are compromised by corporations and corporate interests*
> . . . *are compromised by advertising and commercial interests.*
> . . . *have un-democratic practices.*
> . . . *have un-patriotic practices.*
> . . . *disempower the public.*
> . . . *support the status quo.*
> . . . *are compromised by the big egos or career ambitions of journalists.*
> . . . *are compromised by the anti-religious or immoral attitudes of journalists.*
> . . . *are biased because of the politics of their owners.*
> . . . *are biased because of the politics of their journalists*
> . . . *are motivated too much by profit.*
> . . . *need more government regulation.*

From which medium do you mainly get your news, in the course of a normal day?

> *Magazine—Newspaper—Radio—Television—Internet*

Rate each of these mediums as a means for getting news and information.

> *Very useful—Useful—Somewhat Useful—Not Useful at All*
>
> *Magazine—Newspaper—Radio—Television—Internet*

How often do you read the following publications, either in print or online? Please check the appropriate boxes.

> *Regularly—Sometimes—Hardly Ever—Never*
>
> *Daily newspapers—Mother Jones—Progressive—Alternative newsweekly(ies)— Harper's—Human Events—Time or Newsweek—Atlantic—Economist— Nation—National Review—New Yorker—New Republic—Weekly Standard*

How often do you watch the following news channels, either on TV or online? Please check the appropriate boxes.

> *Regularly—Sometimes—Hardly Ever—Never*
>
> *Community/cable access TV—ABC—CBS—CNN—C-SPAN—Fox— MSNBC—NBC—PBS*

How often do you listen to the following radio programs, whether broadcast, satellite or online? Please check the appropriate boxes.

> *Regularly—Sometimes—Hardly Ever—Never*

Rush Limbaugh—NPR—Sean Hannity—Michael Savage—Glenn Beck—
Laura Ingraham—BBC— Democracy Now!

How often do you listen to the following radio programs, whether broadcast, satellite or online? Please check the appropriate boxes.

Regularly—Sometimes—Hardly Ever—Never

Indymedia—Daily Kos—Huffington Post—Drudge Report—Smoking Gun—Talking Points Memo—Gateway Pundit—Newsbusters—Five Thirty Eight—Hot Air—Powerline—Air America—Politico

What is your political orientation?

Very conservative—Somewhat conservative—Somewhat progressive or liberal—Very progressive or liberal

In your own words, how would you describe "ALTERNATIVE media"? Please explain briefly in the box below.

In your view, what are the major problems with MAINSTREAM media? Please explain briefly in the box below.

APPENDIX D

Additional Qualitative Survey Data

This appendix provides a census of all answers to the open-ended survey question "In your own words, how would you describe ALTERNATIVE MEDIA?" from respondents who did not indicate their political orientations. The responses are edited for grammar, spelling, and punctuation and organized in alphabetical order according to four categories: *economics theme, politics theme, both themes, neither theme (n = 106).*

Responses with an economics theme *(n = 30)*

- A news source not controlled by huge corporate interests with a variety of viewpoints and information sources. Less compromised by ties to big business.
- Alt. media is outside the corporate mega-structures like Hearst, Murdoch, etc.
- Alternative media gives a more open-minded view of reality, still can fall in the "journalist-ego" game, but it offers alternatives to the mainstream media that is usually managed by corporate powers.
- Alternative media is noncorporate, noncommercial, and challenges the status quo. It comes from a variety of sources and perspectives. It includes voices of the poor and conducts true investigative journalism.
- Alternative media provides citizens with facts, ideas, viewpoints, and opinions that are not represented in the mainstream media. Alternative media is more unbiased and truthful, and it is less connected to corporate interests or profit margins than mainstream media.
- Alternative media, to me, is media coming from a variety of sources or viewpoints, as opposed to one big conglomeration. The definition is inherent in

the name-offering alternatives or choices, to what is being thrown in our faces on a regular basis.

- Any source other than the three main television broadcasting companies— ABC, CBS, NBC—and national print publications, both newspaper and magazine.
- I describe alternative media as anything other than mainstream/corporate owned or controlled. Mostly, alternative media is small and focused on issues. They don't attempt to be something for everybody.
- I describe alternative media as the media that seeks to investigate and disseminate investigative truths. Alternative media is the media that is not driven by neither profit or corporate interest. Alternative media strives to investigate and investigate either an objective representation of current events or—be that as it may—"objectively slanted" according to that particular outlet's motive. But alternative media seeks to present the "story not as commercial interest dictates."
- I would describe alternative media as information sources that are generally not produced by corporate or commercial interests. There is a wide range of resources within the category—print, online, radio, television, etc.—with varying degrees of quality and credibility across the board.
- It can be several things: noncorporate, produced from an outsider perspective or a minority point of view.
- Media forms which aren't as in-demand for publicity, and that are separate from large corporations or ad supporters.
- Media that is relatively free of corporate control or supported by readers and listeners.
- Media looking for alternative viewpoints, not primarily associated with big companies governing their storylines.
- Media not part of the corporate empires, independent, and able to work outside of the standard perceptions.
- Media produced with the material created as the end goal, not appeasement of a particular demographic or advertiser base. Fanzines, alt. radio, anyone working to afflict the comfortable with a little much-needed critical thinking.
- Media that is funded and produced outside of the normal confines of Big Corporations as well as media that takes a skewed view of everyday life.
- Media that is not owned by a major corporation.
- Media that is not owned by large corporations.
- Media that is not under the direct control of the major media conglomerates and smaller regional media corporations.
- Media that is objective to the facts, not ran by corporations, big money, or one political group or agenda.
- Media that is owned by large corporations that responds to the bottom line of the dollar and/or someone like Rupert Murdoch.
- Media that isn't funded by big corporations.

- Noncommercial news. More nuanced and detailed reports and not 30-second sound bites and reports on major issues and debates. They cover all stories that are important to many people and not just money [*sic*] stories like Anna Nicole or Brittney Spears.
- Noncorporate/independently owned.
- News media that is not owned by the handful of large corporate conglomerates as described in *The Media Monopoly.*
- Not owned by a major corporation/independently owned. Not on corporate-owned station. Difficulty getting on airwaves/print exposure.
- NOT RUN BY CORPORATE GIANTS.
- Not underwritten by companies driven by the bottom line and paying off debt and/or driven to expose truth.
- Not-for-profit media, not subject to the influence of corporations.

Responses with a politics theme *(n = 12)*

- A breathe of fresh air and a welcomed "ALTERNATIVE" to what has been offered for years. The center-right views are not only informative but free of everyday indoctrination.
- Alternative media is a progressive nontraditional form of media that provides unrepresented information and views from people and areas of the world that are typically not focused on in mainstream media. Alternative media also provides its information through avenues of production (such as zines) that are not utilized by their mainstream counterparts.
- Anything that doesn't tow the party line.
- Fox News is the only channel with fair and balance news. All others are not. Just very liberal and biased.
- Information that has no agenda, able hold objectivity [*sic*], has no political special interest leaning.
- It was such a relief, after feeling isolated, to discover that other people thought for themselves and were willing to take positions that didn't fit into the neocon, mainstream narrative. The journalism done by *Talking Points Memo*, especially, and the *Nation* is heartening.
- Liberal, free, open minded.
- News with a non-US bias, mostly human rights based, and providing a source of news that is comes devoid of an ultra-conservative slant.
- Non-liberal. Mainstream media or the Drive-by Media presents only liberal propaganda with a token conservative. FOX is the only exception. They tell both sides of the story. Of course, there are plenty of Huff Post-type left-wing alternative media online but they are just a more mean-spirited edition of the MSM; really mean-spirited.
- Nonnetwork (cable) news or opinion, or Internet sites that advocate right or left. In my town there is only one alternative print publication.

- The opposite of corporate/mainstream media, noncommercial, often opinionated, but open-minded, humanistic, populist oriented.
- Often not for profit; presenting wide array of voices/viewpoints; liberal in direct challenge to the monopoly of reactionary voices on radio; non–Big Three and Fox.

Responses with both economics and politics themes *(n = 1)*

- Interesting in that you put this question in the back. Alternative media is pretty much anything not based in conservatism, neo-conservatism, or tightly structured by financial interests. MSNBC is the only "mainstream" media that actually crosses the threshold of alternative/mainstream types, because of its liberal format.

Responses with neither economic nor politics theme *(n = 63)*

- A context in which radicalism is possible, but not always probable.
- A useful way to stay informed about local and national issues, and to obtain reviews of movies, plays, and other forms of entertainment.
- Alternative media actively challenges the status quo by offering minority and subversive opinion and reporting.
- Alternative media are media that are generated by people themselves.
- Alternative media comes closer to an unadulterated exchange of ideas or a public forum/space.
- Alternative media gives facts without embellishment and without telling me how I'm supposed to think and what conclusions I must reach.
- Alternative media is a good source for a variety of opinions and issues.
- Alternative media is media that either (1) provides an alternative perspective to mainstream media or (2) is produced by alternative information providers than mainstream media.
- Alternative media is what happens when people become frustrated at not finding information that feels valid. You go looking for a better source.
- Alternative media offers a fresh viewpoint, one I agree with highly, that is different than the status quo. The alternative media I interact with is firmly on the side of the "little people," a viewpoint I don't find reflected in my conservative local newspaper. I trust what I read in the alternative media.
- Alternative media represents any media outside of the mainstream American media . . . radio, TV, print.
- Alternative media tells the truth, supports free enterprise, limited government, individual freedom, traditional American Values, and a strong defense. Alternative media supports the Constitution structured by the founders.
- Alternative media would be anything that isn't heavily established media, usually media other than cable news.

- Alternative media, in general, covers stories that are not a primary focus of the mainstream media, or covers them from a different angle.
- Any media that is off the beaten track and gives honest news coverage.
- Anything other than mainstream.
- Anything other than news on main channels of TV.
- Awesome.
- *Berkeley Barb* was my first experience. Any publication willing to publish Charles Bukowski has to be good. Benj. Franklin is at the top of my list. Any media that cuts through the stereotypes to deliver the message instead of the narcissism.
- Blogs, weekly newspapers, non-syndicated radio.
- Channels for reporting, analysis, and opinion that resist the mainstream media's economic and ideological pressures, investigate and challenge the institutions whose dominance the mainstream media tend to take for granted, and present points of view that are marginalized in the mainstream media (often, but not always, unjustifiably and unfairly).
- Different music style.
- Expanding in influence and importance.
- Giving a voice to marginalized and unpopular viewpoints and telling the stories of people who have no power or money.
- Great and the only people who tell the truth!
- Growing more credible, making inroads into mainstream, needing to stay clear of hyperbole.
- I look at alternative media as a way to see the issues of the day from a different angle. I don't have to agree with the view from that angle, but it does allow for me to come to a more informed opinion.
- I love ALTERNATIVE MEDIA and if I'm not able to read these various sources I almost always skim their articles each week/month to see if there is something that I must read. They provide a more realistic view of the world instead of a view that is manufactured to achieve specific ends.
- I would describe alternative media as a vast variety of information given to the public in multiple different publications—whether online, magazine, newspaper, etc.
- Is media that is outside of the mainstream.
- Issue-focused, longer/more detailed, in-depth analysis.
- It is more available to amateurs and, therefore, provides a broad spectrum of viewpoints; however, one must always read it with a skeptic mindset, examining facts quoted, vetting the facts, and being sure the conclusion drawn is supported. Because it is free and readily available, it can be a means of social awakening and activism.
- It is that which provides in-depth information and/or analysis of events which are desirable to the target audience, upon which their support—and therefore, existence—usually rests. While this is what "mainstream" does

too, what makes it different perhaps is that the audiences of "alternative" media are more deeply vested, participatory, or interested in current events in general, because they have already made the judgment call that what's available through the "MSM" is too this or that. Also, "independent" may be considered a synonym for "alternative" in this regard.

- It provides a voice for those who would not normally be focused on by the mainstream media. This is done by focusing on certain issues from a different perspective and providing a different point of view.
- Less constrained than MSM, thus allowing reporters/editorialists to practice their craft to its potential.
- Limited access/distribution either because of small scale or too specialized for wider interest.
- Low production quality, women with unkempt hair and deadpan delivery (TV only). In print, perhaps a more "hip" style. It seems the topics covered in alt. media often differ from those of mainstream. When topics do overlap, alt. media might tend to have more pronounced opinions about the issues.
- Media (sources of information) not yet accepted/adopted/recognized as part of the "mainstream."
- Media aimed more at a niche than the general public, though accessible to the general public.
- Media offering perspective based upon trying to get to the truth with a minimum amount of interference with political or financial interests biasing the viewpoint. Speaking truth to power.
- Media other than traditional newspapers, magazines, and television.
- Media that does its best to explain the facts of major events from a perspective outside the mainstream, while at the same time capitalizing on new and/or emerging technologies to do so. Form is not necessarily important, however; traditionally presented or otherwise, content reigns supreme.
- Media that is alternative to mainstream media in point of view.
- Media that is created outside of the power structure, or that criticizes the power structure.
- Media that is delivered through nontraditional means—that is, the Internet. Also alternative media is one that tries to examine issues in depth, tries to put issues into an historical context.
- Media that may not be as credible or hosts of alternative media may be mostly humorous.
- Media that offer a perspective not often found in traditional media.
- Media that provides you with points of view that may be unpopular in the mainstream. Media that questions accepted ideas.
- Newcomers trying to add a different perspective.
- News reporting via Internet, TV, or print that presents info with a bias.
- Nonprint, non-nightly news. More informal reporting, more open about biases.

- Non-scripted, uncensored commentary that is not controlled by the major broadcast networks.
- Not a great word; alternative implies they live in a separate universe. They actually live in this world but provide a different, truer view of What Goes On. Sort of like breaking away from the blinders of Plato's Cave.
- Not network TV, or a newspaper or mag in business before 1992.
- Objective, independent.
- Open-minded coverage that allows a story to unfold without judgment or stereotype of the situation or people in the story.
- Other than mainstream media.
- Other than major networks and/or big city newspapers.
- Relatively new news source, not linked to big business or legacy power sources.
- Sources of information which allows the individual to investigate and separate "evidence" from "hype" in while striving to reach their own conclusions.
- Spreaders of truth. I'm sick to death of being lied to already. ENOUGH!!
- That's an interesting question. I wondered how the writers of this survey define "alternative" media. Are *Daily Kos* and the *Drudge Report* still alternative? They've been around for a while. Is *Salon.com* alternative? For the purposes of this survey I've considered all the websites I read other than *NYTimes.com* or Google News to be alternative.
- The old media that is on the fringes now that the new mainstream media has arrived. Examples are: ABC, NBC, CBS, CNN, FOX news as well as NPR.

BIBLIOGRAPHY

"2017 Edelman Trust Barometer." January 21, 2017. www.edelman.com/research/2017-edelman-trust-barometer.

Abercrombie, Nick, and Brian Longhurst. *Audiences: A Sociological Theory of Performance and Imagination*. Thousand Oaks, CA: Sage, 1998.

Aday, Sean. "Chasing the Bad News: An Analysis of 2005 Iraq and Afghanistan War Coverage on NBC and Fox News Channel." *Journal of Communication* 60, no. 1 (2010): 144–64.

Adorno, Theodor, and Max Horkheimer. *The Dialectic of Enlightenment*. New York: Herder and Herder, 1972.

Advertising Age. "Media Companies Ranked 1 to 50 (Special Report)." August 22, 2005: 3.

Alexander, Jeffery, and Ronald Jacobs. "Mass Communication, Ritual, and Civil Society." In *Media, Ritual, and Identity*, edited by James Curran and Tamar Liebes. London: Routledge, 2002.

Alterman, Eric. *What Liberal Media? The Truth About Bias and the News*. New York: Basic Books, 2003.

Anderson, Benedict. *Imagined Communities: Reflections on the Origin and Spread of Nationalism*. New York: Verso, 1991.

Andersson, Linus. "There Is No Alternative: The Critical Potential of Alternative Media for Challenging Neoliberal Discourse." *tripleC: Cognition, Communication, Co-operation* 10, no. 2 (2012): 752–64.

Ang, Ien. *Watching Dallas: Soap Opera and the Melodramatic Imagination*. London: Metheun, 1985.

Anglin, Andrew. "A Normie's Guide to the Alt-Right." *Daily Stormer*, August 31, 2016. www.dailystormer.com/a-normies-guide-to-the-alt-right/.

Annenberg Public Policy Center. "*Daily Show* Viewers More Knowledgeable about Presidential Campaign, National Annenberg Election Survey Shows." Philadelphia: University of Pennsylvania Press, 2004. http://cdn.annenbergpublicpolicycenter.org/wp-content/uploads/2004_03_late-night-knowledge-2_9-21_pr2.pdf.

Armstrong, David. *A Trumpet to Arms: Alternative Media in America*. Boston, MA: South End Press, 1981.

Atkinson, Joshua. *Alternative Media and Politics of Resistance: A Communication Perspective*. New York: Peter Lang, 2010.

———. "Conceptualizing Global Justice Audiences of Alternative Media: The Need for Power and Ideology in Performance Paradigms of Audience Research." *The Communication Review* 8 (2005): 137–57.

Atkinson, Joshua, and Debbie Dougherty. "Alternative Media and Social Justice Movements: The Development of a Resistance Performance Paradigm of Audience Analysis." *Western Journal of Communication* 70, no. 1 (2006): 64–88.

Atkinson, Joshua, and Suzanne Valerie Leon Berg. "Narrow Mobilization and Tea Party Activism: A Study of Right-Leaning Alternative Media." *Communication Studies* 63, no. 5 (2012): 519–35.

———. "Right-Wing Activism: The Next Challenge for Alternative Media Scholarship." In *Activist Media and Biopolitics: Critical in the Age of Biopower*, edited by Wolfgang Sutzl and Theo Hug. Innsbruck: Innsbruck University Press, 2012.

Atton, Chris. *An Alternative Internet*. Edinburgh, UK: Edinburgh University Press, 2004.

———. *Alternative Media*. Thousand Oaks, CA: Sage, 2002.

———. "Far-Right Media on the Internet: Culture, Discourse, and Power." *New Media and Society* 8, no. 4 (2006): 573–87.

———. "News Cultures and New Social Movements: Radical Journalism and the Mainstream Media." *Journalism Studies* 3, no. 4 (2002): 491–505.

———. "Reshaping Social Movement Media for a New Millennium?" *Social Movement Studies* 2, no. 1 (2003).

Atton, Chris, and Nick Couldry. "Introduction." *Media, Culture and Society* 25, no. 3 (2003): 579–86.

Atton, Chris, and James F. Hamilton. *Alternative Journalism*. Thousand Oaks, CA: Sage, 2008.

Atton, Chris, and Emma Wickenden. "Sourcing Routines and Representation in Alternative Journalism: A Case Study Approach." *Journalism Studies* 6, no. 3 (2005): 347–59.

Bagdikian, Ben. *The New Media Monopoly*. Boston, MA: Beacon Press, 2004.

Bailey, Olga Guedes, Bart Cammaerts, and Nico Carpentier. *Understanding Alternative Media*. Maidenhead, UK: Open University Press, 2008.

Barassi, Veronica. "Ethnographic Cartographies: Social Movements, Alternative Media, and the Spaces of Networks." *Social Movement Studies* 12, no. 1 (January 2013): 48–62.

Barker, Martin. "I Have Seen the Future and It Is Not Here Yet . . .; Or, On Being Ambitious for Audience Research." *The Communication Review* 9 (2006): 123–41.

Batsell, Jake. *Engaged Journalism: Connecting With Digitally Empowered Audiences*. New York: Columbia Journalism Review Books, 2015.

Baum, Matthew. "Sex, Lies, and War: How Soft News Brings Foreign Policy to an Inattentive Public." *American Political Science Review* 96, no. 1 (March 2002): 91–109.

Baym, Geoffrey. "*The Daily Show*: Discursive Integration and the Reinvention of Political Journalism." *Political Communication* 22, no. 3 (2005): 259–76.

Bellah, Robert, Richard Madsen, William Sullivan, Ann Swidler, and Steven Tipton. *Habits of the Heart: Individualism and Commitment in American Life*. Berkeley: University of California Press, 1985.

Benford, Robert, and David Snow. "Framing Processes and Social Movements: An Overview and Assessment." *Annual Review of Sociology* 26 (2000): 611–39.

Benkler, Yochai, Robert Faris, and Hal Roberts, *Network Propaganda: Manipulation, Disinformation and Radicalization in American Politics*. New York: Oxford University Press, 2016.

Benkler, Yochai, Hal Roberts, and Ethan Zuckerman. "Study: Breitbart-Led Right-Wing Media Ecosystem Altered Broader Media Agenda." *Columbia Journalism Review*, March 3, 2017. www.cjr.org/analysis/breitbart-media-trump-harvard-study.php.

Bennett, Lance W. *News: The Politics of Illusion*. Chicago, IL: University of Chicago Press, 2016.

Bennett, Lance W., and Shanto Iyengar. "A New Era of Minimal Effects? The Changing Foundations of Political Communication." *Journal of Communication* 58, no. 4 (2008): 707–31.

Benson, Rodney. "Commercialization and Critique: California's Alternative Weeklies." In *Contesting Media Power: Alternative Media in a Networked World*, edited by Nick Couldry and James Curran, 111–27. Lanham, MD: Rowman and Littlefield, 2003.

Berelson, Bernard. "What Missing the Newspaper Means." In *Communications Research 1948–49*, edited by Paul Lazarsfeld and Frank Stanton. New York: Harper, 1949.

Berlet, Chip. "Who's Mediating the Storm? Right-Wing Alternative Information Networks." In *Media, Culture, and the Religious Right*, edited by Linda Kintz and Julie Lesage, 249–73. Minneapolis: University of Minnesota Press, 1998.

Bernstein, Joseph. "Alt-White: How the Breitbart Machine Laundered Racist Hate." *BuzzFeed*, October 5, 2017.

Bicket, Douglas, and Melissa Wall. "BBC News in the U.S.: A 'Super-Alternative' News Medium Emerges." *Media, Culture, and Society* 31, no. 3 (2009): 365–84.

Bird, Elizabeth S. "Are We All Produsers Now?" *Cultural Studies* 25, nos. 4–5 (2011): 502–16.

———. *For Enquiring Minds: A Cultural Study of Supermarket Tabloids*. Knoxville: University of Tennessee Press, 1992.

———. "News We Can Use: An Audience Perspective on the Tabloidization of News in the U.S." *Javnost—The Public* 5, no. 3 (1998): 33–49.

———. "Seeking the Audience for News: Response, News Talk, and Everyday Practices." In *The Handbook of Media Audiences*, edited by Virginia Nightingale, 489–508. Wiley-Blackwell, 2014.

Bird, Elizabeth S., and Robert Dardenne. "Rethinking News and Myth as Storytelling." In *The Handbook of Journalism Studies*, edited by Karin Wahl-Jorgensen and Thomas Hanitzsch. London: Routledge, 2008.

Bourdieu, Pierre. "The Aristocracy of Culture." *Media, Culture, and Society* 2, no. 3 (1980): 225–54.

———. *Distinction: A Social Critique of the Judgement of Taste*. Cambridge, MA: Harvard University Press, 1984.

———. *In Other Words: Essays Towards a Reflexive Sociology*. London: Polity Press, 1990.

Bowman, Shayne, and Chris Willis. *We Media: How Audiences Are Shaping the Future of News and Information*. Reston, VA: The Media Center at the American Press Institute, 2003. www.hypergene.net/wemedia.

Boyle, Michael. "Media and Protest: Implications of Mainstream and Alternative Media for Student Protest Participation." Paper presented to the Association for Education in Journalism and Mass Communication, August 2005.

Boyle, Michael, and Mike Schmierbach. "Media Use and Protest." *Communication Quarterly* 57, no. 1 (2009): 1–17.

Bruns, Axel. *Blogs, Wikipedia, Second Life, and Beyond: From Production to Produsage*. New York: Peter Lang, 2008.

Calhoun, Craig (ed.). *Habermas and the Public Sphere*. Cambridge, MA: MIT Press, 1993.

Cammaerts, Bart, Alice Mattoni, and Patrick McCurdy. *Mediation and Protest Movements*. Bristol, UK, and Chicago: Intellect Ltd., 2013.

Cappella, James, and Kathleen Hall Jamieson. *Spiral of Cynicism: The Press and the Public Good*. New York: Oxford University Press, 1997.

Carey, James. *Communication as Culture: Essays on Media and Society*. Boston, MA: Unwin Hyman, 1989.

Carragee, Kevin. "Interpretive Media Study and Interpretive Social Science." *Critical Studies in Mass Communication* 7, no. 2 (June 1990): 81–96.

Chadwick, Andrew. *The Hybrid Media System*. New York and London: Oxford University Press, 2013.

Chan, Joseph Man, and Chin-Chuan Lee. "Journalistic 'Paradigms' of Civil Protests: A Case Study in Hong Kong." In *The News Media in National and International Conflict*, edited by Andrew Arno and Wimal Dissanayake, 183–201. Boulder, CO: Westview Press, 1984.

Chomsky, Noam. *Media Control: The Spectacular Achievements of Propaganda*. Boston, MA: Seven Stories, 2002.

———. *Necessary Illusions: Thought Control in Democratic Societies*. Boston, MA: South End, 1989.

Clark, Jessica, and Tracy Van Slyke. "Welcome to the Media Revolution." *In These Times* 30, no. 7 (July 2006): 20–7.

Clarke, John. "Ordinary People." *Communication, Culture, and Critique* 6 (2013): 208–26.

Coates, Ta-Nehisi. "Four More Years? Bile for Bush Fuels a Boom in Readers, Advertising for Lefty Magazines." *Village Voice*, August 24, 2004.

Coleman, Gabriella. *Hacker, Hoaxer, Whistleblower, Spy: The Many Faces of Anonymous*. New York: Verso Books, 2014.

Coleman, Stephen, Nancy Thumim, Chris Birchall, et al. *The Mediated City: The News in a Post-Industrial Context*. London: Zed Books, 2016.

Condit, Celeste. "The Rhetorical Limits of Polysemy." *Critical Studies in Mass Communication* 6, no. 2 (1989): 103–22.

Converse, Philip. "The Nature of Belief Systems in Mass Publics." In *Ideology and Discontent*, edited by David Apter, 206–61. New York: Free Press, 1964.

Corner, John. "Codes and Cultural Analysis." *Media, Culture, and Society* 2 (1980): 73–86.

———. "Meaning, Genre, and Context: The Problematics of 'Public Knowledge' in the New Audience Studies." In *Mass Media and Society*, edited by John Curran and Michael Gurevitch, 267–84. London and New York: Arnold, 1991.

Corner, John, and Kay Richardson. "Documentary Meanings and the Discourse of Interpretation." In *Documentary and the Mass Media*, edited by John Corner, 141–60. London: Edward Arnold, 1986.

Couldry, Nick. *Why Voice Matters: Culture and Politics after Neoliberalism*. Thousand Oaks, CA: Sage, 2010.

Couldry, Nick, and James Curran. *Contesting Media Power: Alternative Media in a Networked World*. Lanham, MD: Rowman and Littlefield, 2003.

Curran, James, and Tamar Liebes (eds.). *Media, Ritual, and Identity*. London: Routledge, 1998.

Davis, Richard. *Typing Politics: The Role of Blogs in American Politics*. Cary, NC: Oxford University Press, 2009.

Davison, Phillips W. "The Third-Person Effect in Communication." *Public Opinion Quarterly* 47 (1983): 1–15.

Dayan, Daniel, and Elihu Katz. *Media Events.* Cambridge, MA: Harvard University Press, 1992.

De Certeau, Michel. *The Practices of Everyday Life.* Los Angeles, CA: University of California Press, 1984.

Delgado, Gary. *Organizing the Movement.* Philadelphia, PA: Temple University Press, 1986.

Deuze, Mark. "Ethnic Media, Community Media, and Participatory Culture." *Journalism* 7, no. 3 (2006): 262–80.

Domingo, David, and Ari Heinonen. "Weblogs and Journalism: A Typology to Explore the Blurring Boundaries." *Nordicom Review* 29, no. 1 (2008): 3–15.

Downing, John. "Alternative Media and the Boston Tea Party." In *Questioning the Media: A Critical Introduction*, edited by Downing, Ali Mohammadi, and Annabelle Sreberny-Mohammadi, 180–91. Newbury Park, CA: Sage, 1990.

———. "Audiences and Readers of Alternative Media: The Absent Lure of the Virtually Unknown." *Media, Culture, and Society* 25, no. 5 (2003): 625–45.

Downing, John, with Tamara Villareal Ford, Genève Gil, and Laura Stein. *Radical Media: Rebellious Communication and Social Movements.* Thousand Oaks, CA: Sage, 2001.

Drummond, Philip, and Richard Paterson. *Television and Its Audience.* London: British Film Institute, 1988.

Duncombe, Stephen. *Zines and the Politics of Alternative Culture.* New York: Verso, 1997.

Dworkin, Mark, Lois Foreman-Wernet, and Brenda Dervin. "Sense-making and Television News: An Inquiry Into Audience Interpretations." *The Electronic Journal of Communication / La Revue Electronique de Communication* 9, nos. 2, 3, 4 (1999).

Edgerly, Stephanie. "Red Media, Blue Media, and Purple Media: News Repertoires in the Colorful Media Landscape." *Journal of Broadcasting and Electronic Media* 59, no. 1 (2015): 1–21.

Edwards, David, and David Cromwell. *Guardians of Power: The Myth of the Liberal Media.* London: Pluto Press, 2005.

Eliasoph, Nina. *Avoiding Politics: How Americans Produce Apathy in Everyday Life.* New York: Cambridge University Press, 1998.

———. "Routines and the Making of Oppositional News." *Critical Studies in Mass Communication* 5, no. 4 (1988): 313–34.

Eliasoph, Nina, and Paul Lichterman. "Culture in Interaction." *American Journal of Sociology* 108, no. 4 (2003): 735–94.

Entman, Robert. "Framing: Toward Clarification of a Fractured Paradigm." *Journal of Communication* 43, no. 4 (2003): 51–8.

Entman, Robert, and Nikki Usher. "Framing in a Fractured Democracy: Impacts of Digital Technology on Ideology, Power and Cascading Network Activation." *Journal of Communication* 68 (2018): 298–308.

Eveland, William, and Douglas McLeod. "The Effect of Social Desirability on Perceived Media Impact: Implications for Third-Person Perceptions." *International Journal of Public Opinion Research* 11 (1999): 315–33.

Ewart, Jacqui, Michael Meadows, Susan Forde, and Kerrie Foxwell. "Through the Ears of the Audience: Emerging Definitions of News from Community Radio Audiences." Paper presented to the Journalism Education Conference, Griffith University, November–December 2005.

Figenschou, Tine Ustad, and Karoline Andrea Ihlebæk. "Challenging Journalistic Authority: Media Criticism in Far-Right Alternative Media." *Journalism Studies* 19 (2018).

Fillieule, Olivier. "'Plus Ça change, Moins Ça Change': Demonstrations in France During the Nineteen-Eighties." In *Acts of Dissent*, edited by Dieter Rucht, Rood Koopmans, and Friedhelm Neidhardt, 199–226. Lanham, MD: Rowman and Littlefield, 1999.

Fish, Stanley. *Is There a Text in This Class? The Authority of Interpretive Communities.* Cambridge, MA: Harvard University Press, 1980.

Fiske, John. *Television Culture.* New York: Routledge, 1987.

———. *Understanding Popular Culture.* Winchester, MA: Unwin Hyman, 1989.

Forde, Susan. *Challenging the News: The Journalism of Alternative and Community Media.* Houndmills, UK, and New York: Palgrave MacMillan, 2001.

Fraser, Nancy. "Rethinking the Public Sphere: A Contribution to the Critique of Actually Existing Democracy." In *Habermas and the Public Sphere*, edited by Craig Calhoun. Cambridge, MA: MIT Press, 1993.

Freedman, Des. "A Return to Prime-Time Activism: Social Movement Theory and the Media." In *Media Activism in the Digital Age*, edited by Victor Pickard and Guobin Yang. New York: Routledge, 2017.

Friedland, Lewis A. "Electronic Democracy and the New Citizenship." *Media, Culture, and Society* 18, no. 2 (1996): 185–212.

Fuchs, Christian. "Against Henry Jenkins. Remarks on Henry Jenkins' ICA Talk 'Spreadable Media'." May 30, 2011. http://fuchs.uti.at/570/.

———. "Alternative Media as Critical Media." *European Journal of Social Theory* 13, no. 2 (2010): 173–92.

Furnham, Adrian, and Helen Cheng. "Lay Theories of Happiness." *Journal of Happiness Studies* 1, no. 2 (2000): 227–46.

Gamson, William. *Talking Politics.* Cambridge, UK: Cambridge University Press, 1992.

Gamson, William, David Croteau, William Hoynes, and Theodore Sasson. "Media Images and the Social Construction of Reality." *Annual Review of Sociology* 18 (1992): 373–93.

Gamson, William, and Andre Modigliani. "Media Discourse and Public Opinion on Nuclear Power: A Constructionist Approach." *American Journal of Sociology* 95, no. 1 (1989): 1–37.

Gans, Herbert. *Deciding What's News: A Study of CBS Evening News, NBC Nightly News, Newsweek, and Time.* New York: Vintage Books, 1979.

———. *Democracy and the News.* New York: Oxford University Press, 2003.

Gerbaudo, Paolo. *Tweets in the Streets: Social Media and Contemporary Activism.* New York: St. Martin's Press, 2012.

Gerbner, George, Larry Gross, Michael Morgan, Nancy Signorelli, and James Shanahan. "Growing Up with Television: Cultivation Processes." In *Media Effects: Advances in Theory and Research*, 19–42, edited by J. Bryan and D. Zillmann. Mahwah, NJ: Erlbaum, 2002.

Gibbs, Patricia. "Alternative Things Considered: A Political Economic Analysis of Labour Processes and Relations at a Honolulu Alternative Newspaper." *Media, Culture, and Society* 25, no. 5 (2003): 587–605.

Gil De Zúñiga, Homero, Nadine Strauss, and Brigitte Huber. "The Proliferation of the 'News Finds Me' Perception Across Societies." *International Journal of Communication* 14 (2020): 1605–33.

Gillmor, Dan. *We the Media: Grassroots Journalism by the People, for the People.* Cambridge, MA: O'Reilly Media, 2004.

Gitlin, Todd. "Media Sociology: The Dominant Paradigm." *Theory and Society* 6 (1978): 205–53.

———. *The Sixties: Years of Hope, Days of Rage*. New York: Bantam, 1987.

———. *The Whole World Is Watching: The Mass Media in the Making and Unmaking of the New Left*. Berkeley, CA: University of California Press, 1980.

Glaser, Barney, and Anselm Strauss. *The Discovery of Grounded Theory: Strategies for Qualitative Research*. Chicago, IL: Aldine Publishing, 1967.

Glessing, Robert. *The Underground Press in America*. Bloomington, IN: Indiana University Press, 1970.

Goffman, Erving. *Forms of Talk*. Philadelphia, PA: University of Pennsylvania Press, 1981.

———. *Frame Analysis: An Essay on the Organization of Experience*. Cambridge, MA: Harvard University Press, 1974.

———. *Interaction Ritual: Essays on Face-to-Face Behavior*. Garden City, NY: Anchor Books, 1967.

———. *The Presentation of Self in Everyday Life*. Garden City, NY: Anchor Books, 1959.

Gray, Ann. "Reading the Audience." *Screen* 28 (1987): 24–35.

———. *Video Playtime: The Gendering of a Leisure Technology*. London: Routledge, 1992.

Gray, Jonathan. "The News: You Gotta Love It." In *Fandom: Identities and Communities in a Mediated World*, 2nd ed., edited by Jonathan Gray, Cornel Sandvoss, and C. Lee Harrington. New York: NYU Press, 2007.

Guess, Andrew. "(Almost) Everything in Moderation: New Evidence on Americans' Online Media Diets." *American Journal of Political Science* (forthcoming).

Gunther, Albert, and J. Douglas Storey. "The Influence of Presumed Influence." *Journal of Communication* 53 (2003): 199–215.

Haas, Tanni. *The Pursuit of Public Journalism: Theory, Practice, Criticism*. New York and Abingdon, UK: Routledge, 2012.

Habermas, Jürgen. "Further Reflections on the Public Sphere." In *Habermas and the Public Sphere*, edited by Craig Calhoun, 421–61. Cambridge, MA: MIT Press, 1993.

———. *The Structural Transformation of the Public Sphere: An Inquiry Into a Category of Bourgeois Society*. Cambridge: MIT Press, 1989.

Hackett, Robert, and Pinar Gurleyen. "Beyond the Binaries? Alternative Media and Objective Journalism." In *The Routledge Companion to Alternative and Community Media*, edited by Chris Atton, 54–65. Oxford, UK, and New York: Routledge, 2015.

Hájek, Roman, and Nico Carpentier. "Alternative Mainstream Media in the Czech Republic: Beyond the Dichotomy of Alternative and Mainstream Media." *Continuum: Journal of Media and Cultural Studies* (2015): 365–82.

Hall, Stuart. "Encoding and Decoding in the Television Discourse." Edited version published in *Culture, Media, Language*, edited by Stuart Hall, Dorothy Hobson, Andrew Lowe, and Paul Willis. London: Hutchinson, 1980 (1973).

Haller, André, and Kristoffer Holt. "Paradoxical Populism: How PEGIDA Relates to Mainstream and Alternative Media." *Information, Communication, and Society* 22, no. 12 (2019).

Halloran, James, Philip Elliott, and Graham Murdock. *Demonstrations and Communication: A Case Study*. Harmondsworth, UK: Penguin, 1970.

Hamilton, James F. *Democratic Communications: Formations, Projects, Possibilities*. Washington, DC: Lexington Books, 2008.

———. "Theory Through History: Exploring Scholarly Conceptions of U.S. Alternative Media." *The Communication Review* 4 (2001): 305–26.

Hamilton, James T. *All the News That's Fit to Sell: How the Market Transforms Information Into News*. Princeton, NJ: Princeton University Press, 2004.

Hansen, Anders, Simon Cottle, Ralph Negrine, and Chris Newbold. *Mass Communication Research Methods*. New York: NYU Press, 1998.

Harcup, Tony. *Alternative Journalism, Alternative Voices*. Abingdon, UK, and New York: Routledge, 2013.

———. "Asking the Readers: Audience Research into Alternative Journalism." *Journalism Practice* 10, no. 6 (2016): 680–96.

———. "'I'm Doing This to Change the World': Journalism in Alternative and Mainstream Media." *Journalism Studies* 6, no. 3 (2005): 361–74.

———. "'News with a Kick': A Model of Oppositional Reporting." *Communication, Culture and Critique* 7, no. 4 (2014): 559–77.

———. "'The Unspoken—Said': The Journalism of Alternative Media." *Journalism: Theory, Practice, and Criticism* 4, no. 3 (2003): 356–76.

Harlow, Summer. "Recognizing the Importance of Alternative Media: Role Perceptions and Journalistic Culture in Brazil." *Journalism Studies* 20, no. 1 (2017): 117–35.

Harlow, Summer, and Dustin Harp. "Alternative Media in a Digital Era: Comparing News and Information Use Among Activists in the U.S. and Latin America." *Communication and Society/Comunicacion y Sociedad* 26, no. 4 (2013): 25–51.

Harp, Dustin. *Desperately Seeking Women Readers: U.S. Newspapers and the Construction of Female Readership*. Lanham, MD: Lexington Books, 2017.

Harp, Dustin, and Mark Tremayne. "The Gendered Blogosphere: Examining Inequality Using Network and Feminist Theory." *Journalism and Mass Communication Quarterly* 83, no. 2 (2006): 247–67.

Hemmer, Nicole. *Messengers of the Right: Conservative Media and the Transformation of American Politics*. Philadelphia: University of Pennsylvania Press, 2016.

Herbst, Susan. *Reading Public Opinion: How Political Actors View the Democratic Process*. Chicago: University of Chicago Press, 1998.

Herman, Edward. *The Myth of the Liberal Media*. New York: Peter Lang, 1999.

Herman, Edward, and Noam Chomsky. *Manufacturing Consent: The Political Economy of the Mass Media*, 2nd ed. New York: Pantheon, 2002.

Hertog, James, and Douglas McLeod. "Anarchists Wreak Havoc in Downtown Minneapolis: A Multi-Level Study of Media Coverage of Radical Protest." *Journalism and Communication Monographs* 151 (1995).

Hindman, Matthew. *The Myth of Digital Democracy*. Princeton, NJ: Princeton University Press, 2009.

Hobbs, Renee. "Literacy: Understanding Media and How They Work." In *What Society Needs from Media in the Age of Digital Communication: Media XXI*, edited by Robert Picard, 133–59. New York and Barcelona: Social Trends Institute, 2016.

———. *Mind Over Media: Propaganda Education for a Digital Age*. New York: Norton, forthcoming. wwnorton.com/books/9780393713503.

Hobson, Dorothy. *Crossroads: The Drama of a Soap Opera*. London: Methuen, 1982.

Hocke, Peter. "Determining the Selection Bias in Local and National Newspaper Reports of Protest Events." In *Acts of Dissent*, edited by Dieter Rucht, Rood Koopmans, and Friedhelm Neidhardt, 131–63. Lanham, MD: Rowman and Littlefield, 1999.

Holiday, Ryan. *Trust Me, I'm Lying: Confessions of a Media Manipulator*. New York: Portfolio, 2013.

Holt, Kristoffer. "Alternative Media and the Notion of Anti-Systemness: Towards an Analytical Framework." *Media and Communication* 6, no. 4 (2018): 49–57.

Holt, Kristoffer, Tine Ustad Figenschou, and Lena Frischlich. "Key Dimensions of Alternative News Media." *Digital Journalism* 7, no. 7 (2019): 860–9.

Holt, Kristoffer, and André Haller. "What Does 'Lügenpresse' Mean? Expressions of Media Distrust on PEGIDA's Facebook Pages." *Politik* 4, no. 20 (2017).

Howard, Philip, and Andrew Chadwick. *The Routledge Handbook of Internet Politics.* Abingdon, UK, and New York: Routledge, 2009.

Howley, Kevin (ed.). *Understanding Community Media.* London: Sage, 2009.

Iyengar, Shanto. *Is Anyone Responsible? How Television Frames Political Issues.* Chicago: University of Chicago Press, 1991.

Iyengar, Shanto, and Donald Kinder, *News That Matters: Television and American Opinion.* Chicago: University of Chicago Press, 1987.

Jacobs, Ronald, and Eleanor Townsley, *Space of Opinion: Media Intellectuals and the Public Sphere.* New York: Oxford University Press, 2011.

Jamieson, Kathleen Hall, and Joseph Capella. *Echo Chamber: Rush Limbaugh and the Conservative Media Establishment.* New York: Oxford University Press, 2010.

Jenkins, Henry. *Textual Poachers: Television Fans and Participatory Culture.* New York: Routledge, 1992.

Jensen, Klaus Bruhn. *Making Sense of the News.* Aarhus, Denmark: Aarhus University Press, 1986.

———. "Television Futures: A Social Action Methodology for Studying Interpretive Communities." *Critical Studies in Mass Communication* 7 (1990): 129–46.

Johnson, Michael. *The New Journalism: The Underground Press, the Artists of Nonfiction, and Changes in the Established Media.* Lawrence: University Press of Kansas, 1971.

Just, Marion, Ann Crigler, Dean Alger, and Timothy Cook. *Crosstalk: Citizens, Candidates, and the Media in a Political Campaign.* Chicago: University of Chicago Press, 1996.

Kaniss, Phyllis. *Making Local News.* Chicago: University of Chicago Press, 1991.

Karpf, David, Daniel Kreiss, Rasmus Kleis Nielsen, and Matthew Powers. "The Role of Qualitative Methods in Political Communication Research: Past, Present, and Future." *International Journal of Communication* 9 (2015): 1888–906.

Katz, A.J. "Evening News Ratings, Week of May 6." *Adweek,* May 14, 2019. www.adweek.com/tvnewser/evening-news-ratings-week-of-may-6-2.

Katz, Elihu, and Paul Lazarsfeld. *Personal Influence: The Part Played by People in the Flow of Mass Communications.* Abingdon, UK, and New York: Routledge, 2017 [1955].

Kearney, Michael. "Trusting News Project Report." *Reynolds Journalism Institute,* July 25, 2017. www.rjionline.org/reporthtml.html.

Kellner, Douglas. *Media Culture: Cultural Studies, Identity, and Politics Between the Modern and the Postmodern.* New York: Routledge, 1995.

Kenix, Linda Jean. *Alternative and Mainstream Media: The Converging Spectrum.* London: Bloomsbury Academic, 2012.

———. "Blogs as Alternative." *Journal of Computer-Mediated Communication* 14, no. 4 (2009): 790–822.

———. "Commercialism and the Deconstruction of Alternative and Mainstream Media." In *The Routledge Companion to Alternative and Community Media,* edited by Chris Atton, 66–76. Oxford, UK, and New York: Routledge, 2015.

———. "Independent Websites Not So Different From Group-Owned." *Newspaper Research Journal* 35, no. 2 (2014): 24–39.

Kilgo, Danielle, and Summer Harlow. "Protests, Media Coverage, and a Hierarchy of Social Struggle." *The International Journal of Press/Politics* 24, no. 4 (2019): 508–30.

Kim, Eun-gyo, and James F. Hamilton. "Capitulation to Capital? OhMyNews as Alternative Media." *Media, Culture, and Society* 28, no. 4 (2006): 541–60.

Kim, Yonghwan, Hsuan-Ting Chen, and Homero Gil de Zúñiga. "Stumbling upon News on the Internet: Effects of Incidental News Exposure and Relative Entertainment Use on Political Engagement." *Computers in Human Behavior* 29, no. 6 (2013): 2607–14.

Kintz, Linda, and Julie Lesage. *Media, Culture, and the Religious Right.* Minneapolis: University of Minnesota Press, 1998.

Klein, Naomi. *No Logo: Taking Aim at the Brand Bullies.* New York: Picador USA, 1999.

Kperogi, Farooq. "Cooperation with the Corporation? CNN and the Hegemonic Co-optation of Citizen Journalism through iReport.com." *New Media and Society* 13 (2011): 314–29.

———. "News With Views: Post-objectivism and Emergent Alternative Journalistic Practices in America's Corporate News Media." *Review of Communication* 13 (2013): 48–65.

Krieg, Alice. "Vacance Argumentative: L'Usage du (Sic) dans la Contemporaine." *Mots: Les Langages du Politique* 58 (1999): 11–34.

Kull, Steven, Clay Ramsay, and Evan Lewis. "Misperceptions, the Media, and the Iraq War." *Political Science Quarterly* 118, no. 4 (Winter 2003/2004): 569–98.

Ladd, Jonathan. "Affective and Perceptive Polarization among Party Activists." Working paper. Previous version presented at 2016 annual meeting of the American Political Science Association, Philadelphia, January 5, 2018. www.jonathanladd.com.

———. *Why Americans Hate the Media and How It Matters.* Princeton, NJ: Princeton University Press, 2012.

Lamb, Eleanor. "Power and Resistance: New Methods for Analysis across Genres in Critical Discourse Analysis." *Discourse and Society* 24, no. 3 (2013): 334–60.

Larsen, Bent Steege, and Thomas Tufte. "Rituals in the Modern World: Applying the Concept of Ritual in Media Ethnography." In *Global Media Studies: Ethnographic Perspectives*, edited by Patrick Murphy and Marwan Kraidy, 90–106. New York: Routledge, 2003.

Laufer, Peter. *Slow News: A Manifesto for the Critical News Consumer.* Corvallis: Oregon State University Press, 2011.

Le Masurier, Megan. "Slow Journalism: An Introduction to a New Research Paradigm." *Journalism Practice* (2016). https://doi.org/10.1080/17512786.2016.1139902.

Lewis, Justin. *The Ideological Octopus: An Exploration of Television and Its Audience.* New York: Routledge, 1991.

Lewis, Justin, Karin Wahl-Jorgensen, and Sanna Inthorn. "Images of Citizenship on Television News: Constructing a Passive Public." *Journalism Studies* 5, no. 2 (2004): 153–64.

Lewis, Roger. *Outlaws of America: The Underground Press and Its Context.* Middlesex, UK: Penguin, 1972.

Lichterman, Paul. *The Search for Political Community: American Activists Reinventing Commitment.* New York: Cambridge University Press, 1996.

Liebes, Tamar, and Elihu Katz. *The Export of Meaning.* Oxford: Oxford University Press, 1991.

Lieuvrouw, Leah. *Alternative and Activist New Media.* Malden, MA: Polity, 2011.

Lindlof, Thomas. "Media Audiences as Interpretive Communities." *Communication Yearbook* 11 (1987): 81–107.

Lindlof, Thomas, and Debra Grodin. "When Media Use Can't Be Observed: Some Problems and Tactics of Collaborative Audience Research." *Journal of Communication* 40, no. 4 (1990): 8–28.

Livingstone, Sonia. "Engaging With Media: A Matter of Literacy?" *Communication, Culture, and Critique* 1, no. 1 (2008): 75–86.

————. "Giving People a Voice: On the Critical Role of the Interview in the History of Audience Research." *Communication, Culture, and Critique* 3 (2010): 566–71.

————. *Making Sense of Television: The Psychology of Audience Interpretation*. New York: Routledge, 1998.

————. "Relationships between Media and Audiences: Prospects for Audience Reception Studies." In *Media, Ritual, and Identity*, edited by James Curran and Tamar Liebes. London: Routledge, 1998.

Lule, Jack. *Daily News, Eternal Stories: The Mythological Role of Journalism*. New York: Guilford Press, 2001.

Lull, James (ed.). *World Families Watch Television*. Newbury Park, CA: Sage, 1988.

Madianou, Mirca. "The Elusive Public of TV News." In *Audiences and Publics: When Cultural Engagement Matters for the Public Sphere*, vol. 2, edited by Sonia Livingstone. Bristol: Intellect Books Ltd, 2005.

————. "Shifting Identities: Banal Nationalism and Cultural Intimacy in Greek Television News and Everyday Life." In *Discursive Constructions of Identity in European Politics*, edited by Richard Mole. Basingstoke, UK, and New York: Palgrave Macmillan, 2007.

Malone, Martin. *Worlds of Talk: The Presentation of Self in Everyday Conversation*. Malden, MA: Polity, 1997.

Mansbridge, Jane. "Complicating Oppositional Consciousness." In *Oppositional Consciousness*, edited by Jane Mansbridge and Aldon Morris, 238–64. Chicago, IL: University of Chicago Press, 2001.

Marcuse, Herbert. *Counterrevolution and Revolt*. Boston, MA: Beacon, 1972.

Marwick, Alice, and Rebecca Lewis. *Media Manipulation and Disinformation Online*. New York: Data and Society Research Institute, 2016.

Mathison, David. *Be the Media: How to Create and Accelerate Your Message, Your Way*. Tiburon, CA: Natural E Creative, 2009.

Mazepa, Patricia. "Regressive Social Relations, Activism, and Media." In *Alternative Media in Canada*, edited by Kirsten Kozolanka, Patricia Mazepa, and David Skinner, 244–63. Vancouver: University of British Columbia Press, 2012.

McChesney, Robert. *Digital Disconnect: How Capitalism is Turning the Internet Away from Democracy*. Boston, MA: New Press, 2014.

————. "The Internet and U.S. Communication Policy-making in Historical and Critical Perspective." *Journal of Communication* 46, no. 1 (1996): 98–124.

————. *The Problem of the Media: U.S. Communication Politics in the 21st Century*. New York: Monthly Review, 2004.

————. *Rich Media, Poor Democracy: Communication Politics in Dubious Times*. New York: The New Press, 2015 (1999).

McCurdy, Patrick. "Mediation, Practice, and Lay Theories of Media." In *Mediation and Protest Movements*, edited by Bart Cammaerts, Alice Mattoni, and Patrick McCurdy, 57–74. Bristol, UK, and Chicago: Intellect Ltd., 2013.

McLeod, Douglas. "News Coverage and Social Protest: How the Media's Protest Paradigm Exacerbates Social Conflict." *Journal of Dispute Resolution* 185 (2007).

McLeod, Douglas, and Benjamin H. Detenber. "Framing Effects of TV News Coverage of Social Protest." *Journal of Communication* 49, no. 3 (1999): 3–23.

McLeod, Douglas, and James Hertog. "Social Control, Social Change, and the Mass Media's Role in the Regulation of Protest Groups." In *Mass Media, Social Control, and Social Change: A Macrosocial Perspective*, edited by David Demers and K. Viswanath, 305–32. Ames: Iowa State University Press, 1999.

McLeod, Douglas, and Dhavan Shah. *News Frames and National Security: Covering Big Brother.* New York: Cambridge University Press, 2015.

McMillian, John. *Smoking Typewriters: The Sixties Underground Press and the Rise of Alternative Media in America.* New York: Oxford University Press, 2011.

Meikle, Graham. *Future Active: Media Activism and the Internet.* New York: Routledge, 2002.

Merton, Robert, Marjorie Fiske, and Patricia Kendall. *The Focused Interview: A Manual of Problems and Procedures.* New York: The Free Press, 1990.

Meyrowitz, Joshua. "Power, Pleasure, Patterns: Intersecting Narratives of Media Influence." *Journal of Communication* 58, no. 4 (December 2008): 641–63.

Min, InCheol. "Perceptions of the Audience by the Alternative Press Producers: A Case Study of the Texas Observer." *Media, Culture, and Society* 26, no. 3 (2004): 450–58.

Mindich, David. *Tuned Out: Why Americans Under 40 Don't Follow the News.* New York: Oxford University Press, 2005.

Morley, David. *The Nationwide Audience.* London: British Film Institute, 1980.

———. "The Nationwide Audience: A Critical Postscript." *Screen Education* 39 (1981): 3–14.

———. *Television, Audiences, and Cultural Studies.* London: Routledge, 1992.

———. "Unanswered Questions in Audience Research." *The Communication Review* 9 (2006): 101–21.

Morley, David, and Charlotte Brunsdon. *Everyday Television: Nationwide.* London: British Film Institute, 1978.

Murray, Catherine, Kim Christian Schrøder, Kirsten Drotner, and Steve Kline. *Researching Audiences: A Practical Guide to Methods in Media Audience Analysis.* London: Bloomsbury, 2003.

Nadler, Anthony. *Making the News Popular: Mobilizing U.S. News Audiences.* Chicago: University of Illinois Press, 2016.

Nagle, Angela. *Kill All Normies: Online Culture Wars From 4chan and Tumblr to Trump and the Alt-Right.* London: Pluto Press, 2017.

Nah, Seungahn, and Deborah Chung. "When Citizens Meet Both Professional and Citizen Journalists: Social Trust, Media Credibility, and Perceived Journalistic Roles among Online Community News Readers." *Journalism* 13, no. 6 (2012): 714–30.

Neiwert, David. *Alt-America: The Rise of the Radical Right in the Age of Trump.* New York: Verso, 2017.

Neuman, W. Russell. *The Digital Difference: Media Technology and the Theory of Communication Effects.* Cambridge, MA: Harvard University Press, 2016.

———. *The Future of the Mass Audience.* New York: Cambridge University Press, 1991.

Neuman, W. Russell. Marion Just, and Ann Crigler. *Common Knowledge: News and the Construction of Political Meaning.* Chicago: University of Chicago Press, 1992.

New York Times. "Young Adults Suffering From News Fatigue, Study Says." June 2, 2008.

Nicholson, Benedict. "These Were the Top Publishers on Facebook in January 2020." *Newswhip,* March 2, 2020. www.newswhip.com/2020/03/these-were-the-top-publishers-on-facebook-in-january-2020/.

Nord, David Paul. *Communities of Journalism: A History of American Newspapers and Their Readers.* Champaign-Urbana: University of Illinois Press, 2001.

Örnebring, Henrik, and Anna Maria Jönsson. "Tabloid Journalism and the Public Sphere." *Journalism Studies* 5, no. 3 (2004): 283–95.

Padovani, Cinzia. "The Media of the Ultra-Right: Discourse and Audience Activism Online." *Journal of Language and Politics* 15, no. 4 (2016): 399–421.

Paul, Bryant, Michael B. Salwen, and Michel Dupagne. "The Third-Person Effect: A Meta-Analysis of the Perceptual Hypothesis." *Mass Communication and Society* 3, no. 1 (2000): 57–85.

Peck, Abe. *Uncovering the Sixties: The Life and Times of the Underground Press.* New York: Pantheon, 1985.

Perloff, Richard. "The Third-Person Effect." In *Media Effects: Advances in Theory and Research*, edited by Jennings Bryant and Dorf Zillman, 489–506. Mahwah, NJ: Erlbaum, 2002.

Peterson, Mark. "Getting the News in New Delhi." In *The Anthropology of News and Journalism*, edited by S. Elizabeth Bird. Bloomington: Indiana University Press, 2009.

Pew Research Center. "Americans Still Prefer Watching to Reading the News—And Mostly Still Through Television." December 3, 2018. www.journalism. org/2018/12/03/americans-still-prefer-watching-to-reading-the-news-and-mostly-still-through-television.

———. "Campaign Leads the Pack as Campaign News Source." February 7, 2012. www. pewresearch.org/politics/2012/02/07/cable-leads-the-pack-as-campaign-news-source.

———. "News Audiences Increasingly Politicized." June 8, 2004. www.people-press. org/2004/06/08/news-audiences-increasingly-politicized.

———. "Self-Censorship: How Often and Why." April 30, 2000. www.pewresearch. org/politics/2000/04/30/self-censorship-how-often-and-why.

———. "Trump, Clinton Voters Divided in Their Main Source for Election News." January 18, 2017. www.journalism.org/2017/01/18/trump-clinton-voters-divided-in-their-main-source-for-election-news.

———. "Understanding the Participatory News Consumer." March 1, 2010. www. pewinternet.org/2010/03/01/understanding-the-participatory-news-consumer.

Phillips, Whitney. *This Is Why We Can't Have Nice Things: Mapping the Relationship Between Online Trolling and Mainstream Culture.* Cambridge, MA: MIT Press, 2015.

Philo, Greg. *Seeing Is Believing: The Influence of Television.* London: Routledge, 1990.

Pickard, Victor. "Assessing the Radical Democracy of Indymedia: Discursive, Technical, and Institutional Constructions." *Critical Studies in Media Communication* 23, no. 1 (2006): 19–38.

———. "Coronavirus is Hammering the News Industry. Here's How to Save It." *Jacobin*, April 20, 2020.

———. *Democracy Without Journalism?* New York: Oxford University Press, 2020.

Pickard, Victor, and Guobin Yang (eds.). *Media Activism in the Digital Age.* New York: Routledge, 2017.

Pickerell, Jenny. *Cyberprotest: Environmental Activism Online.* Manchester, UK: Manchester University Press, 2003.

Platon, Sarah, and Mark Deuze. "Indymedia Journalism: A Radical Way of Making, Selecting, and Sharing News?" *Journalism* 4, no. 3 (2003): 336–55.

Postman, Neil. *Amusing Ourselves to Death: Public Discourse in the Age of Show Business.* New York: Penguin Books, 1985.

Postman, Neil, and Steve Powers. *How to Watch TV News.* New York: Penguin Books, 1992.

Potter, Claire Bond. *Political Junkies: From Talk Radio to Twitter, How Alternative Media Hooked Us on Politics and Broke Our Democracy.* New York: Basic Books, 2020.

Pritchard, David, Christopher Terry, and Paul Brewer. "One Owner, One Voice? Testing a Central Premise of Newspaper-Broadcast Cross-Ownership Policy." *Communication Law and Policy* 13 (2008): 1–27.

Radway, Janice. *Reading the Romance: Women, Patriarchy, and Popular Literature*. Philadelphia: University of Pennsylvania Press, 1991.

Rauch, Jennifer. "Activists as Interpretive Communities: Rituals of Consumption and Interaction in an Alternative Media Audience." *Media, Culture, and Society* 29, no. 6 (2007): 994–1013.

———. "Are There Still Alternatives? Relationships Between Alternative and Mainstream Media in a Converged Environment." *Sociology Compass* 10, no. 9 (2016): 756–67.

———. "Comparing Progressive and Conservative Audiences for Alternative Media and Their Attitudes toward Journalism." In *Alternative Media Meets Mainstream Politics: Activist Nation Rising*, edited by Joshua Atkinson and Linda Jean Kenix, 19–37. Lanham, MD: Lexington Books, 2019.

———. "Constructive Rituals of Demediatization: Spiritual, Corporeal, and Mixed Metaphors in Popular Discourse About Unplugging." *Explorations in Media Ecology* 13, no. 3+4 (2014): 237–52.

———. "Exploring the Alternative-Mainstream Dialectic: What 'Alternative Media' Means to a Hybrid Audience'." *Communication, Culture, and Critique* 8, no. 1 (2015): 124–43.

———. "Hands-on Communication: Zine Circulation Rituals and the Interactive Limitations of Web Self-Publishing." *Popular Communication: International Journal of Media and Culture* 2, no. 3 (2004): 153–69.

———. "Participation Beyond Production: Possibilities for Reception and Ritual in the Study of Activist Audiences." In *Audience and Interpretation in Media Studies*, edited by Radhika Parameswaran, vol. 3 in *The International Encyclopedia of Media Studies*, edited by Angharad N. Valdivia, 489–509. Oxford: Wiley-Blackwell, 2013.

———. "Rooted in Nations, Blossoming in Globalization? A Cultural Perspective on the Content of a 'Northern' Mainstream and 'Southern' Alternative News Agency." *Journal of Communication Inquiry* 27, no. 1 (2003): 87–103.

———. *Slow Media: Why Slow Is Satisfying, Sustainable and Smart*. New York: Oxford University Press, 2018.

———. "Superiority and Susceptibility: How Activist Audiences Imagine the Influence of Mainstream News on Self and Others." *Discourse and Communication* 4, no. 3 (2010): 263–77.

Rauch, Jennifer, Sunitha Chitrapu, Susan Tyler Eastman, John Christopher Evans, Christopher Paine, and Peter Mwesige. "From Seattle 1999 to New York 2004: A Longitudinal Analysis of Journalistic Framing of the Movement for Democratic Globalization." *Social Movement Studies* 6, no. 2 (2007): 131–45.

Ricketts, Aidan. *The Activist's Handbook: A Step-by-Step Guide to Participatory Democracy*. London: Zed, 2012.

Rodriguez, Clemencia. *Citizens' Media Against Armed Conflict: Disrupting Violence in Colombia*. Minneapolis: University of Minnesota Press, 2011.

———. *Fissures in the Mediascape: An International Study of Citizens' Media*. Creskill, NJ: Hampton Press, 2001.

Roodhouse, Elizabeth. "The Voice from the Base(ment): Stridency, Referential Structure, and Partisan Conformity in the Political Blogosphere." *First Monday* 14, no. 9 (2009). https://journals.uic.edu/ojs/index.php/fm/article/view/2624/2289.

Rosen, Jay. "The People Formerly Known as the Audience." *PressThink* (blog), June 27, 2006. http://archive.pressthink.org/2006/06/27/ppl_frmr.html.

Rosenstiel, Tom, and Marion Just. "Five Ways to Build Viewership." *Columbia Journalism Review/Project for Excellence in Journalism* (November/December 2002): 92–3. www.journalism.org/resources/research/reports/localTV/2002/viewership.asp.

Rothenbuhler, Eric. *Ritual Communication: From Everyday Conversation to Mediated Ceremony.* Thousand Oaks, CA: Sage, 1998.

Rucht, Dieter. "The Quadruple A: Media Strategies of Social Movements Since the 1960s." *Cyberprotest: New Media, Citizens, and Social Movements,* edited by Wim van der Donk, Brian Loader, Paul Nixon, and Dieter Rucht, 25–48. London and New York: Routledge, 2004.

Ruddock, Andy. "Scientific Criticism? A Critical Approach to the Resistive Audience." *Atlantic Journal of Communication* 6, no. 1 (1998): 59–80.

———. *Understanding Audiences: Theory and Method.* London: Sage, 2001.

Russell, Adrienne. *Journalism as Activism: Recoding Media Power.* Cambridge, UK: Polity, 2016.

Ryan, Charlotte. "It Takes a Movement to Raise an Issue: Media Lessons From the 1997 U.P.S. Strike." *Critical Sociology* 30, no. 2 (2004): 483–511.

———. *Prime-Time Activism.* Boston, MA: South End Press, 1991.

Salzman, Jason. *Making the News: A Guide for Activists and Nonprofits.* Cambridge, MA: Westview Press, 2003.

Sandoval, Marisol, and Christian Fuchs. "Towards a Critical Theory of Alternative Media." *Telematics and Informatics* 27 (2010): 141–50.

Schrøder, Kim Christian. "Making Sense of Audience Discourses." *European Journal of Cultural Studies* 3, no. 2 (2000): 233–58.

Schudson, Michael. *Discovering the News: A Social History of American Newspapers.* New York: Basic Books, 1978.

———. *The Power of News.* Cambridge, MA: Harvard University Press, 1995.

Seiter, Ellen. *Television and New Media Audiences.* Oxford: Oxford University Press, 1999.

Shaw, Randy. *The Activist's Handbook: Winning Change in the Century,* 2nd ed. Oakland: University of California Press, 2013.

Shoemaker, Pamela, and Stephen Reese. *Mediating the Message: Theories of Influences on Mass Media Content.* White Plains, NY: Longman, 1996.

Sigal, Leo. *Reporters and Officials: The Organization and Politics of Newsmaking.* Lexington, MA: D.C. Heath, 1973.

Slater, Michael. "Operationalizing and Analyzing Exposure: The Foundation of Media Effects Research." *Journalism and Mass Communication Quarterly* 81, no. 1 (2004): 168–83.

Smith, Jackie, John McCarthy, Clark McPhail, and Boguslaw Augustyn. "From Protest to Agenda Building: Descriptive Bias in Media Coverage of Protest Events in Washington D.C." *Social Forces* 79, no. 4 (2001): 1397–423.

Sobieraj, Sarah. *Soundbitten: The Perils of Media-Centered Political Activism.* New York: NYU Press, 2011.

Solutions Journalism Network. "What Is Solutions Journalism?" https://thewholestory.solutionsjournalism.org/what-is-solutions-journalism-c050147bb1eb.

Stewart, Charles. "The Master Conspiracy of the John Birch Society: From Communism to the New World Order." *Western Journal of Communication* 66, no. 4 (2002): 424–47.

Stolte, John, Gary Alan Fine, and Karen Cook. "Sociological Miniaturism: Seeing the Big Through the Small in Social Psychology." *Annual Review of Sociology* 27 (2001): 387–413.

Streitmatter, Rodger. *Mightier Than the Sword: How the News Media Have Shaped American History,* 2nd ed. Boulder, CO: Westview Press, 2001.

Swidler, Ann. "Culture in Action: Symbols and Strategies." *American Sociological Review* 51 (1986): 273–86.

Syvertsen, Trine. *Media Resistance: Protest, Dislike, Abstention*. Cham, Switzerland: Palgrave Macmillan, 2017.

Tewksbury, David, Andrew Weaver, and Brett Maddex. "Accidentally Informed: Incidental News Exposure on the World Wide Web." *Journalism and Mass Communication Quarterly* 78, no. 3 (2001): 534.

Thornton, Sarah. *Club Cultures: Music, Media, and Subcultural Capital*. Hanover, NH: Wesleyan/New England, 1996.

Toff, Benjamin, and Antonis Kalogeropoulos. "All the News That's Fit to Ignore: How the Information Environment Does and Does Not Shape News Avoidance." *Public Opinion Quarterly*, July 10, 2020. https://doi.org/10.1093/poq/nfaa016.

Toft, Amoshaun. "Cross-Talk in Political Discourse: Strategies for Bridging Issue Movements on *Democracy Now!*" In *'Doing Politics': Discursivity, Performativity, and Mediation in Political Discourse*, edited by M. Kranert and G. Horan, 301–29. Amsterdam: John Benjamins, 2018.

———. "Network Structures in Cross-Movement Talk: *Democracy Now!*, 2003–2013." *Social Movement Studies* 19, no. 3 (2020): 342–61.

Trilling, Damian, and Klaus Schoenbach. "Skipping Current Affairs: The Non-Users of Online and Offline News." *European Journal of Communication* 28, no. 1 (2013): 35–51.

Tuchman, Gaye. *Making the News: A Study in the Construction of Reality*. New York: The Free Press, 1978.

Turner, Victor. "Liminal to Liminoid, in Play, Flow, and Ritual: An Essay in Comparative Symbology." In *Play, Games, and Sports in Cultural Contexts*, edited by Janet Harris and Roberta Park, 53–92. Champaign, IL: Human Kinetics Publishers, [1983] (2003).

Turow, Joseph. *Breaking Up America: Advertisers and the New Media World*. Chicago: University of Chicago Press, 1997.

Vallone, Robert, Lee Ross, and Mark Lepper. "The Hostile Media Phenomenon: Biased Perception and Perceptions of Media Bias in Coverage of the Beirut Massacre." *Journal of Personality and Social Psychology* 49, no. 3 (1985): 577–85.

van Zoonen, Liesbet. "The Women's Movement and the Media: Constructing a Public Identity." *European Journal of Communication* 7, no. 4 (1992): 453–76.

Viguerie, Richard, and David Franke. *America's Right Turn: How Conservatives Used New Alternative Media to Take Power*. Chicago: Bonus Books, 2004.

Wahl-Jorgensen, Karin, and Thomas Hanitzsch. "Introduction: Why and How We Should Do Journalism Studies." In *The Handbook of Journalism Studies*, edited by Karin Wahl-Jorgensen and Thomas Hanitzsch, 3–16. London: Routledge, 2008.

Waltz, Mitzi. *Alternative and Activist Media*. Edinburgh: Edinburgh University Press, 2005.

Warner, Jamie. "Political Culture Jamming: The Dissident Humor of *The Daily Show*." *Popular Communication* 5, no. 1 (2007): 17–36.

Warzel, Charlie. "The Right Is Building a New Media 'Upside-Down' to Tell Trump's Story." *BuzzFeed*, January 23, 2017.

Wendling, Mike. *Alt-Right: From 4chan to the White House*. London: Pluto Press, 2018.

Woodstock, Louise. "The News-Democracy Narrative and the Unexpected Benefits of Limited News Consumption: The Case of News Resisters." *Journalism* 15, no. 7 (2013): 834–49.

Wyatt, Wendy. *Critical Conversations: A Theory of Press Criticism*. Creskill, NJ: Hampton Press, 2007.

Young, Dannagal. "*Daily Show* Viewers More Knowledgeable About Presidential Campaign." *National Annenberg Election Survey*, September 21, 2004. https://cdn.annenberg publicpolicycenter.org/wp-content/uploads/2004_03_late-night-knowledge-2_9-21_pr2.pdf.

———. *Irony and Outrage: The Polarized Landscape of Rage, Fear, and Laughter in the U.S.* New York: Oxford University Press, 2019.

Zald, Mayer, and John McCarthy (eds.). *The Dynamics of Social Movements: Resource Mobilization, Social Control, and Tactics.* Cambridge, MA: Winthrop, 1979.

Zaller, John. "A New Standard of News Quality: Burglar Alarms for the Monitorial Citizen." *Political Communication* 20 (2003): 109–30.

Zelizer, Barbie. "Journalists as Interpretive Communities." *Critical Studies in Mass Communication* 10, no. 3 (1993): 219–37.

Zimmerman, Don, and D. Lawrence Wieder. "The Diary-Interview Method." *Urban Life* 5, no. 4 (1977): 479–98.

INDEX

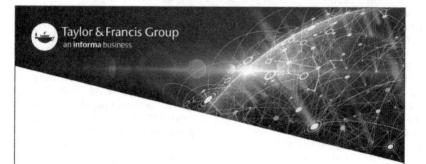